Fethullah Gülen's Teaching and Practice

Paul Weller

Fethullah Gülen's Teaching and Practice

Inheritance, Context, and Interactive Development

To
Rishon

from

Paul

Murk 2022

palgrave
macmillan

Paul Weller
Faculty of Theology and Religion
Regent's Park College — University of Oxford
Oxford, UK

ISBN 978-3-030-97362-9   ISBN 978-3-030-97363-6 (eBook)
https://doi.org/10.1007/978-3-030-97363-6

Cover illustration: Image courtesy of the Alliance for Shared Values

This Palgrave Macmillan imprint is published by the registered company Springer Nature Switzerland AG.
The registered company address is: Gewerbestrasse 11, 6330 Cham, Switzerland

This book is dedicated to Muhammed Çetin,
A former doctoral student of mine at the University of Derby
who first introduced me to the teaching and practice of Fethullah Gülen.

PREFACE

This book focuses on the teaching and practice of Fethullah Gülen—one of the most prominent contemporary Hanafi Sunni Muslim scholars of Turkish origin, who has, by word and deed, inspired what eventually became a global movement known to those within it as Hizmet (meaning 'service'). At the same time, for some circles in Turkish society, he has always been a controversial figure while, most recently, following the events of 15 July 2016 in Turkey and their aftermath (hereafter referred to in abbreviated form as 'July 2016' and in which over 300 people were killed and over 2000 injured), he, and movement inspired by him, stand accused by the Turkish President, Recep Tayyip Erdoğan, the Turkish government, and Turkish state authorities, of having planned and been ultimately responsible for those events, even though Gülen and Hizmet strongly deny this.

This is the first monograph of its kind completely researched and written following the July 2016 events in Turkey and their aftermath. The book has a distinctive methodological approach which sets out to understand and articulate the iterative development of Gülen's teaching and practice by reference to, and interaction with his biography, including its changing and varied geographical and temporal contexts but, especially, through his ongoing dynamic, contextual, dialogical mutual interaction with those engaged in Hizmet from around the world.

The book is intended as a mutually illuminating companion volume to Paul Weller's (2022) *Hizmet in Transitions: European Developments of a Turkish Muslim-Inspired Movement*, also published by Palgrave Macmillan which, in relation to Europe, is a case study of such an interaction. While both books can be read independently, when read together in a complementary way, they add more detailed information and texture to some things that are not appropriate to discuss in equal detail across both books. Taken together, they even more strongly illuminate the dynamic interrelationships between Fethullah Gülen's teaching and practice; how that teaching and practice has historically developed and is still developing in a contextually informed way; and how those inspired by its inheritance have taken it forward within different contextual trajectories which, in an overall hermeneutical circle, in turn has informed Fethullah Gülen's Islamically rooted but also continually contextually developing reflective teaching and practice.

Oxford, UK   Paul Weller

ACKNOWLEDGEMENTS

GENERAL ACKNOWLEDGEMENTS

Primary research for this book was carried out during 2017–2020. Bearing in mind the pressures that have been brought to bear upon those associated with Hizmet not only in Turkey, but also beyond it and which, for some among those interviewed and/or their families, friends, and colleagues, have ranged from loss of employment; expropriation of property and funds; imprisonment; the need to undertake irregular and sometimes dangerous migration; threats of violence to persons, family, and property; as well as state attempts to extradite, acknowledgements for their kind assistance are especially due to the twenty-nine people who were interviewed for this book.

Together with Fethullah Gülen himself, from among his close associates who were content for quotations from what they said to be associated with their names across this book and its complementary volume (Weller 2022), acknowledgements are due to nine individuals. These are Muhammed Çetin, Enes Ergene, Mustafa Fidan, Reşit Haylamaz, Ahmet Kurucan, Mustafa Özcan, Hamdullah Öztürk, Şerif Ali Tekalan, and Hakan Yeşilova.

Haylamaz and Özcan have been with Fethullah Gülen since close to the start of his public work, as was Fidan, who was one of Gülen's early business supporters. Tekalan first met Gülen in 1971 when Tekalan was a medical student who later became an otolaryngologist by profession and then President (2010–2016) of the Hizmet-related Fatih University in Istanbul. Kurucan, widely known within Hizmet as 'Ahmet Abi,' was a student of

Gülen. Although Gülen had students dating back to the 1960s, on 23 October 1985, he formed a new circle of which Kurucan was a part. Öztürk was a later student of Gülen's, Ergene is author of a book on Fethullah Gülen and Hizmet, and Yeşilova is editor of Hizmet's *Fountain* magazine. Çetin was (with the support of Fethullah Gülen and Hizmet, under circumstances discussed further in Weller 2022, Sect. 4.4) a Member of Parliament in Turkey between 2011 and 2014.

The great majority of these interviews took place in the USA in December 2017 (with the exception of that with Tekalan, which took place in the UK in April 2019). The great majority were also conducted in Turkish, supported by Turkish-English-Turkish translation and interpretation undertaken within research ethics-approved protocols. This included two interviews with Fethullah Gülen himself, to whom special thanks must be recorded for allowing me to interview him towards the end of 2017, at a time when he was not physically well.

Among individuals publicly associated with Hizmet organisations in Europe who were interviewed and were also generally content for quotations from what they said to be associated with their names across the book and its complementary volume (Weller 2022), were twelve people, the majority of whose interviews took place in English which, it should be noted, was in most cases not their first or, in some cases, even their second language.

These were Selma Ablak (a member of the Hizmet *overleg*, or co-ordinating body, in the Netherlands); Alper Alasag (also a member of the Hizmet *overleg* in the Netherlands); Abdulkerim Balcı (a leading member of the Hizmet-related London Advocacy, United Kingdom); Sadik Çinar (Executive Director of the Dialogue Society, United Kingdom); Asen Erkinbekov (working with the Platforme de Paris, France); Mustafa Gezen (previously in the leadership of the Dialog Forum, Denmark); Özcan Keleş (Chair of the Dialogue Society's Board of Trustees and, until 2014, Executive Director of its staff team); Ercan Karakoyun (a leader in the Forum Dialog, Berlin, Germany); Termijón Termizoda Naziri (President of the Arco Forum, from Spain); Ramazan Özgü (responsible within Hizmet for dialogue activities, legal questions, and asylum-seeker matters in Switzerland, and an *abi*—or member of the informal leadership structure of Hizmet—in the Zurich region); Özgür Tascioglu (Secretary General of Fedactio, Belgium); and Erkan Toğuşlu (responsible for the Gülen Chair, at the Catholic University of Leuven, and also a volunteer in Fedactio, Belgium). Interviews with those from the UK and Switzerland took place in person in the countries concerned in 2018, while the others were conducted over Skype during 2018–2019.

While readers of the complementary volume (Weller 2022) to this book may have noted that it is dedicated to one of these interviewees (Özcan Keleş), neither the fact nor the content of that dedication should be taken as an evaluative endorsement of all or any of the particular positions taken by Keleş in relation to the movement. Rather, in both books, these are presented alongside those of other interviewees with the aim of giving readers insight into a range of positions being taken and the debate that is ongoing on within Hizmet—partly in relation to reports of its past, but especially concerning its present and future possible trajectories. At the same time, Keleş' (2021) unpublished thesis on *The Knowledge Production of Social Movement Practice at the Intersection of Islam and Human Rights: The Case of Hizmet*, and to which this author was kindly given privileged access just prior to submitting the manuscript, is a piece of work that this author evaluates highly as a very important specialist contribution to the field which also, in due course when it is translated into published form, is likely to have a wider impact in facilitating an understanding of both Hizmet and Fethullah Gülen.

Acknowledgements are also due to three male Hizmet-related asylum-seekers (identified in the text as AS1, AS2, and AS3) and one female Hizmet-related asylum-seeker (identified in the text as AS4), who is married to AS3, all of whom were based in Switzerland at the time the interviews took place in December 2018. These interviewees, not unsurprisingly, requested and were granted anonymity. All of the asylum-seeker interviews were conducted in English.

This was also the case, as was the grant of anonymity, for three other individuals, all of whom were male: one is publicly associated with Hizmet in Europe, identified in the text as HE1, and whose interview took place over Skype in August 2019; one is a Hizmet participant in Italy, identified in the text as HE2 and who was interviewed over Skype in September and October 2019; and one is a participant observer of Hizmet in the Netherlands, identified in the text as HE3, whose interview took place over Skype in August 2019. A request for anonymity was also made and granted in relation to the attribution of some specific quotations from a male interviewee from among the associates of Fethullah Gülen and which are identified in the text as being contributed by CA1.

All interviewees were given the opportunity to review and, if necessary, correct and/or clarify written draft transcripts of the digital recordings of their interviews. At the same time, it should be noted that the interviewees have not reviewed or approved the selected quotations used by the author from their transcripts or how those selections have been deployed in the text, the responsibility for which lies with the author's professionalism in terms of a best understanding of the overall contributions and intentions of the interviewees and a commitment to as far as possible try to avoid being unrepresentative or unbalanced in use of the materials concerned.

Given that English was not the first language of the vast majority of those interviewed, in the presentation of quotations from such interviewees, there are sentences that are not completely correct in terms of English grammar or structure. However, where what seemed to be the intended meaning of the interviewee is intelligible, the decision was made not to correct the text but to leave it as it is, thereby reflecting something of its originally oral flavour.

Finally, acknowledgements are due to members of the research project's reference group. Across the lifetime of the project, this included: Revd. Professor Dr. Paul Fiddes, Professor of Systematic Theology and formerly Research Director, Regent's Park College, University of Oxford; Revd. Dr. Nicholas Wood, formerly Fellow in Religion and Culture and previously Director of the Oxford Centre for Christianity and Culture, Regent's Park College; Dr. Minlib Dalhl, OP, formerly Research Fellow in the Study of Love in Religion, Regent's Park College; Dr. Anthony Reddie, Director of the Oxford Centre for Religion and Culture, Regent's Park College; Mahmut Gunyadin from the Dialogue Society, Oxford; Dr. Fatih Isik and Dr. İsmail Mesut Sezgin—Dialogue Society volunteers; Mr. Sadik Cinar, Executive Director, the Dialogue Society; Mr. Cem Erbil, Academic Director, the Dialogue Society; and Mr. Ozan Keleş, Chair of the Dialogue Society.

Copyright Permissions

The vast majority of this book's content is formed from new primary research data. However, acknowledgements are also due to authors and publishers whose work this book quotes under the generally recognised provisions for "fair dealing… for the purposes of criticism or review." Every attempt has been made to exclude copyright material in this book that may go beyond such provisions. If, in error, the author has inaccurately or not fully referenced any material, if this is brought to the author's attention, any such mistakes will be rectified in any future editions.

Personal and Professional Thanks

The author wishes to record his personal and professional thanks to other colleagues at Regent's Park College, Oxford, and beyond, who supported him by showing an interest in his work on this book and the research that underlies it. This includes the former College Principal, Revd. Dr. Robert Ellis, who supported bringing the project to the College, and Ms. Nichola Kilpin, the College's Finance Officer, who administered the project funds granted through the Dialogue Society, behind which were individual anonymous donors, without whose financial support neither the research project underlying these two books would not have been possible, nor their publication in Open Access format would have been possible.

Personal thanks are due to the author's wife, Marie Adenau, for her patience with, and interest in, this book and its companion volume, as well as the author's wider work on Fethullah Gülen and Hizmet.

Finally, professional thanks are due to colleagues at Palgrave Macmillan for their patient support and work in bringing this book to publication, including especially to Philip Getz, Senior Editor, Palgrave Macmillan; Amy Invernizzi, Assistant Editor, Philosophy and Religion, Palgrave Macmillan; Jack Heeney, Editorial Assistant—Literature and Theatre & Performance, Palgrave Macmillan; and Immy Higgins, Editorial Assistant—BEST (Books Editorial Service Team) Springer Nature.

TURKISH WORDS

Since Turkish is the first language of both Fethullah Gülen and many of those inspired by his life, teaching, and practice (including many of those in Europe), and it remains an important language in Hizmet's overall milieu, generally speaking key Turkish language terms and concepts are, on first use in this book, referred to in their original Turkish form, followed by an English language translation and/or explanation.

Turkish words are generally used in their modern Latin script form, without diacritics apart from those that are normally present in modern Turkish writing (ö, ü, ğ, ç) which contains several letters that are not present in the English alphabet. These are pronounced as follows:

Ç, ç "ch" as in "chime"
ğ which lengthens the sound of the vowel that appears before it; except that when it appears between two vowels, it is not pronounced
I, ı the sound of the "a" as pronounced in "attack"
Ö, ö same as the sound of "u" in "Turkey"
Ş, ş "sh" as in "shoot"
Ü, ü "u" as in "tube"

CONTENTS

ABOUT THE AUTHOR

Paul Weller When conducting the research that lies behind the writing of this book, and during its substantive writing, Paul Weller was part-time Research Fellow in Religion and Society and Associate Director (UK) of the Oxford Centre for Religion and Culture, Regent's Park College, a Baptist Permanent Private Hall of the University of Oxford, where he is an Associate Member of the Faculty of Theology and Religion. He retired from his employed Research Fellowship at the end of November 2021, and from 1st December, his research fellowship became a non-Stipendiary one. He is also Emeritus Professor of the University of Derby and a Visiting Professor in the Research Institute for Peace, Security, and Social Justice of Coventry University.

CHAPTER 1

Introduction

1.1 THE FOCUS OF THE BOOK

This book focuses upon and explores the life and iterative development of the teaching and practice of Muhammed Fethullah Gülen—a traditionally trained Islamic scholar of Turkish origin from within the Hanafi school of Sunni Islam. From his life, teaching, and practice, many hundreds of thousands of Muslims and others have taken inspiration to engage in what those involved in it call Hizmet (a Turkish word *hizmet*, meaning service), which expanded initially across Turkey; into post-Soviet Central Asia and Europe; and also around the globe.

The book examines Gülen's life and teaching in a highly contextualised way in relation to the social, historical, political, and religious environments in which he has lived and with which he has engaged. But in addition, as will become clear in the following chapters, it is also especially done through engaging with the impact of Gülen upon those inspired by his teaching and, in turn, their interactive engagement with him and the further development of his teaching arising out of that. Thus, although sections of this book might seem to be as much about Hizmet as they are about Fethullah Gülen, this is because the book takes an approach that, just as Hizmet cannot be properly understood without an understanding of the person and teaching of Fethullah Gülen, so also Fethullah Gülen cannot be properly understood as an individual alone, but only contextually and interactively with Hizmet.

© The Author(s) 2022
P. Weller, *Fethullah Gülen's Teaching and Practice*,
https://doi.org/10.1007/978-3-030-97363-6_1

1

For those inspired by his teaching, and for many wider observers, Gülen's teaching differentiates the rich traditional inheritance and spirituality of Islam from contemporary 'Islamism.' He advocates in word and deed for the central importance of education. He argues for engagement with science and the modern world, without being a 'modernist,' and he promotes the necessity of inter-religious dialogue without being a 'liberal.' Gülen is, however, also a figure around whom there has been considerable suspicion, contestation, and controversy, both within Turkish society and beyond. In the late 1990s, these suspicions coalesced into a legal process against him (Harrington 2011) on charges, citing video evidence, that he had been plotting to overthrow the secular state. These charges continued to be pursued after he had moved to the USA in 1999 and where, in the context of both this, and of health-related issues, he has lived ever since.

Although he was first acquitted from these charges in 2006 and then, again, on appeal in 2008, those in Turkey who have been suspicious of him have long characterised him as a threat to the secular state. The election of the AKP (*Adalet ve Kalkınma Partisi* or, in English, "Justice and Development Party") to government in 2002 originally gave new opportunities to both pious Muslims in general and to Hizmet in particular as compared with what had been the case under the previous Kemalist hegemony. However, with the changing configurations of Turkish politics following the emergence in 2013 of corruption charges against leading figures in the ruling party and the government's response to that in closing down Hizmet institutions, and especially its schools, Gülen became the target of personal attacks sponsored and/or supported by the current Turkish authorities.

Geographically speaking, during his life in Turkey, Gülen moved from his rural eastern Turkish origins in Ezerun; to the Turkish-European western borderlands in Edirne; and then to the cosmopolitan cities of Izmir and Istanbul. In terms of political context, he experienced the radical fissures and upheavals of the Cold War period when Turkey often seemed to teeter on the brink of civil war between armed factions of the political left and right, resulting in military coups during which he became a wanted person.

The Hizmet movement inspired by him expanded into Europe and the Turkic Central Asian states of the former Soviet Union, and then globally. Following a period during which, in Turkey, there was a relatively close relationship between Hizmet and the AKP in terms of at least a confluence of perceived interest on some major issues (see Weller 2022, Sects. 4.1 and 4.2), from around 2013 onwards the current Turkish authorities increasingly accused Gülen and the Hizmet movement of having created what they identified under the derogatory and threatening name of the *Paralel Devlet Yapılanması* (PDY or, in English, "Parallel State Structure").

Even more intensely, since July 2016, Gülen has been charged with being the leader of what the government identifies as *Fethullahçı Terör Örgütü* (FETÖ or, Fethullahist Terrorist Organization), claiming that Gülen and Hizmet were behind these events, which accusations they strongly deny. Also following the events of July 2016, The Presidency of the Religious Affairs of the Republic of Turkey (2017), the Diyanet, attacked Gülen in theological terms and charged him with being a "cult leader" (p. 5) who, over a number of decades, has "operated under the mask of an educator" (p. 7) and who takes "some of the concepts used in the Sufi tradition and employs them out of context to brainwash his followers" (p. 9).

In the light of all these developments, the Turkish state authorities have undertaken an almost complete dismantling of the network of Hizmet-related organisations within Turkey itself while imprisoning thousands of individuals, and pressuring governments in many other countries, either to hand over to the Turkish government or to shut down Hizmet-related initiatives such as schools, as in the case of the Hizmet Pak-Turk Schools in Pakistan.

Especially since July 2016, the US Government has also been under pressure from the Turkish Government to extradite Gülen himself. Issues related to this also became caught up in US political and public debate around the relationship between key figures in the former Trump administration and foreign governments, including allegations that General Michael Flynn had been involved in discussing a potential 'rendition' of Gülen to Turkey.

Therefore, in addition to scholarly interest in this figure in the areas of theology; Islamic/Muslim studies; Muslim hermeneutics; politics and international relations, given how the USA, Turkey, and many European countries are members of NATO (The North Atlantic Treaty Organization), and especially bearing in mind Turkey's Eurasian geopolitical context and significance, how this global figure and the movement inspired by him and his teaching emerged into global presence and influence and are now dealing with extra-territorial pressures from the current Turkish government and are charting a course for the future, is of considerable strategic import and broad public and current affairs interest.

Indeed, this book is published at a time that is pivotal for both Gülen and Hizmet who find themselves in a significant transitional period, in relation to both Turkey and the USA where he is currently based, but also because Hizmet's previous profile and ways of operating in Turkey itself has effectively been strangulated, while also coming under economic, political, and religious pressure globally. Within the overall context of what this book and its companion volume (Weller 2022) identify as a 'de-centring' of Hizmet from Turkey, a more open self-criticism (see Sect. 5.4) has emerged within parts of Hizmet relative to its experiences in that country, and there has been a growing re-assessment by many associated with Hizmet about its future trajectory or trajectories.

1.2   A RELIGIOUS STUDIES APPROACH

The disciplinary approach of Religious Studies provides the main framework for this study. Within this approach can be found what is known as the 'insider-outsider' problem in the study of religion (McCutcheon Ed. 1999) in which scholarly problems and opportunities are not seen as being exclusively associated with either 'insider' or 'outsider' perspectives. Indeed, in contrast to much mainstream Sociology of Religion, where religions tend to be approached according to the kind of prior sociological theory adopted for understanding them, or of Theology, which usually entails the making and application of normative evaluative judgements, in the non-confessional study of religion known broadly as 'Religious Studies,' there has been a well-established tradition of a broadly phenomenological approach to the understanding of lived religion among individuals and groups (Smart 1973).

Although this overall approach has been critiqued (Flood 1999), its premise that, as far as possible, one should avoid moving too quickly into imposing one's own interpretative (whether theological or sociological) framework without first having sought to understand phenomena as fully as possible in relation to how they present themselves remains an important one. Taking such an initial approach does not mean that one has completely to avoid the responsibility for making evaluative judgements. This is pertinent to how one approaches and understands the teaching and practice of Gülen not least since, as discussed in more detail both later in this chapter, and also in Sect. 6.1 of this book, there are widely differing evaluative judgements made in relation to his person. But it does mean acknowledging that, in understanding any phenomenon, including that of Gülen personally and that of Hizmet collectively, there is a need to take their self-understandings seriously even if ultimately bringing other evaluative and interpretive frameworks to bear upon them.

Inevitably, not everything can be perfectly or fully translated from one language to another, and one of the key issues that emerges in the book is the role that language, translation, and culture play in the hermeneutics of the contextual reception and further development of Gülen's teaching. Nevertheless, as a starting point, a number of key terms and concepts within the book are referred to in their original Turkish form. This includes, for example, in relation to the person of Gülen, the use by some Hizmet-related interviewees of the Turkish honorific title *hocaefendi* (or *Hojaefendi*) that combines *hoca* (or hoja), referring to a teacher, and *efendi*, which signals a traditional respect for those who preach about Islam. In a publication such as this, which aspires to be an academically informed evaluation, the preference is to refer to him and discuss him simply by his civil family name rather than by using terminology that would inevitably be seen by one side of the debate or the other as either honorific or derogatory, although it should also be acknowledged that, among those inspired by him, it can be seen as discourteous simply to refer to him for conciseness, as is done in these books, as Gülen rather than, for example, as Mr. Gülen.

1.3 Situating in the Wider Literature

Not least because of the controversies that have developed around Gülen, it is important to situate this study of Gülen's teaching and practice transparently within the wider literature about him, including the author's own previous research and publications on Gülen and Hizmet. This includes two previously co-edited books on Hizmet, the first by Weller and Yılmaz (2012a), and which contained two co-authored chapters by the co-editors (Weller and Yılmaz 2012b, 2012c) and two chapters by the author (Weller, 2012a, 2012b); the second co-edited by Barton, Weller, and Yılmaz (2013a), and which contained two co-authored chapters by the co-editors (Barton et al. 2013b; Barton et al. 2013) and one chapter by the author (Weller 2013). In this field, the author has also published a co-authored booklet, Weller and Sleap (2014), as well as four single authored book chapters (Weller 2006, 2015a, 2015b, 2017), one of which specifically focused on the development of Hizmet in the UK. In addition, the author was Director of Studies for a University of Derby doctoral thesis discussing the Hizmet movement in relation to social movement theory written by Muhammed Çetin (2008) to whom this book is dedicated.

There is a large amount of literature on Gülen, his teaching and prac- tice—let alone on the Hizmet that has been inspired by this, the latter literature for which is explored in greater detail in this book's companion volume (Weller 2022, Sect. 1.3). Even prior to July 2016, Gülen and Hizmet were a focus of controversy as embodied and reflected in the wide range of publications which form part of the context for the debates that rage around them. Particularly, but not only, in the Turkish language there are a considerable number of publications, albeit of a more journalistic or popularist kind, that are fundamentally designed to attack and discredit Gülen, rather than to evaluate him and his teaching in a sober and prop- erly critical way.

Doğan Koç's (2012) book examines such literature from its earliest appearance in Turkish, in the early 2000s, up to the time of his book's publication when such things were also increasingly appearing in English, especially online. In relation to such works, Koç highlights the different and sometimes mutually contradictory portrayals used in Turkish and English language publications. He explains that while some early Turkish examples of that literature charged that Gülen was intent on establishing an Islamic state to replace the Turkish Republic, by the end of the 1990s onwards, most were relying on the: "…image of the American puppet, the accusation that interfaith dialogue serves the Vatican, and the suggestion that Gülen's alleged Zionism will subvert Islam" (p. 12), with some going even so far as to claim that Gülen is not even a Muslim and secretly works for the Papacy. In English language works of a similar character, Gülen is portrayed as an Islamic 'Trojan Horse' danger to the West, as being at one and the same time "anti-Western and anti-Semitic, and his promotion of tolerance, understanding and interfaith dialogue is simply meant to dis- guise his true intentions of establishing a secret caliphate" (p. 23) through the use of what in Arabic is known as *taqiyya*, or religiously sanctioned dissimulation.

In relation to how these tropes came into existence, operate and are spread, Koç points out that up to the time of his writing, "the Turkish defamations appear primarily in printed materials, such as books, maga- zines and newspapers, the English defamations appear almost exclusively online" (p. 54), with the latter facilitating rapid reproduction. From examining literature of this kind, Koç presents evidence that "One can predict how Gülen is defamed with a 87% accuracy only by looking at the language of the article, regardless of the authors" and that, therefore "The results suggest that Gülen is defamed strategically, not randomly" such that "The authors of such incendiary articles shape their depiction of Gülen according to the primary fears and suspicions of their particular audiences". This analysis leads to the conclusion that: "Therefore the authors who wish to denigrate the work of Gülen and the Hizmet movement resort to these contradictory defamations and model their accusations on the primary fears of their audience rather than any gathered evidence." (p. 36). As an example of such, Koç devotes a chapter (pp. 57–70) to analysing Rachel Sharon-Krespin's (2009) article on "Fethullah Gülen's Grand Ambition: Turkey's Islamist Danger" and discusses evidence for that article's pivotal role in the subsequent appearance of a much larger numbers of similar articles in English than was the case prior to it.

There is also a wide range of literature that reflects the sometimes quite radically different religious, political, and academic disciplinary approaches and evaluations of both Gülen and Hizmet. These include hundreds of journal articles, conference proceedings papers, and book chapters, as well as Masters' and Doctoral theses, representing a variety of disciplinary approaches. A range of scholarly publications about Gülen is reflected in the Oxford University Press' online bibliography of *Muhammed Fethullah Gülen* by Alparslan Açıkgenç (2011). However, since this was last updated only in 2011, its coverage is now somewhat dated. More recently, the scholar Karel Steenbrink (2015) wrote what he calls an introductory "bibliographical essay" on "Fethullah Gülen, Hizmet and Gülenists" (pp. 13–46), while a 2016 edition of the *Hizmet Studies Review* (linked with the movement-funded Gülen Chair at the Catholic University of Leuven, as discussed in Weller 2022, Sect. 3.4) was devoted to a *Hizmet Index, 1996–2015*.[1]

An important part of the research project that underlies this book was the undertaking of a systematic review of research and other literature with which this volume and its companion volume engages. Indeed, the present author is currently working together with İsmail Şezgin on a 'spin off' annotated bibliographical project,[2] with the aim of creating a new and comprehensive annotated bibliography of publications on Hizmet and Gülen, initially in English and Turkish, but with the possibility of extending coverage also to other languages.

The previous section of this chapter noted the so-called 'insider-outsider' problem in the study of religion (McCutcheon ed. 1999). In relation to work by some Hizmet 'insiders,' Yavuz (2013) argues in a footnote that, "their works while informative tend to lack a critical edge" (p. 251). This debate is arguably further complicated by contention over the role and status of 'external' scholars who have presented papers at what Tittensor (2014) calls the "deeply problematic and ultimately counterproductive" flurry of "in-house books and conferences," and which he sees as "little more than a public relations campaign that seeks to capture the field" (p. x).

Indeed, in a more recent book chapter on "Secrecy and Hierarchy in the Gülen Movement and the Question of Academic Responsibility," Tittensor (2018) goes on to develop further his concerns in this regard referring to what he describes as "a major push by the GM to effectively co-opt Western scholars into writing 'academic lite' articles that overlook its more problematic aspects" (pp. 217–218). However, to put the specificity of this issue into some wider context, around two or three decades ago, similar debates took place in relation to the work of scholars working to understand the Unificationist movement and who took part in conferences out of which came related publications that were sponsored by that movement—the various dimensions of, and issues related to which, are discussed in a paper by one of those scholars, George Chryssides (2004) who reflects honestly that "The researcher's role involves several areas of conflict, which are difficult, if not impossible, to resolve" (np).

Clearly, as with conferences in many disciplinary fields where scholars are given an honorarium for preparing and presenting a paper, there are ethical issues to consider in relation to expectation and independence. However, while respectful of Tittensor's work on Hizmet, and understanding the potential grounds for his concerns, this author does not ultimately share Tittensor's scepticism about the nature of such conferences or the value of the literature produced out of them. This is not only because of what could be seen as the potentially self-interested reason that the author's two previous co-edited books on Hizmet originated largely from papers presented at movement-sponsored conferences, albeit that the ultimately published books and two of the book chapters were published by 'mainstream' scholarly publishers. Rather, it is that in the current book and its companion volume, all scholarly publications—including those published by publishers related to Hizmet and those published by commercial academic publishing houses; those written by 'insiders,' as well as those written by 'outsiders'; those that aspire to objectivity and those which are clearly of a strong positionality—are all seen as offering different kinds of valuable insight into Gülen's teaching and practice and how it is received by others, including by those that he, his person, teaching and practice has inspired.

Indeed, despite Tittensor's (2018) strictures in relation to movement-funded conferences and publications, he concluded his own discussion of academic responsibility in relation to studies of Hizmet with the words, "I wish to stress that I am not seeking to impugn the scholarship or the place of insider research but simply counsel that it is important that scholars maintain a critical distance." (p. 232). And in relation to such concerns, it is this author's experience of participating in editorial work for Hizmet conferences that he has been freely able to review and score papers for inclusion or otherwise and also that, in the conferences it sponsors and in other ways, Hizmet has consistently given invitations to 'outsiders' to offer critiques with a consistency and to a degree that is not common among religious groups. For those of us who are outside Islam or Hizmet, the fact that we may not always take the opportunities afforded to us to make our honest, and including properly critical, input is not the fault of Hizmet, but is rather a matter of our scholarly and/or religious/ethical responsibility.

Of course, to operate in a way in which one can read and evaluate texts at multiple levels requires a methodologically sophisticated and critical hermeneutical engagement with the texts concerned. In relation to the Hizmet movement, such a theoretical discussion linked with worked examples can be found in Florian Volm's (2017) German language book, *Die Gülen-Bewegung im Spiegel von Selbsdarstellung und Fremdrezption* (or, in the author's English translation of this, *The Gülen Movement in the Mirror of Self-Representation and External Reception*). Taking an approach of this kind, while no scholarly literature will be excluded from consideration in this book, there will be a transparent acknowledgement of both the locus and type of the publications concerned.

In considering published works in English with a specific focus on Gülen himself, as distinct from a discussion of the Hizmet inspired by his teaching and practicec, in particular with reference to the movement in Europe, is more the focus of this book's companion volume (Weller 2022), it should be noted that a number of short biographies of Gülen exist (see Sect. 2.1). Some of these tend towards the hagiographical. However, Professor Jon Pahl of the Lutheran Theological Seminary in

Philadelphia worked for some years on a more properly scholarly biography of Gülen, bringing to bear Pahl's skills as an historian of religion. His book *Fethullah Gülen: A Life of Hizmet* was published in 2019 by the Blue Dome Press (a publishing house associated with the movement). Among other monographs coming from publishing houses connected with Hizmet and which focus on Gülen himself and his teaching are Carroll (2007); Albayrak (2011); Khan (2011); Ergil (2012); Kurt (2013); Wagner (2013); Grinell (2014); Dumanlı (2015); Mercan (2016); and Ashrati (2017).

The only scholarly single author book treatments in English that centrally focus on Gülen, his thinking, and practice, and which are published by publishing houses not associated with Hizmet, are Robinson (2017), which focuses specifically on the ethical aspects of his teaching; and Valkenberg (2015), which is a Christian theological evaluation of Gülen and his teaching. There is also Harrington's (2011) discussion of the Turkish legal processes and trials around Gülen, and Koç's (2012) previously mentioned discussion of defamatory works about Gülen. Other monographs which do discuss Gülen's thinking, teaching, and practice, but do so in a way that ultimately focuses more on the movement he inspired include, for example, Yavuz's (2013) seminal work, *Towards an Islamic Enlightenment: The Gülen Movement.*

Closest to the current book, both because of their publishers, their focus, and their approaches, are the monographs above from Robinson and Valkenberg, while Pahl's book is perhaps the closest of all in terms of substance. As with the current book and its companion volume (Weller 2022), and in contrast to much academic work on Gülen coming from a more sociological and especially political science disciplinary perspective, Robinson, Valkenberg and Pahl's books emphasise, the fundamentally *religious* nature of Gülen and his teaching.

Alongside these authored and edited books are many hundreds of journal articles and book chapters representing a variety of disciplinary approaches and evaluative stances in relation to Gülen and Hizmet. From among these, one new edited collection of book chapters should be particularly noted—both because of its publication following July 2016 and also because of the critical (albeit varied) perspectives it contains on the question of the involvement or otherwise of the Gülen and the Hizmet movement in those events. This is *Turkey's July 15th Coup: What Happened and Why?*, edited by Hakan Yavuz and Bayram Balcı (2018), albeit that the essays in it are more concerned with Turkey than directly with Gülen's teaching.

In addition to all the above publications there is, of course, also a range of other publications, from magazine through to newspaper articles which also form part of the context for the debates that rage around this Turkish and global figure and the movement inspired by him. Since these in themselves form part of what might be called relevant "social data," they will also be taken account of and engaged with where appropriate, albeit also on a basis informed by transparency concerning their locus and modes of production.

1.4   Evidence, Aims, and Methods

Research and scholarship undertaken into movements and people subject to religious and political contention can be subject to many challenges, some of which are informed by real issues; while others can be more to do with perceptions, whether accurate or inaccurate; and still others (including also among scholars) can be the product of ideological or prejudicial stances in relation to which there has been insufficient reflexive and self-critical awareness.

In the Preface to his book on Hizmet, Tittensor (2014) explains his aim to "make a serious empirical contribution" that provides "insight into the lived realities of those that work within the movement and those that are touched by it" (p. x). By gathering primary research data through interviews with Gülen and his close associates this book, like Tittensor's, aims also to provide such empirically informed insight into the lived realities of Fethullah Gülen, those who have been close to him and others who have been inspired by him.

Alongside being able to draw upon two decades worth of informal knowledge of, and conversations and interaction with those associated with Hizmet, this was achieved by means of conducting twenty-nine semi-structured in-depth narrative interviews which, through participants' stories, collated evidence of underpinning cultural milieux, social contexts, and personal attitudes. One limitation of the fieldwork, and therefore potential criticism of the book that must be acknowledged and taken seriously, is that the vast majority of the formal interviews that inform this book took place with men. This partly reflects the reality that, as discussed in Weller 2022, Sect. 5.7, Hizmet is still quite strongly reflective of patriarchy in terms of both its Turkish and Muslim heritages. When coupled with the choice made to give significant voice to those who have been Fethullah Gülen's historically close associates and to interviewees in Europe who have had public roles within Hizmet-related groups (primarily on the grounds that in the post-2016 context interviewees already known to be publicly aligned with Hizmet might be less hesitant to go on the record) this inevitably had further gender-related consequences.

Recognising the gender balance limitations of the interviews, the author has tried in terms of other published sources, to pay special attention to those that concern the position and perspectives of women within the movement (for example: Curtis 2010, 2012; Hassencahl 2012; Pandaya 2012; and Rausch 2012, 2014). Nevertheless, despite these mitigating factors, it remains the case that it is likely that both companion volumes will, in due course, need complementing, critiquing, and quite probably correcting by primary interviews with emergent women leaders in Hizmet, and also by more conscious and systematically applied specifically feminist perspectives and approaches, some work on which has been commenced, among others, by Raja (2013) and Fougner (2017).

Despite these acknowledged limitations, it is to a large degree the raw nature of the contributions made by interview participants, and who in this book are frequently 'given voice' directly in quotations, as well in summarised form, that brings a particular focus and power to the wider discussions of the book. Of course, when it comes to a more analytical consideration of the raw interview data and observations of the researcher, neither can straightforwardly and without qualification be taken as having any especially privileged status that is not itself subject to further analysis. Therefore, as a matter of transparency, it should be stated that this research was conducted in the course of the author's employment at Regent's Park College in the University of Oxford. It was funded through charitable donations made for this purpose to the College by anonymous donors and channelled via the Dialogue Society, a UK registered charity (No. 1117039) which, on its website, acknowledges its inspiration from Gülen.[3] The Dialogue Society therefore has had a material interest in this book and research that lies behind it. That interest was also represented in the project's reference group, of which some representatives of the Dialogue Society were a part, along with senior scholars from the College.

However, in relation to research on religion (as in other fields) in a university context, it is quite possible to have an ultimate funding source for research that may or may not have expectations for, and/or be welcoming or not of the work that is actually produced, while having confidence in the academic integrity and rigour of the publication and its underlying research. In contrast with consultancy, in which the integrity of the research depends on the nature of the contractual relationship that is directly between the commissioner of the research and the person, persons or company that conducts it, higher education institutions have systems in place that control for potential challenges to the integrity of externally funded research, and the funders of research who work through higher education institutions accept such controls.

In this instance, the funding agreement with the College for the research included a clear statement relating to the College's academic independence and the author's academic freedom, thus safeguarding the independence, integrity, and results of the project. In addition, the project went through a rigorous research ethics scrutiny and approval process at the University of Oxford, as one of the world's leading research universities, and which took account of the University's Conflict of Interest policy. Within these processes, the funding source and arrangements governing the research were made transparent and the approaches to be taken to the research were set out and discussed in a detailed way, resulting in the formal ethical approval that undergirds the rigour and integrity of the research.[4]

However, it remains the case that those who conduct research and write for publication are necessarily affected by their disciplinary, religious, and civil society backgrounds and commitments. Transparency in relation to such is particularly important when research deals with individuals and groups that have been the focus of controversy. In this case, it should therefore be made clear that the author works broadly in the study of religion rather than that of political science, the latter of which, along with sociology, are the disciplines from within which many scholars have hitherto approached these matters. When dealing with phenomena which, at the least, present themselves to others in terms of a religious inspiration, the epistemological presuppositions and social understandings that the researchers inevitably bring to their disciplines and the subject matter of their research entail both potential benefits and limitations. One of the lessons that has been pressed home by, among others, advocates of feminist and decolonising epistemologies and methodologies is that, however rigorously scholars seek to operate within their disciplinary norms, neither they nor their disciplinary traditions are neutral—even, and perhaps are especially not so, when they purport to be.

Thus, in terms of personal positionality it should be acknowledged that the author is a religious believer and practitioner, albeit within (the Baptist tradition of) Christianity rather than within Islam. Thus, for all that it is the case that the research lying behind this book and its companion volume draws on social scientific methodologies and literatures, informed by over two decades of personal knowledge of, and interaction with, Hizmet and an extensive engagement with the literature about Fethullah Gülen and Hizmet, it is ultimately the author's professional judgement that, in order to understand Fethullah Gülen and Hizmet in as fully an adequate a way as possible, one needs to recognise and to acknowledge the primarily religious register in which they at least understand themselves to be operating.

According to the African scholar, Achille Mmembe (2016), it is both possible and important to work within a "a process of knowledge production that is open to epistemic diversity" (p. 37). At the same time, in advocating this, Mbembe is quick to anticipate the critique that such an approach might lead to an epistemological, cultural, and ethical relativism by arguing that such an approach "does not necessarily abandon the notion of universal knowledge for humanity," but rather that pluriversity itself embraces the possibility of a universal knowledge for humanity *"via a horizontal strategy of openness to dialogue among different epistemic traditions"* (italics in the original).

In terms of the relationship between one's position and approach as a scholar and one's engagements and responsibilities as a citizen, the author should also acknowledge both currently being—and also having been for a number of years—a member of the Board of Advisors of the Dialogue Society. A readiness to act in such a capacity is, of course, distinct from being in membership or having similar categories of direct personal alignment. Nevertheless, readiness to act in this capacity signals the fact that, evaluatively speaking, overall the author takes a critically sympathetic approach to the practice of Hizmet and the teaching of Fethullah Gülen. It also means that, in addition to any ways in which one's academic work may impact upon and influence the development of Hizmet, that in the context of the Board of Advisors role the present author has, on occasion, either individually and/or as part of the wider Board, made recommendations to it on matters that are discussed later in this book, including that of transparency around the inspiration for the Dialogue Society's work as having been drawn from the person and teaching Fethullah Gülen (Weller

2022, Sect. 5.4), and encouragement to the Society to engage with other organisations of Muslim inspiration (Weller 2022, Sect. 5.6).

Such a role also enables the possibility of having an awareness of, and perhaps more access to, some important and sometimes sensitive internal discussions and debates. At the same time, ethically, it is important to differentiate such informal knowledge from data that is collected when one is acting formally as a researcher which is only used here within the principles and practice of 'informed consent.'

Finally, in the light of a note on the *Turkishinvitations* website that "there is no such thing as a free Turkey trip,"[5] the author should also acknowledge that, in 2008, he also took part in a study visit to Turkey and Hizmet institutions there at the invitation of the UK's Dialogue Society. Nevertheless, as with the author's previously noted experience concerning Hizmet-sponsored conferences, participation in such a trip certainly did not preclude the asking of sharp and robust questions. Details of some of those that were posed by the author in an 18 July 2008 paper, circulated to participants as part of the preparations for the trip, are set out in detail in Sect. 6.1 of this book.

As Tittensor (2014) acknowledged when arguing for the importance of trying to make an empirically based contribution, his approach was also "not value-neutral" (p. x). In all of this, therefore, awareness of oneself and transparency before others is the main means by which there can be control for potentially illegitimate bias. This is, in turn, a part of what the widely acknowledged parent of the discipline of Religious Studies, Ninian Smart (1973), used to called the importance of "axioanalysis" in the study of religion. Of this, he argued that particularly in relation to any attempt at a cross-cultural approach to religion, one "should stimulate some degree of self-awareness. It is as though we should undergo axioanalysis – a kind of evaluational equivalent to psychoanalysis: what has been called more broadly 'values clarification'. Or perhaps we might call it 'own-worldview analysis.' " (p. 265). Especially in such hotly debated areas as those that are under discussion in this book, both contributors to the research, and researchers themselves are inevitably also actors in a social process.

In relation to this, HE1 (see Acknowledgements), an anonymous interviewee publicly associated with Hizmet in Europe, said, "For me it was really a good reflection," commenting further that he otherwise "didn't have time for." Finally because of the extensive number of imprisonments without trial, deprivation of employment and assets, and actions pursuing guilt by mere association with Fethullah Gülen and/or Hizmet which followed the July 2016, in contrast with Tittensor's (2018) counsel that "it is important that scholars maintain 'a critical distance' " as between "two polar-opposite narratives" (p. 232) of what "actually transpired" (p. 218), there is at least a case that one might argue that such a context calls rather for scholars to be ready to take the risk of adopting a clear overall position in terms of becoming consciously (rather than, in any case actually being so, but unconsciously) a social actor in relation to the human issues at stake.

Adopting such a conscious position of scholar as also social actor entails a readiness to accept the responsibility that in doing so, it is in principle possible that one's evaluations and associated choices might be wrong. Therefore, in moving beyond critical distance alone and incorporating positionality in a way that is academically and ethically responsible, this can only be attempted on the basis of being as informed as possible through aspiring to gain as much empirical insight as possible into lived realities of what is being researched, alongside being as self-aware as possible of one's own value and epistemological positionalities through the application to oneself and one's academic approach of a rigorous axioanalysis.

Notes

1. Issue Number 4.
2. This project is also being conducted (2019–20) at Regent's Park College, University of Oxford. Like the project behind this book and its companion volume, it is also being funded through the Dialogue Society including through a contribution from crowd funding, see https://www.youtube.com/watch?v=oVvFkDKQsOM.
3. http://www.dialoguesociety.org/about-us.html, 2021.
4. University of Oxford Humanities and Social Sciences Divisional Research Ethics Committee Reference No: R52855/RE001.
5. https://turkishinvitations.weebly.com/the-interfaith-dialog-bubble.html, 3.10.2010.

References

Açıkgenç, Alparslan. (2011, last modified). *Muhammed Fethullah Gülen*. Oxford Bibliographies Online. Oxford: Oxford University Press.
Albayrak, Ismail (2011). *Mastering Knowledge in Modern times: Fethullah Gülen as an Islamic Scholar*. New York: Blue Dome Press.

Ashrati, Sulayman (2017). *A Contemporary Renaissance: Gülen's Philosophy for a Global Revival of Civilization.* New York: Blue Dome Press.

Barton, Greg, Weller, Paul and Yılmaz, İhsan. (Eds) (2013a). *The Muslim World and Politics in Transition: Creative Contributions of the Gülen Movement.* London: Bloomsbury.

Barton, Greg, Weller, Paul and Yılmaz, İhsan (2013b). Fethullah Gülen, the Movement and This Book: An Introductory Overview. In Greg Barton, Paul Weller, İhsan Yılmaz (Eds.), *The Muslim World and Politics in Transition: Creative Contributions of the Gülen Movement,* (pp. 1–12). London: Bloomsbury.

Barton, Greg, Yılmaz, İhsan, and Weller, Paul (2013c). Towards a Conclusion: Fethullah Gülen, the Hizmet and the Changing 'Muslim World'. In Greg Barton, Paul Weller, İhsan Yılmaz (Eds.), *The Muslim World and Politics in Transition: Creative Contributions of the Gülen Movement* (pp. 209–216). London: Bloomsbury.

Carroll, Jill (2007). *A Dialogue of Civilizations: Gülen's Islamic Ideals and Humanistic Discourse.* New Jersey: The Light.

Çetin, Muhammad (2008). *Collective Identity and Action of the Gülen Movement: Implications for Social Movement Theory.* Doctoral Thesis. Derby: University of Derby.

Chryssides, George (2004). 50 Years Unification: Conflicts, Responsibilities and Rights. Paper presented at 2004 CESNUR international conference at Baylor University, Waco, Texas, June 18–20, https://www.cesnur.org/2004/waco_chryssides.htm.

Curtis, Maria (2010). Reflections on Women in the Gülen Movement: Muslim Women's Public Spheres, Yesterday, Today, and Tomorrow. In Gurkan Çelik and Martien Brinkman (Eds.), *Mapping the Gülen Movement: A Multidimensional Approach, Conference Papers from Felix Meritis, Amsterdam, The Netherlands, October 7th 2010,* (pp. 162–86). Amsterdam: Dialog Academie and VISOR Institute for the Study of Religion, Culture and Society.

Curtis, Maria (2012). Among the Heavenly Branches: Leadership and Authority among Women in the Gülen Hizmet Movement. In Tamer Balcı and Christopher Miller (Eds.), *The Gülen Hizmet Movement: Circumspect Activism in Faith Based Reform* (pp. 119–154). Newcastle: Cambridge Scholars Publishing.

Dumanlı, Ekrem (2015), *Time to Talk: An Exclusive Interview with Fethullah Gülen,* New York: Blue Dome.

Ergil, Doğu (2012). *Fethullah Gülen and the Gülen Mmovement in 100 questions.* New York: Blue Dome Press.

Flood, Gavin (1999). *Beyond Phenomenology: Rethinking the Study of Religion.* London: Bloomsbury.

Fougner, Tore (2017). Fethullah Gülen's Understanding of Women's Rights in Islam: A Critical Reappraisal, *Turkish Studies, 18* (2), 251–277. https://doi. org/10.1080/14683849.2016.1245582

Grinell, Klas (2014). *Reflections on Reason, Religion, and Tolerance: Engaging with Fethullah Gülen's Ideas.* New York: Blue Dome Press.

Harrington, James (2011). *Wrestling with Free Speech, Religious Freedom and Democracy: The Political times and Trials of Fethullah Gülen.* Lanham, Maryland: University Press of America.

Hassencahl, Fran (2012). Framing Women's Issues in the Fountain Magazine. In Sophia Pandaya and Nancy Gallagher (Eds.), *The Gülen Hizmet Movement and Its Transnational Activities: Case Studies of Altruistic Activism in Contemporary Islam* (pp. 117–132). Boca Raton: Brown Water Press.

Khan, M. Maimul Ahsan (2011). *The Vision and Impact of Fethullah Gülen: A New Paradigm for Social Activism.* New York: Blue Dome Press.

Koç, Doğan (2012). *Strategic Defamation of Fethullah Gülen: English Versus Turkish.* Lanham, Maryland: University Press of America.

Kurt, Ercan (2013). *A Fethullah Gülen Reader: So That Others May Live.* New York: Blue Dome Press.

McCutcheon, Russell. (Ed.) (1999). *The Insider/Outsider Problem in the Study of Religion: A Reader.* London: Continuum.

Mbembe, Achille Joseph (2016). Decolonizing the University: New Directions. *Arts and Humanities in Higher Education, 15* (1), 29–45. https://doi. org/10.1177/1474022215618513

Mercan, Faruk (2016). *No Return from Democracy: A Survey of Interviews with Fethullah Gülen.* New York: Blue Dome Press.

Pahl, Jon (2019). *Fethullah Gülen: A Life of Hizmet.* New York: Blue Dome Press.

Pandaya, Sophia (2012). Creating Peace on Earth through Hicret (Migration): Women Gülen Followers in America. In Sophia Pandaya and Nancy Gallagher (Eds.), *The Gülen Hizmet Movement and Its Transnational Activities: Case Studies of Altruistic Activism in Contemporary Islam* (pp. 97–116) Boca Raton: Brown Water Press.

Presidency of the Religious Affairs of the Republic of Turkey, The (2017). *Gülenist Terrorist Organization: A Sponsored Exploitation of Islam and Muslims.* Volume 1 of 2. Trans. Hans E. Strauss. No place of publication given.

Raja, Aamir Hanif (2013). Role of Women in Hizmet and Feminist Movement: A Comparative Analysis. *Pakistan Journal of Social Sciences, 33* (2), 321–329. https://www.bzu.edu.pk/PJSS/Vol33No22013/PJSS_Vol33%20No%20 2_2013_08.pdf

Rausch, Margaret (2012). Gender and Leadership in the Gülen Movement: Women Affiliates' Contributions to East-West Encounters. In Sophia Pandaya and Nancy Gallagher (Eds.), *The Gülen Hizmet Movement and Its Transnational Activities: Case Studies of Altruistic Activism in Contemporary Islam* (pp. 133–159). Boca Raton: Brown Water Press,

Rausch, Margaret (2014). " 'A Bucket with a Hole': Hizmet Women and the Pursuit of Personal and Professional Progress Through Sohbetler (Spiritual Conversations). *Hizmet Studies Review*, *1* (1), 73–79.

Robinson, Simon (2017). *The Spirituality of Responsibility: Fethullah Gülen and Islamic Thought.* London: Bloomsbury.

Sharon-Krespin, Rachel (2009). Fethullah Gülen's Grand Ambition: Turkey's Islamist Danger. *Middle East Quarterly*, Winter, 55–66. https://www.meforum.org/2045/fethullah-gulens-grand-ambition

Smart, Ninian (1973). *The Phenomenon of Religion.* Basingstoke: Macmillan.

Steenbrink, Karel (2015). Fethullah Gülen, Hizmet and Gülenists. A Bibliographical Essay. In Gürkan Çelik, Johann Leman and Karel Steenbrink (Eds.), *Gülen-Inspired Hizmet in Europe: The Western Journey of a Turkish Muslim movement* (pp. 13–46). Brussels: Peter Lang.

Tittensor, David (2014). *The House of Service: The Gülen Movement and Islam's Third Way.* Oxford: Oxford University Press.

Tittensor, David (2018). Secrecy and Hierarchy in the Gülen Movement and the Question of Academic Responsibility? In Hakan Yavuz and Bayram Balcı (Eds), *Turkey's July 15th Coup: What Happened and Why?* (pp. 217–236). Salt Lake City: University of Utah Press.

Valkenberg, Pim (2015). *Renewing Islam by Service: A Christian View of Fethullah Gülen and the Hizmet Movement.* Washington D.C.: Catholic University of America Press.

Volm, Florian (2017). *Die Gülen-Bewegung im Spiegel von Selbsdarstellung und Fremdrezption: Eine Textuelle Performanzanalyse der Schiften der BerfürterInnen (Innenperspektive) und KritikerInnen (Aussenspeckive)* [English translation by the author of this book: *The Gülen Movement in the Mirror of Self-Reflection and External Reception: A Textual Performance Analysis of the Writings of the Proponents (Internal Perspective) and Critics (External Perspective)].* Baden Baden: Ergon Verlag.

Wagner, Walter (2013). *Beginnings and Endings: Fethullah Gulen's Vision for Today's World.* New York: Blue Dome Press.

Weller, Paul (2006). Fethullah Gülen, Religions, Globalization and Dialogue. In Robert Hunt and Yüksal A. Aslandoğan (Eds.), *Muslim Citizens of the Globalized world: Contributions of the Gülen Movement* (pp. 75–88). Somerset: New Jersey, The Light Inc. and IID Press.

Weller, Paul (2012a). Dialogue and Transformative Resources: Perspectives from Fethullah Gülen on Religion and Public Life. In Paul Weller İhsan Yılmaz (Eds.), *European Muslims, Civility and Public Life: Perspectives on and From the Gülen Movement* (pp. 3–19). London: Continuum.

Weller, Paul (2012b). Robustness and Civility: Themes from Fethullah Gülen as Resource and Challenge for Government, Muslims and Civil Society in the United Kingdom. In Paul Weller and İhsan Yılmaz, *European Muslims, Civility and Public Life: Perspectives on and From the Gülen Movement* (pp. 143–59). London: Continuum.

Weller, Paul (2013). Fethullah Gülen, Turkey and the European Union. In Greg Barton, Paul Weller and İhsan Yılmaz (Eds.), *The Muslim World and Politics in Transition: Creative Contributions of the Gülen Movement* (pp. 108–125). London: Bloomsbury.

Weller, Paul (2015a). The Gülen Movement in the United Kingdom. In Gürkan Çelik, Johan Leman and Karel Steenbrink, *Gülen-Inspired Hizmet in Europe: The Western Journey of a Turkish Muslim Movement* (pp. 239–251). Brussels: Peter Lang.

Weller, Paul (2015b). Islam in Turkey as Shaped by the State, its Founder and its History: Insight Through Baptist Eyes and Three Key Muslim Figures. In Raimundo Barreto Jnr, Kenneth Sehested, Luis Rivera-Pagán and Paul Hayes (Eds.), *Engaging the Jubilee: Freedom and Justice Papers of the Baptist World Alliance (2010–2015)* (pp. 193–209). Falls Church, Virginia: Baptist World Alliance.

Weller, Paul (2017). Religious Freedom in the Baptist Vision and in Fethullah Gülen: Resources for Muslims and Christians. In John Barton (Ed.), *A Muslim Sage Among Peers: Fethullah Gülen in Dialogue with Christians* (pp. 133–156). Blue Dome, New Jersey.

Weller, Paul (2022). *Hizmet in Transitions: European Developments of a Turkish Muslim-Inspired Movement*. London: Palgrave Macmillan.

Weller, Paul and Sleap, Frances (2014). *Gülen on Dialogue*. London: Centre for Hizmet Studies.

Weller, Paul and Yılmaz, İhsan (Eds.) (2012a). *European Muslims, Civility and Public Life: Perspectives on and From the Gülen Movement*. London: Continuum.

Weller, Paul and Yılmaz, İhsan (2012b). Fethullah Gülen, the Movement and This Book: An Introductory Overview. In Paul Weller and İhsan Yılmaz (2012b). *European Muslims, Civility and Public life: Perspectives on and From the Gülen Movement* (pp. xxi–xxxiv). London: Continuum.

Weller, Paul and Yılmaz, İhsan (2012c). Conclusion: Fethullah Gülen and the Hizmet: Towards an Evaluation. In Paul Weller and İhsan Yılmaz (Eds.), *European Muslims, Civility and Public Life: Perspectives on and From the Gülen Movement* (pp. 199–210). London: Continuum.

Yavuz, Hakan (2013). *Toward an Islamic Enlightenment: the Gülen Movement*. Oxford: Oxford University Press.

Yavuz, Hakan and Balcı, Bayram (Eds.) (2018). *Turkey's July 15th Coup: What Happened and Why?* Salt Lake City: University of Utah Press.

PART I

Turkish Muslim Scholar, Preacher, and Activist

CHAPTER 2

Person, Places, and Development

2.1 Biographies of Fethullah Gülen

In a footnote, Hakan Yavuz (2013) identified Latif Erdoğan (1995), writing in Turkish, and also Ali Ünal and Alphonse Williams (2000), writing in English, as the main sources for Gülen's biography, noting that both Erdoğan and Ünal are "very close to Gülen" (p. 252) although Erdoğan (who is not related to Turkish President Recep Tayyip Erdoğan) has since broken with Gülen. There is, however, also the somewhat unusual book by Farid al-Ansari (2015), originally published in 2011 in Arabic and now available in English. Like the biography by Erdoğan and the Alphonse and Williams book, al-Ansari's book is published by the movement press. In fact, Blue Dome has promoted al-Ansari's book with a cover sticker that states it is a "novel," while in its Preface, the author al-Ansari says that the text he has produced "might be considered a novel, a biography, a poem or a history book" but that he himself was "not exactly sure what it should be considered." What, however, he does say that he knows is that the book is "a story of a spirit in anguish" connected with "the heart of a man from Anatolia whose radiance has abundantly flowed upon the whole world!" (np).

Since Yavuz's summary of these biographical sources, and in contrast with al-Ansari's more subjectively reflective meditation, Jon Pahl (2019), an American historian of religion, has more recently written a full-length biography in English, which has also been published by the movement's Blue Dome Press. Overall, in relation to Gülen's biography, Gülen's close

© The Author(s) 2022   25
P. Weller, *Fethullah Gülen's Teaching and Practice*,
https://doi.org/10.1007/978-3-030-97363-6_2

associate and interviewee Ahmet Kurucan (see Acknowledgements) says: "One could classify his lifetime into several stages starting from Erzurum first; then Edirne second; then he moved to Izmir; then he came to Istanbul – and I split Istanbul into two: before 1992 and after 1992 until 1999 when he moved to the US is the final stage in the United States."

2.2   Erzurum: Traditional Contextualisation

Muhammed Fethullah Gülen was born in the small village of Korucuk, in the Erzurum region of eastern Turkey on 27 April 1941. An editorial note in al-Ansari (2015) states of his given name Fethullah that it has "roots in the Arabic words *fath* and *Allah*, meaning 'Conquest of Allah' or 'Opening the Door to Divine Mercy and Benevolence'." (p. 1). In Korocuk, the contextualisation of the growth and development of his thinking and acting was primarily one of a deeply nurturing environment rooted in the traditions of Anatolian Islam. Gülen's father Ramiz was an *imam* and, by the age of ten, the young Fethullah had read the Qur'an. As Gülen's close associate and interviewee, Hamdullah Öztürk (see Acknowledgements) explained:

> One should take account of the importance of the home Gülen was raised. Especially his grandmother had a great influence on him. She was a woman of great love for God and the Prophet. She was immersed to the point of intoxication for the love of God and the divine. So, his subconscious developed with that love from early years of his childhood. When his grandmother heard the name of God twice, she would pass out. He grew up with that huge love for the divine. His father was an *imam* in this *tekke*, a Sufi lodge of Alvarli Efe who was like a spiritual prototype for Gülen. So, when his thoughts and spiritual world were being shaped, his first role models and prototypes were the Prophet, his Companions and other saintly leaders. These prototypes were the ones who were able to produce a civilization out of sand, out of the desert. Also, his family genealogy has this connection to the two great *pashas*, two uncles of his mother, one was a great *pasha* in Edirne, in the most western part of Turkey next to Greece. He was a general. And the other was also a general, in Medina. They both defended those cities in the First World War. So, there is this noble historical backdrop to his identity as well.

When interviewed, Gülen explained about the effect of upon him within this period of one other key Islamically prototypical person, as follows:

> In my childhood I have seen one such person, who is the *imam*, Mohammed, of the town, or the village, of Alvar, although I was not in an age or development to be his student, he always treated me as if I were his student. And love of God, and love of the Prophet, and love of the whole creation could be seen in his person, in his life. He often cried upon recitation of certain verses or prophetic sayings. And if somebody said something inappropriate about the Prophet or about God almost his heart stopped, he was so sensitive.

Even more personally, he then went on to explain the influence of some key members of his own family, and especially that of his grandfather, Ahmet Efendi, as well as of his own parents, Ramiz and Razia:

> Among my family, extended family members, my mother's father Ahmet Efendi was a person who, nobody recalls any incident in which he harmed or disturbed anybody. He was very sensitive, very caring person. And according to my family members he was reciting the whole Qur'an every three days. So he was compassion personified. For a long while I've never noticed him actually getting angry. My father's father was a very serious person, so much that when he was walking by a gathering, people would, if they were sitting, they would stand up, they respected him so much. He was a very serious person, but he also was very caring and did not hurt or harm anybody. My father and mother also exemplified this spirit. I cannot claim that I have actually inherited their sensitivity or devotion.

Öztürk recounts that, "It was in the second or third grade that Fethullah Gülen stopped going to public school." While some have pointed to such a short period of formal education as a basis for attacking Gülen, Öztürk's evaluation of this is that "This is how, I believe, he was protected from the dictates of the education system of the Turkish Republic. There was no religion at all, basically. They were basically shaping, forming the generation to a certain goal: that ideology had that vision." Öztürk says that Gülen then went on to study in a *madrassah*, of which Öztürk said "Many of the literature that were being taught there were irrelevant to our times, they were written centuries back, but they kept on studying the same literature, over and over."

By the age of 14, Gülen had preached his first sermons. After graduating from a private divinity school in Erzurum, he was licensed under Turkey's Diyanet system to act as an *imam*, including to preach and to teach. However, as Öztürk explains "What he experienced in Erzurum was extremism, extreme conservatism, which really was very tough to break through, that constituted a set of its own problems." Kurucan says of Gülen at this time that:

> So, in Erzurum what you would really see is a very deeply pious Hojaefendi, with really orthodox understanding which is no different from the rest of the community of scholars all the time that he was in that Erzurum province. So, he was very conservative in those years. In my terminology, we cannot say if someone is really like reactionary. He is living in the past, he is not in the 20th century. Very orthodox.

Öztürk notes, though, that it was also during this period that Gülen heard of Bediüzzaman Said Nursi (1873–1960), who had been a renewing influence in Islam in relation to modernity (Mardin 1989; Turner and Hurkuç 2008) so that, "When a student of Nursi with the name Muzaffer came to the town, Gülen and his *madrassah* friends, were invited by Mehmet Kırkıncı to attend his reading circle." However, Öztürk went on to note that when the time came for the second circle meeting, only Gülen turned up and that this was because "They did not agree with the way in which the *Hadith* and traditions were being interpreted in Nursi's works. They could not reconcile what they learned at *madrassah* with how Nursi interprets this knowledge; only Gülen was able to make that transition." Therefore, he also stayed overnight with the students, watching them in their night prayers and, from his observation of this he concluded that it was possible, also today, to live like the original Companions of the Prophet Muhammad. As Öztürk summarised it:

> That's the first time he can see people really acting out the stories that he heard from his father, from that *imam*, from his grandmother: that these people are really leaving the world behind, as the Prophet did going out to exile to another city, and keeping himself separated, free, from those worldly aspirations. So, this is really a possible thing.

This was, in many ways the biographical origin of the expansion of Gülen's vision, from Erzerum to the world, with Öztürk recalling of him that:

> This is the first time that encounter took place of a man who grew up with the stories of that noble history, stories of people who really created that huge, honourable civilization out of the desert sand, and with the people who can really achieve the same thing, perhaps, in the modern times. I even heard him say once that he was always dreaming of such a world even from his early childhood. That connection of the human being with the life, and that connection of the life with the universe, that triangle: human being, life and the universe, he saw with the teachings of Nursi that could be done not only by religious studies, but also through the study of the universe, through natural science.

2.3   EDIRNE: SECULAR AND PLURAL CONTEXTUALISATION

From 1963 to 1966, Gülen moved to live in Edirne and Kırklareli, near the Bulgarian border. Edirne, formerly known as Adrianople, was between 1369 and 1453 the capital city of the Ottoman Empire. In terms of Turkey's geographical, intellectual, and spiritual landscape, this represented a radically different environment: geographically in the European, rather than in the Asian part of Turkey; intellectually in organic contact with Western ideas; and in overall atmosphere, more secular.

This environment fed into a different kind of contextualisation of Gülen's thought and action. This was in the sense that, in contrast with the perhaps more 'taken for granted' inheritance and environment represented by Korucuk and Erzurum, Edirne represented an environment of challenge to a 'received Islam' in which very little could be taken for granted. As characterised by Öztürk, "Hojaefendi with his piety, that godliness, praying all the time, was praised, and people really praised the way he lived in Erzurum." But then "After Erzurum, from the far east of Turkey he goes to the far west of the country to Edirne, which is the opposite to all he grew up with." It is generally seen as an area where not many people practice religion and where there can also be anti-religious currents. It was also in Edirne that Gülen "comes face to face with the police – he has become *persona non grata*, with the way he came from Erzurum, as a pious man. They actually kept a policeman at his doorstep to cut his access to the rest of the community." Thus, in this environment, in many ways, began the history of tension between Gülen's life, teaching, and work and those elements of the Turkish state that were, at very least, suspicious of him.

It was in this context that, as Öztürk further explains, Gülen "was able to see whether his studies from the past could really respond to the world he was now facing in Edirne." Having experienced the conservatism of Erzurum, "In Erdirne in the west, he saw another domain of problems which actually was arising from antagonism towards religion, an animosity towards faith and practice." The challenge and opportunity of contextualisation between these different geographical and ideological locations arguably lies at the personal and experiential roots of Gülen's development of a life, teaching, and inspiration geared towards charting what Ahmet Kuru (2003) has called Gülen's search for a "middle way" in the relationship between Islam and modernity.

Edirne was also the place where Gülen had his first direct and significant experience of encounter with religious plurality in terms of meeting with individuals and communities from other than Muslim religious traditions. Edirne is, for example, an important place for Bahá'ís, being where the founder of the Bahá'í faith, Bahá'u'lláh (whose house in Edirne can still be visited today), lived in exile between 1863 and 1868 before being further banished to the Ottoman penal colony in Akka (now in the modern state of Israel). The Bahá'í tradition can—for many contemporary Sunni Muslims, as for the historical Ottoman Empire—be at the least controversial because of its claims to bring further revelation beyond that conveyed through Moses, Jesus, and Muhammad, but Öztürk recalled that, while there, "Gülen visited their places of worship and he met them." Öztürk also noted that "He met the Jewish leaders, he went to their synagogues to observe the way they prayed." Edirne is the site of Kal Kadoş Agadol (or Great Synagogue) which was originally opened for worship on the eve of Pesach in April, 1909, replacing 13 previous synagogues that had been destroyed in the city's great fire of 1905. At its peak in the early twentieth century, the Jewish community in Edirne had around 20,000 members until it shrank and the synagogue fell into disrepair and was closed in 1983, before eventually being restored and re-opened in 2015 as both a cultural museum and a dedicated place of worship.[1]

Such encounters informed what Gülen's close associates evaluate as having been a significant period of reflection. As Gülen's close associate and interviewee Şerif Ali Tekalan (see Acknowledgements) put it "While staying in Edirne, he stayed in the window of the mosque where he was doing his duty and thought about what he should do." What came out of this reflection was a new approach to preaching. Indeed, it is arguable that in order really to understand Gülen, one needs to understand him as a preacher who is communicatively—and hence dialogically—engaged with the congregations and other groups to which he preaches. In relation to this kind of preaching, Tekalan explained that:

> These sermons were completely different from those of others in terms of the subjects, presentations and methods of the sermons. Sermons not only in Edirne but also in other cities were performed in the same way. It was like a college course for students and followers. The existence of God, prophethood, the afterlife and similar subjects, examples, questions and answers were both historical and true. For those who had little knowledge of religion these sermons were satisfactory. It showed that religion was not only historical and philosophical for both ordinary and intellectual people, but also it is something that can be practiced in everyday lives and that it is feasible.

But Tekalan also notes that, rather more distinctively among Turkish *imams*, Gülen's preaching was not limited to the physical and spiritual environment of mosque buildings, but took place "also in coffee houses, movie theatres and houses. He was trying to tell people these truths, no matter when or where." In addition, the content of what Gülen was preaching and discussing was very different to what might today be called an 'Islamist' vision of engagement with, and transformation of, society through the adoption of *Shariah* of the kind that some were also at that time promoting both on the streets and in some intellectual circles. As CA1 put it when reflecting on his neighbourhood during his youth, "In our area there was this people, this very orthodox people, who voted for this Erbakan group" who was known as "the father of political 'Islamism'" and of whom, as CA1 describes it, "they were chanting in the streets, shouting out from their cars in the streets, with their flags, and I said is this what Islam is? I hate this."

This period also saw Gülen's first experience of imprisonment. This came about because, after two years in Edirne, it was time for him to undertake his obligatory military service, for which he was sent to İskenderun. While there, because of a sermon that he preached he found himself facing charges. Although ultimately acquitted (in what was the first instance of a pattern to be repeated throughout his life), he was held for ten days in a military prison as a disciplinary punishment. After his military service, Gülen then stayed with his family in Erzurum for a year.

2.4   Izmir: Creative Contextualisation Through Differentiation

In 1966, Gülen was appointed to Izmir's Bornova mosque. Izmir is Turkey's third largest city and, as Tekalan put it, the city "was different in terms of culture and behaviour," it being "a more secular city." In relation to this move to Izmir, Öztürk explains of Gülen that "he actually didn't want to go. He was appointed there upon someone's reference." But in terms of a religious interpretation of why this happened, Öztürk also says that, "But I believe this was a response to his inner call from his early years, that longing for that generation which yielded a civilization out of sand in a glorious history. I believe this is related to his strong connection to God."

In Izmir, Gülen was confronted with two contextual polarisations of that period in Turkey. The first, as explained by Öztürk, was that of religion and science since "he met with the academy, with the students from universities, and also with the hippy generation of 1968, you know. There was this huge conflict in the universities where people were polarised across religion and science conflict. That was one thing." The other polarisation was that of politics and ideology and so, as summarised by Öztürk:

> His idealist aspirations meet the real hurricane in Izmir. He is truly introduced to western philosophy and literature in Izmir. So, in 1971, when there was this military intervention he actually shares the same cell with the extreme leftists in the prison. So, they shared the same space and he came to know them much better of course.

In terms of connecting with people and of the principle of contextualisation that informed his overall approach, "He was following the same direction here, just like he did with Erdirne. He was trying to find a way to get to people." In the course of this, although following and further developing the same basic method of dialogical engagement, this was now in the context of a cosmopolitan coastal city which was also a crucible of commercial, social, cultural, and political energy. And it was here that what the heading to this section of the chapter calls a "creative contextualisation"—including through differentiation from other movements rooted in Islam—took place, and which stimulated the further development of Gülen's thought, teaching, and action into the possibility of a still wider work and vision. As Öztürk evaluated this period:

> I believe that this is a huge opportunity for Hojaefendi to be here after Edirne and Izmir, to have lived here for this many years: to see that level, the height that human intellect has come, and how we can, or any person who has been nourished by the Qur'an and Prophet's example, contribute to this civilization.

Within that overall context, a number of individuals began collectively to coalesce around Gülen's teaching and proposals for practice. By then he was becoming known among those inspired by him by the honorific title of *hocaefendi* (see Sect. 1.2). As this occurred, both Gülen and those inspired by his teaching began to differentiate themselves more clearly from the *cemaat* (or, community) of those inspired by Nursi, and Hizmet started to develop its own distinctive forms of self-organising. This included, firstly, the opening of the so-called *ışık evleri* (lighthouses), and secondly, the adoption of communication methods with the wider society via use of what, at that time, was the technologically cutting-edge medium of audio cassette recordings of Gülen's sermons. These were, significantly, free from the control and constraints of the state media but they were also ideally suited to the transmission of core messages within the process of the creation of a dynamic and rapidly emerging socio-religious movement. Indeed, it was in such a context that many of the 'weeping sermons' for which Gülen later became so well-known were spread (Sunier and Şahin 2015).

Gülen and Hizmet were seeking to find their own point of balance in relation to the political parties and groups of the time. During this period, the MSP (the Millî Selâmet Partisi, or in English "National Salvation Party") began to gain in strength and prominence. While Necmettin Erbakan recommended his followers to relate to Gülen and help him, in 1977, Gülen criticised the boycott of the Turkish Islam Institutes and criticised the New Asia group for being too political. A sign of Hizmet's growing distinctiveness was the foundation, in 1978, of the journal *Sızıntı* (or *Fountain*) published by the Türkiye Öğretmenlar Vafi (or, in English, Turkish Teacher Foundation).

Open debate with the MSP followed after Gülen, in a 24 June 1980 sermon criticised the MSP and the National Paper (*Milli Gazete*), albeit without specifically naming them, even though during this period the leadership of the MSP had not openly criticised Gülen. During this latter period in Izmir, Gülen frequently obtained medical reports excusing him from duty, until in November 1980 he was appointed to Çanakkale. However, he again obtained a medical report as a result of which he did not commence his assignment there and, on 20 March 1981, he resigned from his office as a recognised preacher.

In Izmir, as a student, Tekalan lived together with a small group of other students in one of Hizmet's houses before such forms of living became known as *ışık evleri*. As Tekalan explains it: "There was no such name at that time" but we were "all college students" and "were staying together. We prepared our meals ourselves, prayed together and studied together." And Tekalan recalls that, "At that time, Gülen was coming to Bornova to sermons, and we were visiting him, and he was coming to our house time to time. We had many questions about religion, and he was answering our questions. We had a great discussion with him." Following the initial establishment of these houses, Gülen's close associate and interviewee, Mustafa Özcan (see Acknowledgements) says that:

> Starting with seventy-one and towards the end of the decade, at that time there were sixty-seven city provinces in Turkey and forty-five out of sixty-seven cities that in a sense were in competition to establish such student hostels because they saw that it's working and that their own kids are benefiting in their cities, in the sense that there is this student hostel establishment and progress.

2.5   ISTANBUL: WITHDRAWAL AND COSMOPOLITAN ENGAGEMENT

By 1980, Gülen had relocated to Istanbul, the cosmopolitan city of Turkey straddling Europe and Asia and the influences flowing between them. Initially, in the context of the impact flowing from the 1980 military coup he was, of necessity, withdrawn from public life for around six years. For much of the time in Istanbul he lived, as Jon Pahl's, 2019 biography of him put it "hiding in plain sight" (p. 190) in a small flat on the fifth floor of a Hizmet dormitory, though from time to time he needed to leave and find refuge in other parts of Turkey, including in a house in Erzurum that his brother had secretly built. But as Pahl's biography of Gülen put it, Gülen's fifth floor flat in Istanbul soon became a metaphor for how, what the novelist Orhan Pamuk, Pahl (2019), called 'the melancholy of Istanbul' in due course "turned into both a deep personal peace and an expanding network of people" (p. 189).

Alongside his own personal devotions, study and reading, for those who knew where to find him, Gülen offered a breadth and depth of teaching that both laid the foundations of much of the next phase of his teaching and work as well as extending them. Pahl explained the significance of what occurred in this period and in this place in the following way: "It is an axiom of contemporary cultural studies that place matters. So it should be no surprise that over time the 5th Floor became to people of Hizmet much more than just an apartment" (p. 205). As an example of the significance attributed to this, as al-Ansari (2015) put it in his 'biographical novel,' it was here that Gülen found:

> ...retreat and revelation, his exile and prison, his companions and gatherings. Month after month he would stay there in this sacred space and not leave it except to go to one of his other small rooms if he received a sign, an indication or a warning that it was necessary for him to leave or to go to another place.

After Turgut Özal arranged for the military charges against Gülen to be dropped, from 1986 onwards, Gülen emerged ever more into a public life and profile in Istanbul. As Tekalan put it in a somewhat succinct and compressed way, generally passing over the years of withdrawal, "When he went to Istanbul, he contacted businessmen, academics, Christian leaders, the Jewish people and many other celebrities."

And indeed, it was during the second part of his period in Istanbul, during the 1990s, that Gülen started particularly to become known for his teaching about, commitment to, and engagement in inter-faith dialogue in both Turkey itself and beyond. Fast-breaking events during Ramadan were one of the key ways in which, on the one hand, Gülen's commitment to build bridges and extend friendship to Jewish and Christian leaders and communities were concretely expressed, but because of their religious and social significance, these *iftars* also acted as public interventions of a kind that provoked reflection in Hizmet and among the wider Muslim population of Istanbul and Turkey.

In January 1998, Gülen publicly broke the fast with the Jewish businesspeople Üzeyir Garih and İshak Alaton, partners in the Turkish business conglomerate Alarko Holdings. Soon after that, Gülen had what Pahl (2019) describes as "a very public meeting" (p. 238) with then chief

Sephardic Rabbi of Israel, Eliyahu Bakshi-Doron, following which "Gülen continued throughout his time in Istanbul to foster good relations with the Jewish community around the globe and in Istanbul" (p. 239), including several meetings with the then Chief Rabbi of Turkey, David Aseo.

Gülen's public meetings with important Turkish Christian leaders evolved out of broadly inclusive Fast-breaking events organised by the Journalists and Writers' Foundation which was, by then, very active in activities concerned with dialogue and which, in February 1995, organised an inter-religious *iftar* for over a thousand people of all Christian, Jewish, and Muslim backgrounds, including religious people and secularists. In April 1996, at the invitation of Patriarch Bartholomew I, the Pharnariot Greek Patriarch of Istanbul, Gülen met the Patriarch for a brief dialogue at the Polat Renaissance Hotel on the Sea of Marmara. In November 1997, Gülen also met with the Vatican Representative to Istanbul, George Marovitch, who was one of those who had attended the Ramadan dinners. This, in turn, opened up the way, in January 1998, for Gülen to receive a message from Pope John Paul II in honour of the month of Ramadan, which was followed a month later by Gülen's travel to Rome to meet the Pope which Pahl describes as "the apex of his *public* activities on behalf of interreligious dialogue" (p. 249). Other highly significant and sensitive meetings with Christian leaders (given the historical context and continuing trauma affecting relations between Turks and Armenians) included meetings with Armenian Patriarchs Karekin II and Mesrob II.

These personal and individual initiatives by Gülen in inter-religious dialogue and inter-community relations, as supported also and built on by the Journalists' and Writers' Foundation, all had widespread effects that went beyond even the importance of the individuals who were directly involved given the broader impacts that arose from their profound active symbolism in the particular socio-religious context of Turkey. But in terms of Hizmet's development more broadly, its educational initiatives in many ways remained the driving motor of Hizmet's expansion throughout Turkey and, in due course, into Europe, Turkish Eurasia, and beyond.

2.6   PIVOTAL ROLE OF EDUCATIONAL INITIATIVES

After the abolition of traditional *madrassahs*, İmam Hatip schools were founded in Turkey for the training of government employed *imams*. In relation to the emergence of Hizmet educational initiatives, Öztürk adds of Gülen that, "While in Izmir, he was *imam* but also the teacher of Qur'an in a Qur'anic school. So, surely he was also supporting the expansion of the numbers of the İmam Hatip schools so that more people can read and understand the Qur'an." Nevertheless, it was also the case that because: "In Izmir he has also encountered with the challenges of modernity" and as a result "He understands that İmam Hatip schools really do not lead you to anywhere where students can find responses to this conflict. Then he thinks a better way would be the kind of schools where people could see that religion and science can go together, that Muslims can also do science; that science is not against religion." Gülen arrived at the view that "İmam Hatip schools would never be able to achieve that," and this led into what Tekalan described as Gülen's "second period". Tekalan identified this as being from 1980 onwards, during which Gülen was starting to place a special emphasis on education, advocating for the establishment of primary schools and high schools. And in this context:

Not only the well off people but even the ordinary lay people, when they see that there are safe havens in a sense for their children to go to the big cities and to attend high schools or the universities, they are encouraged to send their kids to these educational institutions based on the trust that people will take care of them so they will not be prey to terror, atheism, you know, other pervert ideologies in a sense, or addictions and sort of other, you know, misconduct. Believing that they see the students over there, so they will be more encouraged to send these kids to such 'houses' and to such people.

Educational initiatives were therefore the first among the triad of characteristics by which Hizmet in due course became to be more known (Weller 2022, Sects. 2.2, 2.3 and 2.4) within the broad heritage of Nursi that identified ignorance, conflict, and poverty as the three evils facing both Islam and humanity and sought to address them through initiatives in education, dialogue, and the relief of poverty. As Öztürk explained about Gülen:

Even at this time, he travelled all cities, whether in smaller cities or in larger groups he convinced people that we have three enemies – you know it: poverty, ignorance and disunity and he then convinced them with education and you know, being economically developed, and combine efforts, small business people combine efforts in collectives to make investments and to make such efforts against disunity, interaction and mutual respect, you know, in a sense, among that dialogue, interaction, proper interaction, rather than being reactionary.

Those businessmen and students who had, for up to a decade, been learning with and from Gülen, responded to his challenge to support the creation of what he hoped would become what he called a "Golden Generation" (Sunier 2014) of confident and educated young Muslims, through supporting the establishment of schools, beginning with Yamanlar High School in Izmir. Then, according to Tekalan, there was a development of mutually reinforcing initiatives of the kind that characterised the growth and spread of Hizmet in Turkey through nearly four decades until July 2016. Young teachers graduating in a range of subjects were ready to work in Yamanlar High School, and within four or five years, Tekalan said that "this school achieved great results, won prizes in the international science olympics, mathematics, computer science and physics. They always won first prizes in Turkey." As a consequence of this, businessmen and other people in other cities "realized how important it is to have these schools in other cities too, and they've tried to find out how they could open these schools in their own provinces." Therefore, Tekalan says, "They also opened schools, but they needed experienced teachers. Just like at Yamanlar High School in Izmir." As a result of this:

Teachers were sent to these schools from Izmir and other cities of Turkey. The success of these schools was also very good. People across Turkey loved these schools. Why, because these schools not only train students at universities, but also care about educating people with good charitable objects. On the one hand, they taught courses such as physics chemistry very well, but on the other hand they also taught how to live the practices of religion with examples in life.

In relation to those unstable times, close associate of Gülen, Mustafa Özcan explained that the schools started also to include female students in what was a relatively radical development given the inherited context of the time within which:

At that time, among the Muslims, they were concerned and for that reason they prevent their own daughters to go to schools or to attend high schools after the compulsory primary school education, they were not sending their daughters to the secondary schools and high schools, let alone universities. And if the family is a little bit well off, affluent, or a little bit knowledgeable about the social issues and the religion, even they were just defending this as a cause to protect so-called morality, chastity or, you know 'our own values'. Then Hojaefendi came revolutionary in that sense. He convinced all these well-off people, the people leading the communities, and afterwards the normal ordinary people, laymen, to send their daughters to the school to provide them with a proper education and let them study at higher schools for their education.

With regard to the centrality of education in the teaching and practice of Gülen, Özcan explained that, "If you just look at the 1960s and the '70s at that time it was always the same story, coup d'etats, coalitions, failing coalitions, street fights and skirmishes, and interference of the state apparatus in all government issues and the people, but no matter what happened, Hojaefendi didn't give up his idea of education." Although in that early period the Turkish system did not allow the establishment of private schools, Özcan explained of Gülen that:

He came up with the idea to establish 'houses' in which four or five students would share the same flat and the basic necessities will be sponsored or provided by the businessmen as donations, and by charities, so that they can, in a safe environment, properly study their courses. It doesn't mean only Islamic study. It can mean that when they are attending their schools they can also properly study the secular subjects over there.

And, as Öztürk further explained:

At that time, these institutions also set a good example to the other faith communities so even they saw that this is picking up and working, even if just a few communities, religious communities, also follow in the footsteps. But then majority of the people saw that whether they are coming from the rightist background or leftist background, that the street skirmishes and fights are coming from an ideological place and that they cannot trust other people, people from all backgrounds started sending their kids to our hostels and such institutions thinking that they will be honest, they will be just hard working, and they will be at the end be beneficial to their own people and community, the Turkish community in general. So, up to the 1980s, up to the September 12 1980 coup d'état, this system of houses, and of student hostels, and the dormitories became a true model for Turkish people for all groups and communities, and rather than a path for a proper education, it became almost a highway. It developed so much and it was embraced by all people. So, this 1980 coup did not discriminate whether rightest or leftist, whether they are equally culpable, criminal or not. They bulldozed all the groups of the people from the left and the right without any distinction. At that time the basic understanding was that it was only the rich and well-developed people's children were attending the schools and high schools, and the universities were completely exceptional and in the universities only the rich people and influential people's children were attending.

As time went on, however, the military government started to encourage people to establish and develop their own educational institutions. And in this broader setting, the schools were not only attractive to pious and practising Muslim parents and but also secular people were supporting the project by giving their children to Hizmet schools as well. Tekalan set these developments within an interpretive framework that emphasised their religious inspiration although, of course, this development can also be analysed from a socio-economic perspective. Thus, as Tekalan pithily summarised it: "It's like a franchise," while interviewee Ozcan Keleş (see Acknowledgements) from the UK has suggested that "there's also an operational reason for why there was this impetus for creating schools" and that is that:

> The schools were founded by and large by capital investment. Capital investment is solicited from donors. Donors in part express their commitment through donation. So, how do you continue the expression of commitment if you don't continue to open and found new establishments, i.e. buildings?

In other words, in order to operate as educational institutions, school buildings also need equipment, furniture, and book supplies. Therefore, as Keleş explained it, although "ultimately nobody is trying to do nothing for their personal gain. It's not a negative thing, and it's not about becoming rich oneself" and, as close associate of Gülen Reşit Haylamaz (see Acknowledgements) explained the evolution of this system through projects that in due course became institutionalised such as the Kaynak Publishing Group:

> It first started by producing testing materials for the testing/ tutoring schools, weekend schools; there were hundreds, perhaps thousands of them in Turkey, and they definitely needed some testing materials to make it different from the rest of the industry. So what happened is that some of those teachers came together to form a company, a publisher's company, to meet those needs. And as schools started to be opened in different countries, new

needs emerged and our publishing house also tried to meet their needs as much as they could. Other companies like school furniture which came out of the need to furnish our schools with furniture as well as laboratories, which were a huge investment. And our friends, as I understand it, set up this company to supply those needs in the most cost-effective way.

Reflecting on this, Keleş described it is "a pattern" that is related to the Turkish term *metafizik gerilim* (literally translatable as 'metaphysical tension') in which one "encourages people to become overwhelmed by altruism, in order to get them to donate for the founding of a school, what next?"

The pivotally important role of schools like Fatih High School in Istanbul and the Samanyolu High School in Ankara in realising Gülen's aim to encourage the creation of a so-called "Golden Generation" can be seen in the testimonies of many people who later became deeply involved in Hizmet. For example, when asked how he became involved with Hizmet, CA1, explained that:

> The private schools were a new phenomenon in Turkey and Hizmet schools were some of the few ones that were available other than the other very secular schools, which were also very expensive. In our neighbourhood I had my best friend … who was one year older than me and I heard he was accepted by this Fatih College, which was not very far away from where my home was.

He explained that "My family was a very secular family. My father was not a practising person. But he was an honest man, a very virtuous man in many other ways." Of both his family and himself, he said that "we had no idea about the school." In the first instance, he wanted go there for the very ordinary and common reason among children, namely, that his best friend was already a student there. It was only "later on I discovered that there were rumours about the school, because of my wider secular family and there was this pressure from my uncles on my mother not to keep sending me to that school." But despite these rumours, "I really liked the school" and that "They were pushing us to study harder. I really loved the way they taught. I loved the way they taught English a lot. And they were doing it well." Overall, his evaluation was that, "I really enjoyed the environment and I did not see any manifestation of any radicalism or extremism with these people – on the contrary, I saw teachers who were passionately teaching, smiling and young." But as he said, although study-ing there for seven years, in relation to Gülen:

> I heard about him, I think first, when I was in my third or fourth year and there I heard about this preacher who was coming to Istanbul to deliver a sermon and people were speaking about this, and some of my friends invited me to go too, but my parents did not allow me, so I didn't go, which is something I really feel missing in my heart. I never attended any of his ser-mons in a mosque. But I listened to his audio cassettes.

Significantly, this interviewee says, "But more importantly I met with the teachers" of whom he said that he noticed "how they were so kind to parents, how they were so generous in their smile. You could feel the warmth of these people emanating out of their soul. It was nothing artifi-cial. That connection just developed over time." In summary, and in con-trast, he said of these teachers that:

> They were not like other people who would fill our mosques who are usually older men, and who did so mostly because it became a part of their lives. But I saw in these beautiful people, a much greater devotion and a much great connection when they stood for prayer and I really loved praying with them. They recited the Qur'an beautifully which, in a way, that didn't sound to me that beautiful before.

However, he was not a boarding student until his last year and there-fore "I never knew Gülen was behind all those things, Hojaefendi," although, "I later learned that he actually stayed for some time at the top floor of the school which was like a guest room, and Gülen was there, but I never saw him." And this was but one testimony among many. For exam-ple, the asylum-seeker in Switzerland, AS2 (see Acknowledgements), explained that because education had been very important for his parents, back in Turkey he had been sent a school around 200 kilometers distant from his home and which, as he described it, was, "a privileged school, a private school. And it was connected with Hizmet."

As with the previous interviewee, this was despite the fact that his father was not a Hizmet member, but it happened because Hizmet's early initia-tives in education were often highly valued across at least parts of the broader society beyond those who were themselves directly involved with Hizmet. According to this asylum-seeker, his father's view of Hizmet was that "He knows it very well and he loved the guys of the members – they are the right men and good men." Looking back, AS2 said, "So I went there, to that school, connected with Hizmet, and it began like that." In other words, the seeds of what later became networked relationships were planted at that time because "they had a lot of activities as well, so how can I say, this affected me. So, I wanted to continue the relations."

At the same time, while clearly engagement with the community of Hizmet people was strongly socialising in its effects, this was not only a case of an individual being simply attracted to something because of it meeting an otherwise unmet psychological or emotional need. Rather, the same interviewee underlined about that experience of being drawn into the community that, "When I see something nonsensical and illogical I can quit, I can finish the relation and connection." But evaluating his experience in the round, he said "I had known a lot people and I recognised a lot of Hizmet people in that school and later on I connected all my life with them. So it started like that."

Another anonymous Hizmet-related asylum-seeker, AS1 (see Acknowledgements), from Turkey and at present living in Switzerland—recounted of his youth in Turkey that, "I met the Hizmet volunteers first when I was attending the middle school. At that time, I was looking for after school help to prepare myself for the university. At that time, I was attending some activities of the Hizmet followers." From the testimony of this interviewee, it is also clear that Hizmet created networks for those who then went on to universities and he explained that he had become particularly active in Hizmet "during the first years of my university life."

A similar theme is common among other informants and from across different age groups. Thus, interviewee Erkan Toğuşlu (see Acknowledgements) from Belgium, recalled that, "My overall relationship with Hizmet began already in my early childhood, when I saw especially that many people were dedicated to education, in Turkey, for example, in my little town on the eastern side." So, as with many others, contact in the Hizmet schools became the gateway to becoming aware of and to engage with Gülen's teaching as well as getting to know other parts of Hizmet. As Toğuşlu went on to explain further:

> Then later on I discovered many other people who committed themselves also in other areas like, social welfare activities, school education, coming from different backgrounds – from businesspeople to university students, also in terms of age very old people and very young people and they committed themselves to different areas within the movement.

Finally, this led into personal engagement with aspects of the movement, so that "I think that, slowly, I started organising some activities within the Hizmet movement – especially tutoring the young children in Turkey, including giving them some extra educational courses." Asylum-seeker interviewee AS3 (see Acknowledgements) explained that he had previously been to "the Hizmet preparation courses for high school." However, AS3 and his wife, AS4 (see Acknowledgements), only first properly connected with Hizmet when they were university students. This was through the movement's dormitories, of which the husband, AS3, said "I was for one year in a dormitory of the Hizmet movement so I learned many things there." Later on, AS3 also said that, as a couple "Maybe once or twice in a month we met somewhere and talked with each other, or had some social things organised like a picnic or a football match, or like that. Our general social life was around those people. Because of that we were so much talking with them or talking on the telephone." In the light of this, it would seem that the initial attraction of Hizmet included the kind of activities that it sponsored and the warm and honest character of individuals committed to Hizmet as much as the actual teaching of Gülen. Indeed, the couple both affirmed what was explained by AS3 in the following way:

> First, what we liked was people making activities. We are eating, we are having maybe more social things. First of all that: if you like them, if you like to go there. But after liking those people, people try to tell about something more – maybe, if you want to read this book, advising. So first getting to like those people and then learning something about the movement.

As AS1 explained it, after being in a Hizmet school, "When I went to the University I also connected with them and I lived in their dormitory" or lighthouse, in relation to which he explained further that "It was very enjoyable for me. It was very good because there were a lot of kind people. We were reading always books, novels and magazines there. It was a good chance for me to improve myself in both spiritually and intellectually. So, it was an opportunity for me to live there."

As Hizmet schools spread into different parts of the world, including the continent of Europe (Weller 2022), according to interviewee Mustafa Gezen from Denmark (see Acknowledgements), the Hayskolen Hizmet school founded there in 1993 was "my way into the Hizmet movement. I became familiar with people from the school." He also commented that,

"I think you will have heard similar stories about teachers who were great role models through their teaching and actions who gave me as a Danish Kurdish student with roots from Turkey motivation to educate myself." Gezen came from a family that had not had the opportunity of an extended education and, of the teachers that he encountered, he said that they were:

> Great role models and educated; they were people with good manners – you can call it *'akhlaq* in Arabic, something was different. We began to see that this was an amazing way of being a human. So that inspired me a lot and I saw some role models and I am still in touch with a couple of them still.

Gezen further explained that "my contact with Hizmet grew in the high school, and then we were going to camps together, playing football in the camps, although in Gezen's case – rather exceptionally among Hizmet people – he eventually qualified at the University of Copenhagen with a Master's degree in the History of Religions and, on which he commented that he 'had not met many people doing this at the point that I did it'." Looking back on the original creative impulses behind what eventually became a global development, Öztürk noted that:

> Hojaefendi pinpointed one fact about the social movements or collective action then, that people are always a bit hesitant and reserved when they are making progress on jumping from one step to another. So even when people, Hojaefendi came forward with a private school, or secondary or high school initiative, even the believers were a bit hesitant that we cannot do the state job, you know, how can we manage such things, even Hojaefendi admitted that at that time he was having difficulties in convincing people to take up this initiative of establishing private schools. But again, one of the favourable points, at that time since the state encouraged this one, so it was not only Hojaefendi's, in a sense, pipe dream, it was what was needed and required and the state allows this. So in this way people gradually and slowly picked up the initiative of establishing schools.

As Haylamaz reflected, "Many foundations, especially related to education, were opened in almost all provinces of Turkey. These foundations later gave way to schools." As Gülen's influence spread, Haylamaz noted that, "His audio cassettes, video cassettes were all over Turkey, and people listened to him on the radio, and people listened to him via the cassette in their cars" and from this, "you could definitely say they had their own personal inspiration from Hojaefendi, and most of that geared towards education, towards schooling. His call is like the *adhan*, call to prayer; when you hear it you attend to it." Building out from this, Haylamaz noted that there was an organic development within a community of mutual sharing and learning:

> There were different foundations and institutions that were affiliated with Hizmet. For example, I was first working for the Yamanlar College in Izmir, and I was in charge of the dormitory. But I also used to meet with the Principals of other schools, or the directors of other dorms that I knew were affiliated with Hizmet, and we used to organise workshops together so that we knew and learned from one another how to solve problems with better conditions, better facilities, better services to students, how to help them develop certain skills etc. But in those matters where we felt we disagreed, those of us who were closer, we would come and ask Hojaefendi's opinions.

To some extent, especially these early developments from Hizmet partook, at least in part, of what might be called a 'copy-paste' approach that is now increasingly being questioned within Hizmet (Weller 2022, Sect. 6.8). As Haylamaz explained it, "Often a project started in one district, others copied them. For instance, schools like, Fatih, Yamanlar, Samanyolu were very successful and well-established. Schools in other provinces started taking their name and model as a franchise." However, despite this, Haylamaz argued that there was nothing automatic or purely replicative about such a process, explaining that, "And we moved these projects on to other countries, and we had a brainstorming session, and ideas shared with Hizmet people in those countries. And when they agreed with the idea they took on the project, and when they don't, they don't." As a more contemporary example of this process, Haylamaz noted that:

> Last year we wanted to have these reading contests on the life of the Prophet in Egypt, in Indonesia. But our friends there were not able to do it. We hope this time we can do it, and we hope to develop a more agreeable project. We are having conversations with the friends there and we will see if they will be convinced and well, then will take it on, otherwise we will see. When something becomes successful, others model it.

2.7   EUROPE, TURKISH EURASIA, AND BEYOND

Öztürk explained that it was while he was in Izmir that Gülen made his first contacts with Europe: "In 1970s he also travelled in Germany, in the western Europe, so he had an initial encounter with the western world" albeit that this was only for the month of Ramadan during which the Diyanet assigned him as an official *imam* to travel and to preach to the Turkish faithful in Germany. One of the anonymous translators of Öztürk, and who came from the UK, added to this that Gülen visited the UK in 1992, 1994, and 1996, although not for long visits, and that he also visited the Netherlands and France as well as a number of other countries where there were sizeable Turkish populations.

During the time that Gülen visited Germany there was considerable conflict among mosques of different Islamic groups and backgrounds (Weller 2022, Sect. 3.3) and it is possible that this experience had some influence in confirming and strengthening what was a growing conviction that he had originally developed in the Turkish context about the relative importance, contextually, of building schools rather than mosques and which was crystallised into his famously startling and challenging aphorism that "Turkey doesn't need more mosques but more schools." As suggested by Kurucan (for more context, see Weller 2022, Sects. 3.2 and 5.7), it seems likely that his visit to the Netherlands, where the secular women's movement was particularly strong in opening up new social and religious opportunities for women, may have contributed to a new development in Gülen's thinking around the role of women within Hizmet.

Then came another decade of development arising out of the political changes at the end of the Cold War when the former Soviet Union was, in 1991, dissolved and succeeded in terms of legal personality by the Russian Federation and the emergence of other former Soviet Republics as independent post-Soviet states. In relation especially to the former Turkic Republics of the Soviet Union, Tekalan quoted Gülen as saying, "We know the people there, we should go to those countries and share our educational experiences with those people and start to open schools in these countries." In relation to this, close associate of Gülen and interviewee, Hakan Yeşilova (see Acknowledgements) also commented of Gülen that:

> Hojaefendi always said we learned our religion from Central Asian scholars, Bukhari, and they were the ones who really formulated the Hadith

scholarship. And the heritage of Islamic knowledge exists today thanks to their very uniquely delicate, academically sensitive work. So, we owe it back to those nations, they are deprived of anything, and that includes business, most and foremost, education and schools. So, I think, he mobilised his followers to go there to start business as well as to start schools.

As Tekalan emphasised, "These schools were secular schools" and "They weren't religious schools." In Turkey, the curricula of Hizmet schools were in line with the broader Turkish education system. In other countries, a similar programme was used with some enrichments and, as Tekalan reports, "In these countries, people quickly witnessed the success of these people and everyone was very happy with these results" because "As well as the educational achievements of children in these schools, the improvement in their behaviour was also noteworthy." According to Tekalan, these initiatives then developed further into university level with the establishment of Kafkas University in Azerbaijan in 1992, following which universities also opened in Georgia, Turkmenistan, Kazakhstan, Kyrgyzstan, and Russia. In Albania there were two universities—Epoca and Badr University.

In Turkey itself, in 1996, Fatih University was founded of which, as previously noted, Tekalan became President (2010–2016), having previously been a member of the Higher Education Executive Committee (1992–1996) overseeing all the universities in Turkey. He had previously been Chair of the International Association of Universities (also 1992–1996) in relation to which he explained that "We held congresses every year on innovations, accreditation activities and many other topics related to higher education issues" and to these congresses "We were also inviting rectors, university professors. Not just from our own universities, but from Harvard, England and the Far East." In relation to this transition first into the wider Turkic regions of the former Soviet Union, and then into a wider global development, CA1 recounted that:

> I remember seeing these students coming from Central Asia to study at Fatih College when I was a senior there. And I later learned they came under a 'Student Exchange' programme. Some Turkish kids were sent to Central Asia to attend college in those countries. Probably they were again on scholarships by Hizmet philanthropists for I imagine many families would not be able to send their kids to Turkey. It was the time when

these new Republics were emerging, like, Uzbekistan, Turkmenistan, from what used to be the Soviet Union.

In reflection on this, with the benefit of hindsight, Yeşilova summatively commented that, "I think that Hojaefendi always had this in his mind, not to remain in Turkey, but to interact with the rest of the world." Whether or not this was indeed the case, Kurucan says that:

> When Hojaefendi came to Europe, the United States and also Australia, it was a long tour. He went to Germany ...that was the first time in Germany, but that was a limited period for Ramadan and it was, again, intensely related to the Ramadan time. But he was now moving out to see what is happening in the world, to visit friends, or perhaps for other reasons. He is now expanding his vision even more in Europe, in the United States, and in Australia, and I think that was a milestone, where really you could see it had changed his vision.

Following this, Gülen challenged people to travel to the Far East and to the countries of Africa, and eventually Hizmet schools also reached Latin American countries and Australia. From the 1990s onwards, they had also reached European countries of Turkish migration, as well as to the USA where many young people from Hizmet went especially for their postgraduate education.

2.8   'Enemy of the State'

In the eyes of those opposed to Gülen and Hizmet, Gülen's vision of developing a "Golden Generation" of pious young Muslims fully engaged in all contexts and at all levels in society through educational development was interpreted as an attempt to take over the state in a sinister way. Therefore, instead of being seen as a figure offering a route to combining Islamic scholarship, piety, and socially engaged action, he was seen as an 'enemy of the state.' This interpretation can especially be referenced to recordings made and broadcast on Turkish TV on 18 June 1999, of Gülen speaking about Hizmet people "moving through the arteries of the state," but in relation to which, defenders of Gülen argue that the original form and context were tampered with and the intentions misinterpreted. These broadcast recordings were the cited basis for the measures taken against Gülen that were, in the first instance, initiated by Kemalist forces in the state and which led, in 1999, to the commencement of a legal process against Gülen (Harrington 2011), which in turn formed a significant part of the context for his departure from Turkey to the USA in the same year.

Under this process, on 18 March 1999, the Ankara Chief of Police sent a letter to the Presidency of the Inspecting Council and the Presidency of the Intelligence Department on the subject of "Fethullah Gülen and the Light (Işık) Sect." In this, the question was asked whether this grouping had an organisational structure, and whether it aimed at destroying the existing Constitutional order of the State in order to establish a system based on the *shariah*, in particular through a systematic attempt to take over institutions such as the Police Academy. On 3 August 2000, the Ankara Prosecutor asked the court to issue an arrest warrant against Gülen. At a second attempt on 22 August 2020, the Ankara State Security Court accepted an indictment of 22 August 2000 that charged Gülen with an offence under Article 7/1 of the *Anti-Terror Law* which, if proved, carried a sentence of up to 10 years' imprisonment. However, by 28 August, the arrest warrant in absentia was lifted. Nevertheless, a trial commenced in the Ankara State Security Court on 16 October 2000 and ended on 10 March 2003. Under Law 4616, the case was suspended on condition that the same offence would not be committed within the next five years.

After changes in 2003 to Article 1 of the *Anti-Terror Law* which had added a condition that an act of violence needed to have been used in order for it to be treated as a terrorist offence, on 7 March 2006, Gülen's lawyers asked for a retrial on the basis that their client had to be acquitted since there was no evidence that he had ever used violence. This had closely followed a request made by Gülen's defence lawyers to the General Directorate for Security as part of their right to see evaluations made of foundations, associations, and educational institutions cited as being related to Gülen and the answer that had been as received on this as of 3 March 2006, which was signed by the Deputy Director for Security. That answer had stated that the institutions cited could not be evaluated under Article 1 of the *Anti-Terror Law* since there was no evidence that they had gathered in order to change the Constitutional order of the State. Up to a hearing on 5 May 2006 at the Ankara 11th High Criminal Court (which had replaced the Ankara State Security Court), the Prosecutor was still pressing for a conviction, but the court ruled in favour of an acquittal and, on 5 March 2008, the 9th Criminal Bureau of the Supreme Court of Appeals (Court of Cassation) finally confirmed the acquittal.

However, it was also the case that years earlier, Gülen had also been seen by others as an 'enemy of the state.' This was because in each decade during which he lived in Turkey, Gülen's life and work was regularly punctuated by coups and other episodes of military intervention. This included the traditional military coups of 27 May 1960; 12 March 1971; and the 12 September 1980. But also, on 28 February 1997, what some have described as a "post-modern" coup took place, in which the political branch of the military, the National Security Council, issued a Memorandum following which a series of political resignations took place and a range of restrictions were re-imposed on religious practice. In similar vein, in 2007, the General Staff issued an E-Memorandum on its website highlighting its position as a defender of secularism and commenting on the Presidential elections, following which the elections failed and a new General Election took place. Finally, on 15 July 2016, there was what, according to one's evaluative perspective, is generally known as either a "failed coup," a "silent coup," or a "staged coup."

When Gülen was asked in interview about what it meant for him to try to hold onto what he articulated as the central theme of love in his teaching in the context of having lived through such periods of military rule and imprisonment, he explained that:

> I never held through those difficult years, I never held grudges against anybody. I never took account of who did what to me. I forgot them, I forgot what they did. They simply displayed their character through their actions and I was trying to live the example that I had seen in the previous exemplary people. I tried to live my life and to stay true to my values. I lived through the military coup of 1960, 27 May. I lived through the coup of 1971, where I was actually imprisoned.

In the period of military rule following that imprisonment, just as the Hizmet educational institutions were beginning to be developed, Haylamaz pointed out that, "Hojefendi increased his efforts even though he himself was being sought after by the coup junta, even at that time when there was an arrest warrant, when he was in posters along with forty or fifty terrorists who are under capital punishment, Hojafendi was among them." And, as Gülen himself testified of this period, "In 1980 they followed me for six years and then eventually they caught me. But the Prime Minister at the time, Ozal, intervened and simply asked, you know, why are you after this person and they had to release me. But I basically I was evading arrest and detention for six years."

In the case of the events of July 2016, however, Gülen and those inspired by him were themselves directly accused by the Presidency and government of having conspired together with elements in the military to bring about what happened in Turkey on 15 July 2016. Among publications that have straightforwardly supported the government's narrative about this is Mohy (M. I.) Qandour's (2017), *Night of the Generals: The Story of 2016 Failed Military Coup in Turkey*, while Hakan Yavuz and Bayram Balcı (2008) edited collection of essays on *Turkey's July 15th Coup: What Happened and Why?* presents an academically more nuanced and varied picture, albeit with none of the authors fundamentally questioning the government's narrative.

In evaluating the events of July 2016, this author would argue that the gap that exists between this charge and the explicit and on the record teachings of Gülen that pertain to coups, to democracy and to how people should relate to one another in society, is so great that for Gülen to support, and still more to initiate such a coup, would require the employment of a deception of a very substantial and deliberate kind. Although it is not the purpose of this book either to focus on what happened on 15 July 2016 or to arrive at a definitive judgement about it, bearing in mind that there are those who, in connection with this cite the Islamic tradition of *al taqiyya* (which, in certain circumstances, allows the performance of a kind of holy deception), it remains at least theoretically possible that a substantial gap could exist between what is being said in public and plotted in private.

However, in relation to this, another fundamental question to consider is the one that is posed in the sub-title of an article on "The Gülen Community," by Thomas Michel (2017), a Jesuit Christian priest who, from 1981 to 1994, worked as Head of the Vatican's Office for relations with Muslims and also lived and worked in Turkey over many years. In this article, Michel posed the questions of "Who to Believe? Politicians or Actions?" and suggested that the vast majority of people who have practical and concrete experience of Hizmet's initiatives to overcome ignorance, conflict, and poverty do not find this credible. Therefore, overall, in the light of the substantial evidence of Hizmet's multiple services to education, dialogue, and the relief of poverty, and clear evidence that Gülen's teachings are truly rooted in the sources and wellsprings of Islam, and not the kind of modernist reinterpretation that seeks to use Islam as a tool to transform society or the state from above, there seems to this author to be such a gap between this and the claims of the Turkish authorities that, until anyone produces specific evidence to suggest to the contrary, the application to Gülen and to Hizmet of the Christian tradition's evaluative criterion of "by their fruits you will know them" would seem to be appropriate. This is not to say that no individuals who looked to Gülen and/or to Hizmet for inspiration might, in some way, have participated in the events of July 2016. Indeed, as will be seen below, some Hizmet asylum-seekers interviewed by the author have acknowledged this possibility. But, overall, it should be noted that the present author's general evaluation of this is, in the end, more in line with that of Bruno Kahl (2017), the head of the German intelligence service, the Bundesnachrichtungsdienst (BND). Kahl, when interviewed in *Der Spiegel*, said of the charges from the Turkish authorities that Gülen was behind the coup, "Turkey tried to convince us of that at every level. But so far they have not succeeded" while describing the Hizmet movement as "a civilian association that aims to provide further religious and secular education." In relation to these events and the run up to them, asylum-seeker AS4, explained that:

I think nobody in the Hizmet movement has done a crime. But in Turkey, if a group grows up successfully it's dangerous, perhaps people think. And Islamic ways – we come together and talk about Islam, which many people think is dangerous. And the government doesn't look at these groups in a good way. So, it's been a little bit like that in these years.

At the same time, although being clear in not holding Gülen personally, or the movement collectively, responsible for the coup, AS4's husband, AS3, acknowledged that:

Two years before something occurred in the psychology of people even from, a bit from some people in the army, maybe, some people thought we have to do something, even from the movement, I think like that. They can be in that action. It's not easy because they were still in jail and were not in that night in the action. But some small people from the movement were in that.

As AS4, added: "I don't know how it has occurred. But I think about that, that maybe psychologically they thought that we had to do against Erdoğan maybe"—which suggests that at least these asylum-seekers thought that some associated with Hizmet in Turkey may have thought that they needed to be involved in some form of radical intervention before Erdoğan attained an absolute power. At the same time, AS3 also noted that:

> In the government I think they prepared some lists about this. For example, he has links to Fethullah Gülen movement etc – always they are taking notes about this. And then, after this happened in 2016, they have a chance to come against the movement – yes, it's the chance to stop them because they were growing and coming into all parts of the life in Turkey. So they put out the lists that they had prepared before. For example, you put your money into Bank Asya, so you are guilty. But I put my money in Asya Bank, it's not important. The government gives permission for this bank so it is a crime? Yes, it's a crime. And giving your daughter to their school, yes, it's a crime again.

Commenting on AS4's observation that Erdoğan's speedy evaluation of the events of July 2016 having been "a gift from Allah" (Lorentzen 2019), AS3 added the comment that, "It's not easy to make sense of, but Erdoğan was very happy in that night. I saw some pictures. I think was ready for that. He knows something," to which his wife, AS4 added, "It was planned." From AS3's perspective, "It is so similar to German history….Because the media is like this. Also, people like him so much. Also, in Germany people trusted Hitler, like that." Furthermore, with reference to the Reichstag fire that many think was carried out deliberately in order to take power "Also, it looks like Hitler's fire." And there were other eerie parallels, including, for example, the burning of books with AS4 noting that "in these days, many books of Fethullah Gülen and Said Nursi were thrown away," which her husband AS3 explained was because "It was a crime to have them." In relation to this, his wife AS3 said: "And evidence of this terrorist group, no guns, nothing, but books. Terrorist group, you say, and books, how can it be? Because it is not a terrorist group! What can it be, it is very funny." In some ways, of course, the state's response is a reflection of the power of words. But, overall, as AS4 says "we thought it can't be real. It's a bad dream and we will wake up. But, no, it was real things."

Commenting further on this, AS3 said "It can be real but still we don't feel it is real. In the morning we are looking somewhere that someone comes and says it is not real. Two years have passed, but still we want that." And AS4 went on "Like that, and genocide. It's a kind of genocide going on in Turkey now. And we are looking in our mobile phones and it is still continuing. Like us people are suffering, and it's very bad, and we wish and pray to God every day." At this point, AS4 started to cry and became distraught, and therefore AS3 took over to try to explain the kind of impact that has happened: Thus, although Turkey has had a lot of coups, as AS3 noted, in this instance:

> The lists were prepared, because the second day of that night our General Director at my employment even though it was on a Sunday, called me and said "Come here." He had a written paper that was given to him, and he said, "I am so sorry, I am surprised to know this", but a list came here, on Sunday, after the Friday night, and this occurs on Sunday, "And tomorrow, on Monday, you will go to another department and you will be there for a time. You won't continue, and you can't come in on Monday". Because of this we were learning that those lists were ready. And after fifteen days we were working in a place, wondering what would happen to us, and after fifteen days they kick us out. And it is not easy to understand that night. But strange things occurred. But I don't know why they are blaming me that I am a member of an armed movement. Until that time I haven't been in any place that had guns or like that?! Also, I was very good, I thought. I became Deputy Director in my place because they told me you are a good and hard-working man, and we are making you a Deputy Director of this Department. I had many things that I did to my CV and they were good things. But in a night or a day I became terrorist.

And, therefore, overall:

> It is not easy to understand. Many people also can't understand that we are a terrorist, overnight we became like this! It was not a night I think, maybe you know better than us, because the background is old, I don't know also what was happening in the background. But the government doesn't like this movement. Whether the reasons can be understood or not I don't know. But in relation to the Gülen, the President really had a good team for his plan to make all people terrorists. That night was so strange. After that I read some books that any soldier movement didn't operate like that. That one was so different.

NOTE

1. See Jewish Heritage Europe, "Great Synagogue in Edirne, Turkey reopens after restoration", 26.03.2015. https://jewish-heritage-europe. eu/2015/03/26/great-synagogue-in-erdine-turkey-reopens-after-restoration/

REFERENCES

al-Ansari, F. (2015). *The return of the cavaliers: A biography of Fethullah Gülen. The pioneer of the cavaliers who emerged from the hidden realm.* Blue Dome Press.
Erdoğan, Latif (1995). *Fethullah Gülen Hocaefendi: Küçük Dünyam.* Istanbul: AD Yayıncılık.
Harrington, James (2011). *Wrestling with Free Speech: Religious Freedom and Democracy in Turkey.* Plymouth: University Press of America.
Kahl, Bruno (2017). Interview with German Intelligence Chief 'Coup in Turkey Was Just a Welcome Pretext'. In Martin Knobbe, Fidelius Schmid und Alfred Weinzierl (2017). *Der Spiegel* (20.3.17) https://www.spiegel.de/international/germany/german-intelligence-chief-bruno-kahl-interview-a-1139602.html.
Kuru, Ahmet (2003). Fethullah Gülen's Search for a Middle Way Between Modernity and Muslim Tradition. In Hakan Yavuz and John Esposito (Eds), *Turkish Islam and the Secular State. The Gülen Movement* (pp. 115–30). New York, Syracuse University Press.
Lorentzen, Jørgen (2019). *A Gift From God.* Amazon Prime Videos. https://www.amazon.co.uk/Gift-God-J%C3%B8rgen-Lorentzen/dp/B081ZFS3FV
Mardin, Şerif (1989). *Religion and Social Change in Modern Turkey. The Case of Bediüzzaman Said Nursi.* New York: New York State Press.
Michel, Thomas (2017). The Gülen Community: Who to Believe – Politicians or Actions. In The Fountain Special Issue, *What Went Wrong with Turkey? July 15 Coup Attempt. Erdoğan's Rogue State. The Persecution of the Hizmet Movement,* 34–37. https://fountainmagazine.com/special-issue-2017
Pahl, Jon (2019). *Fethullah Gülen, A life of Hizmet: Why a Muslim Scholar in Pennsylvania Matters to the World.* New York: Blue Dome Press.
Qandour, Mohy (M. I.). (2017). *Night of the Generals: The Story of 2016 Failed Military Coup in Turkey.* Livermore: WingSpan Press.
Sunier, Thijl (2014). Cosmopolitan Theology: Fethullah Gülen and the Making of a 'Golden Generation'. *Ethnic and Racial Studies, 37* (12), 2193–2208. https://doi.org/10.1080/01419870.2014.934259

Sunier, Thijl and Şahin, Mehmet (2015). The Weeping Sermon: Persuasion, Binding and Authority Within the Gülen-Movement. *Culture and Religion*, 16 (2), 228–241. https://doi.org/10.1080/14755610.2015.1058533
Turner, Colin and Hurkuç, Hasan (2008). *Said Nursi: Makers of Islamic Civilization*. London: I.B. Tauris.
Ünal, Ali and Williams, Alphonse (2000). *Advocate of Dialogue: Fethullah Gülen.* Fairfax, VA: Fountain Publication.
Yavuz, Hakan (2013). *Toward an Islamic Enlightenment: The Gülen Movement.* Oxford: Oxford University Press.
Yavuz, Hakan and Balcı, Bayram (Eds) (2008). *Turkey's July 15th Coup: What Happened and Why?* Salt Lake City: University of Utah Press.

PART II

Islamic Rootedness, Taboo-Breaking, and Socio-religious Implications

CHAPTER 3

Biography, Context, and Substance in Interplay

3.1   Turmoil as Turkish Context

The distinctiveness of Fethullah Gülen needs to be understood within the context of a Turkish society in ferment between traditionalism and modernity. During the nineteenth century, the Ottoman Empire increasingly came to be referred to as "the sick man" and/or the "sick man of Europe." In the face of the Empire's relative economic, political, and military decline, and seeing the apparent inter-relationship between industrialisation, modernisation, and the development of the new European colonial powers, groups of people within the Ottoman Empire began to look towards "the West" for inspiration. Among these were the so-called "Young Turks" (who officially later became known as the Committee for Union and Progress, or CUP). They favoured the replacement of the absolutist imperial rule with what might now be described as a "constitutional monarchy." Their agitation eventually led to the 1908 so-called "Young Turk Revolution" in which a form of multi-party democracy was established.

But the most far-reaching upheavals and revolutionary changes came about following the First World War (1914–1918) in which the Ottoman Empire was involved in what was ultimately the losing side of the Quadruple Alliance along with Germany, Austro-Hungary, and Bulgaria. The changes that followed were intimately connected with the life and influence of Mustafa Kemal Atatürk (1881–1938) who, having been an officer during the First World Atatürk War, led the Turkish National

© The Author(s) 2022   61
P. Weller, *Fethullah Gülen's Teaching and Practice*,
https://doi.org/10.1007/978-3-030-97363-6_3

Movement in the successful Turkish War of Independence (1919–1922). This was during a period in which the victorious allied powers might have colonised what was left of the Ottoman Empire. Under his leadership, the provisional Government of the Grand Assembly in Ankara was established, followed by the 24 July 1923 *Treaty of Lausanne* and the 29 October 1923 founding of the modern Republic of Turkey. His importance for the national narrative of Turkey is reflected in the title ascribed to him of Atatürk (meaning in English, "Father of the Turks") and to this day, his image remains almost omnipresent in Turkey.

One of the early and far-reaching consequences of the foundation of the modern state of Turkey was the subsequent abolition, in 1924, of the *Caliphate* that had been associated with the Ottoman Muslim rulers. The idea of the *Caliphate* is closely connected with the political unity of the global community of Muslims (the *ummah*), which was understood as having begun with the death of Muhammad and the appointment of the first Caliph, Abu Bakr Siddiqui. Even with the emergence of the Shi'a Muslims and other groups, when Islamic unity was fractured, the term also continued to be applied to the rulers of various historical Sunni Muslim empires including, eventually, the Ottoman Empire. The abolition of the Caliphate therefore represented a major social, political, and religious rupture with the previous order which had an impact on Islam and Muslims both in Turkey itself and also worldwide which echoes down to today as can be seen in the aim of groups such as ISIL/ISIS (Islamic State in the Levant/Islamic State in Syria) to re-establish a *Caliphate.*

By contrast with that inheritance, the ideological perspectives of the form of government adopted in Republic Turkey, and often called "Kemalism," emerged in a historical period where other forms of secular and statist ideology were in the ascendant, such as that of the Bolshevism of the Russian Revolutions of 1917 and which eventually led to the formation, in 1922, of the Soviet Union. In the case of "Kemalism," its key principles can be summarised in what were known as its "Six Arrows." These were: *cumhuriyetçilik* (or, Republicanism); *halkçılık* (or, Populism); *milliyetçilik* (or, Nationalism); *laiklik* (or, Secularism); *devletçilik* (or, Statism); and *devrimcilik* (or, Reformism). In the shaping of modern Turkey, these principles operated on multiple levels in the context of a society in which traditional Islam met revolutionary modernity. As the British historian Arnold Toynbee (1948) put it in a mid-twentieth century essay on "Islam, the West and the Future":

Here, in Turkey, is a revolution which, instead of confining itself to a single plane, like our successive economic and political and aesthetic and religious revolutions in the West, has taken place on all these planes simultaneously and has thereby convulsed the whole life of the Turkish people from the heights to the depths of social experience and activity. (p. 196).

Because of Kemalism's successful resistance against western colonial and imperial powers, the history and inheritance of Turkey is, in many ways, different from the kind of disruption between Islamic traditionalism and secular modernity experienced by most other countries of Muslim majority populations and Muslim former rulers and which was the product of a more purely external and colonial imposition.

The kind of changes that occurred in connection with Kemalism in Turkey were both symbolised by and give effect in, among other things, the so-called *Hat Law* of 1925, which outlawed the wearing of the traditional fez and turban and required that male head coverings should in future be in the western style of hats, which were promoted as an expression of modern civilisation. In 1928, the Arabic script was abolished and replaced with the Turkish script. The Turkish language had been enriched with various sources including many words of Arabic and Persian origin. But its "Turkification" was an important dimension of the nationalist project of the modern Turkish state within which, as in so many other nationalist projects that found their origins in the nineteenth century, the wish for a common language became politically significant. As a by-product of that, Kurdish (which was the historical language of the many people in south-east Turkey and of a significant minority throughout the country) was for many years not recognised by Turkish governments for use in the public sphere—an issue that has continued to be contentious despite some recent developments and openings in that regard.

The overall shift from relative Ottoman traditionalism and plurality to a Turkish nationalist approach built around notions of "oneness" and of modernity has taken place not only in relation to cultural and linguistic matters, but also in relation to religion. Ironically, this is because despite the generally secularist approach of the Kemalists, a complete separation of religion and the state was not established in relation to Turkey's Muslim traditions, networks, organisations, and institutions. Rather, after a period in which there was a Government Ministry of Religious Affairs and Charitable Foundations (1920–1924), a Presidency of Religious Affairs (Diyanet İşleri Başkanlığı) was established under the 1924 *Law 429*. Its remit was to carry out and oversee work concerning the beliefs, worship, and ethics of Islam, to enlighten the public about their religion, and to administer places of worship.

In 1925, what had been the previously very important and extensive network of Sufi Orders in Turkey but which had generally been seen by Kemalists as both corrupt and as hindering the modernisation project of the new Turkish Republic, were abolished and their lodges were turned into museums. One of the by-products of these developments is that the Sunni Muslim orientation of Diyanet and, indeed, of Turkish nationalism in general, in many ways disguises the degree of religious diversity that actually exists among Turks described as Muslims, since according to some estimates perhaps up to as many as 25 per cent of the population are, in fact, Alevis or Bekhtashis—traditions which connect Sufi influences with Shi'a Muslim traditions.

With regard to the relations between believers and non-believers in Turkey, it is important to understand that the form of secularism espoused by Kemalism was not that of the Anglo-Saxon tradition largely of a prag-matic separation of religion and state. Rather, it was a more ideological and radical version that Yavuz and Esposito (Eds. 2003) call a "radical Jacobin laicism" in which secularism is treated "as above and outside poli-tics" and in which, therefore, "secularism draws the boundaries of public reasoning" (p. xvi). One of the consequences of this approach was a series of moves to exclude religious identities and identity markers from public life and institutions. Beyond the previously mentioned *Hat Laws*, was the especially symbolic 1982 ban on women civil servants wearing headscarves which, in 1997, was though a further interpretation of the law, extended to the wearing of headscarves in universities.

Alongside the tensions between traditionalist Islam and revolutionary modernity, Turkish society has also experienced very sharp cleavages and fractures between the political Left and Right which came about partly because of its geopolitical position in the Cold War as located between the Communist "East" and the Capitalist "West," in relation to the latter of which, despite its ruling party having historically been quite "statist" in domestic politics and economics, Turkey has been a member of NATO (the North Atlantic Treaty Organization) since 1952. Especially in the 1970s, external Cold War tensions and internal Turkish conflicts were played out on the streets of Turkish cities in violent confrontations between leftist and rightist forces. This led to several thousand deaths, until the military intervened in a coup in 1980. In some ways, this coup (and the earlier ones in 1960 and in 1974) could be seen as a response to civil disorder of a kind that at times was verging on civil war by the armed forces in their role as historical guarantors of Turkish independence and stability. But the coup resulted in around 50 executions; the imprisonment of around a half million people; and the death of several hundred of these while in prison.

3.2   DISTINCTIVE SCHOLAR, TEACHER, AND INNOVATOR

It was such an overall context of religious and political turmoil that saw the emergence of a vigorous brand of what the subtitle of political scientist Sena Karasipahi's (2000) book on Muslim thinkers in modern Turkey calls "the revolt of the Islamic intellectuals." Among the public figures identified by Karasipahi in her book as belonging to this group, Gülen appears in neither the index nor the bibliography, although Nursi appears in both. The book does, however, discuss six prominent Turkish intellectuals of the 1990s, namely: Ali Bulaç, Rasim Özdenören, İsmet Özel, İhlan Kutluer, Ersin Nazif Gürdoğan, and Abdurrahman Dilipak. These she describes as "influential" and belonging to a "single coherent school with their novel understanding of Islam, which sees Islam not as an alternative but the only and single solution." (p. 1).

   She argued that these Muslim public intellectuals did not seek to be apologetic about backwardness, but strongly critiqued Western civilisation, while also being distinguished by "their attempt to deconstruct traditions and conventional interpretations of Islamic discourse." (p. 2). However, perhaps somewhat ironically, she also considered them to be "products of Kemalist modernization in the post-1950 period" (p. 2) in the sense that "they owe their intellectual endowment and their ability to diffuse their ideas to a large number of people to modernity." (p. 7). To this extent, at least, she argued that "their uniqueness among other Islamist intellectuals lies in their rejection of both 'the Islamization of modernity' and the 'modernization of Islam'." (p. 7). In arguing that, she pointed out that "their arguments and thoughts are not original in comparison to those of Islamist intellectuals in other parts of the Islamic world." (Karasipahi, p. 8).

   At the same time, she argued that an understanding of these figures is of great importance not only because of "the transformation they engendered in Turkish intellectual life in general" (p. 2) but also because she predicted that they would "be the role models for young people – specifically 'upwardly mobile' high school and university students both in provincial towns and in big cities generally from traditional and conservative circles – in the future." (p. 2). It was, of course, such a group of young people that were also part of Gülen's vision for the creation of a "Golden Generation" (Sunier 2014) of pious Muslims who could also be fully active, contributing and holding responsibilities at all levels in all parts of Turkish society. As Haylamaz explained it, it was among such young people, as well as businesspeople who wanted to live an Islamically authentic life, that Gülen and his teaching became inspirational. Thus:

> From the 1960s onwards Hojaefendi emerged as a very influential preacher who travelled around the country and delivered many sermons as an itinerant preacher who also took some personal initiatives to go and meet people. Many were inspired by him, and asked this question: what can I do for these higher, loftier goals that this preacher is asking or calling us to? People from different walks of life have noticed his presence and have taken a direction in their own fields and disciplines to be a part of Gülen's work. You can see this huge diversity of people coming from various backgrounds who have been influenced, or at least inspired according to their own capacity, in different levels, and basically came forward. Some of them became more prominent and emerged in their locality, and they established especially foundations and institutions.

While it might generally be argued that one cannot properly understand the teaching or theology of any religious figure without at least some insight into their biographical, historical, and sociological context and what might be called the 'passive' and sometimes 'unconscious' effects of these, the central argument of both this book and its companion volume (Weller 2022) goes beyond such a position. Rather, it argues that specifically in the case of Gülen and Hizmet, there is an 'active' and at least sometimes also partially 'conscious' co-productive hermeneutical circle at work. This is such that one cannot understand the teaching of Gülen without understanding the context of his life, his person, and the combined effects of the practices he has inspired in others, also as these ultimately loop back and impact upon the further development of Gülen's own teaching. Among those of whom, of course, one needs to take special interactive account, is the influence and teaching of Nursi whom Gülen himself cited when asked about influences on Gülen's emphasis on love as being at the heart of Islam, explaining this as follows:

I have not met Said Nursi in my life, but I met some of his students, whom I thought exemplified this same centre, love centre, especially the Tahiri Mutlu. He was such a person he treated everybody, including young children, with such respect. I met him many times, but he never called me with my name. As a child, you know, it's cultural to call young people or children with their names, but he always referred to me with some kind of an adjective like "Bey", or some other adjective of respect. Hulusi Efendi was another student of Bediüzzaman Said Nursi. So these people I believe represent the spirit, the philosophy of the Prophet's life, and the centre of Islam.

Nursi's work itself, and the relationship between that; the *Nurcu* (the name given to those inspired by and following Nursi's work); and Gülen's own emergent thinking and teaching is integral to the contextual development of Gülen's teaching and practice as well as the characteristic activities of Hizmet as they developed with that teaching. As will be discussed in a more detailed way in Sect. 6.3, the story of the *Nurcu* is in many ways not only of relevance to the historical, ideational, and religious emergence of Gülen, but also to debates about Hizmet's own possible future trajectories.

Nursi is known to his direct followers and also among many other Muslims by the honorific title *Bediuzzaman*, meaning "Wonder of the Age" (Mardin 1989; Turner and Hurkuç 2008). This reflects a widespread belief among Muslims, that in each "age" a Muslim leader arises who is appropriate for that time and who has the task of renewing Islam within it. As a Muslim scholar of ethnically Kurdish background, in contrast to Muslim traditionalists who saw Islamic civilisation as in conflict with modernity, Nursi became generally known for his conviction that it was possible to unite Islam with science in the modern world. However, he did so in a way that is very different to the largely instrumentalised approach of Islamist thinkers who see secularism as the main enemy of Islam, by identifying ignorance, disunity, and poverty as the main enemies of humanity as a whole. In both of these aspects, one can identify themes that were later taken up and further developed by Gülen and Hizmet, especially in terms of concrete social initiatives.

The followers of Nursi are often referred to as a *cemaat* (or, community) and several streams developed among these, both inside and outside Turkey (Doumont 1986). Nursi himself had been deeply influenced by the Naqshibandiyya Sufi order (Weissman 2007) but never joined it, arguing that the decline of Muslims in the face of Western science and modernity called Muslims to other priorities to which he gave expression, during the 1920s and 1930s, in the collection of writings known as the *Risale-i-Nur* (or, *Epistles of Light*). In common with the Islamists, the aim of this writing was, through engaging with the Qu'ran rather than with Muslim traditionalism, to restore the pillars of Islam, and to expound the relationship between the divine, nature, and human beings in its multiple (and not only socio-legal dimensions). Prior to Gülen, Nursi was the last leader of a *cemaat* to meet a Turkish Prime Minister when, in 1960, not long before his death, he met Prime Minister Adnan Menderes.

After Nursi's death, those who followed his teaching were uncertain about how they might continue his legacy and a debate developed in which some advocated that one overall leader should be identified, while others argued for a consultative council to be established. A group from among the longstanding and senior followers elected Zübeyir Gündüzalp to head up the movement, on basis of an evaluation of him as being the most altruistic among them. However, this did not finally resolve the debate and, in time, a tension that has already existed during Nursi's life came out into the open between those who had copied the *Risale* (or tractates) of Nursi by hand and those who preferred the printed version in Latin letters.

Following the 27 May 1960 coup in Turkey, the former tendency became an identifiably separate group under the leadership of Hüsrev Altınbaşak. Others proposed founding a political organisation, and yet another group, associated with Müslüm Gündüz from Elazığ, believed that the time had come to spread the Nur philosophy through an armed struggle. Gündüzalp believed that these conflicting directions could only be resolved by having a strongly centralised administration. In due course, house number 46 in Kirazlı Mescit Street in Istanbul was rented and became the central office of the *Nurcus* in which all key decisions were taken. This ranged from those on the printing of Said Nuri's books through to the opening of new Nur circles, to the extent that sometimes the community even became known by reference to the address of its headquarters—as the Kirazlı Mescit Cemaat.

Many people currently in Hizmet acknowledge a connection with Said Nursi's teaching as, for example, testified to by AS4 when she said that "We read Gülen's books and Said Nursi's books, the *Risal-i-Nur* and we read those especially – and Qur'an, of course." However, it is also the case that historically when Gülen was in Edirne and Kırklareli between 1963 and 1966, he only rarely invoked the name of Nursi. Indeed, in many ways, he behaved distinctively in comparison to all of the *Nurcu* groups. As interviewee Mustafa Fidan (see Acknowledgements)—an early Hizmet participant who became, and has remained close to Gülen— explained it:

> I was one of the early participants of Hizmet, but I had originally met with the *Risal-i-Nur* first and foremost, and what I liked about *Risal-i-Nur* was that the style Bediüzzaman speaks and then writes is much easier, it actually facilitates for us understand the deeper concepts of theology. It is basically showing that "look this thing really makes sense." You're a part of this not because you are a part of a larger culture, but you believe because it makes sense.

In how Fidan explains this, one can see what was attractive to many about both Nursi and Gülen was the emergence of an Islamic praxis that was rooted in seeing the historic religious sources as living contemporary resources for personal and community life rather than primarily in terms of an historical and/or wider 'cultural' inheritance. As one of the products of both a quite secular familial background, but also of a Hizmet school education, Yeşilova explained this attraction and sense by reference to a dream that his father had in which:

> He saw in this dream that he and my younger brother enter a mosque to pray and then somehow my younger brother goes to lead the prayer, and he can see other people unhappy seeing a young man to lead the prayer. My father turns and shouts at them, "Look he is young but he knows Islam better than you."

Commenting on this, Yeşilova reflects that "You can tell from this, if we have to make psychoanalysis of this, many people were unhappy with the way those so-called Muslims were practising Islam and they constrained the religion to their narrow way of living, which when I was very young I did not like at all, and I was not attracted at all." Expressing this in very modern terms concerning the existential meaning of life, Yeşilova testified that:

> I later started listening to Gülen's sermons and I thought as if he had this way back in time and he was making the images of the example of the Prophet and his friends so visual as if he was there. It would not be possible to keep your heart unmoved when you listened to his emotional sermons.

When you listen to him, you feel that there's a meaning to this life. It's not just what you repeat, what your parents used to do, it's something else. So you can see as you listen to him you know you have to do something for this life; you have to do something for people; you have to do something for God; you just cannot stay here as you are, you know.

Tekalan's descriptions of Gülen's early days in Izmir, out of which came the development of the schools by which Gülen and Hizmet became so well known, also show the roots of this kind of religion in Gülen's contextual and dialogical approach to engaging with people, combined with a focus on discernment of the religious heart of things, differentiated it from merely cultural and traditional inheritances. As Tekelan explained it:

I really liked this method. He explained very well what Islam is: What is our responsibility to God? And as a Muslim, of course, what is our responsibility to our service, to our society? What is our responsibility to the will of Allah? Unfortunately, our prayers were not regular as five times a day, as a Muslim should do regularly. But as I got more sound information about Islam, I began to consciously practice my prayers. I have continued to learn gradually what Islam is and what Islam requires, and I still do. I didn't speak Arabic, but I started to understand the Qur'an and Islam better. After the last prayer of the day, Fethullah Gülen was in the mosque, especially on Fridays, for questions from all people, especially those who could not perform his prayer regularly. People would come and write their questions, then they would direct them to Fethullah Gülen and he would answer these questions one by one.

Tekalan then went on to highlight the dialogical and inspirational momentum that emerged out of this such that:

At that time, not only in Izmir, in other cities and later in the countries where Turkish community grew, there were meetings and conferences where people asked him all kinds of questions in mosques and large conference halls. People were asking questions about the Prophet, about religion, about the hereafter, about today's responsibilities. Our friends later published these questions in the form of books and series. I personally learned a lot from these conferences. Not only young people, but the elderly, too, were coming and learning about religion, and those people were learning the right information about Islam. From 1970 to 1980, for about ten years, he explained Islamic issues not only to the university students but also to the people from all walks of life be it in smaller gatherings, or in mosques, then in conference halls and later in homes, coffeehouses.

Summatively speaking, Özcan explained Gülen's overall methodological approach as being that, "Hojaefendi is looking at the issues from the perspective or angle of human beings, the universe, creation and God Almighty the creator and the relation of all these three elements in a sense, in a balanced way. But this balance is established again through, in the light of Qur'an and the *sunnah*." What was particularly attractive about this is, as Özcan put it, that "Hojaefendi is going to the true and authentic, mainstream resources of Islam" but also that he does this "according to the needs and the requirements of this age."

Indeed, this is of crucial significance in understanding the importance of Gülen's teaching since, as Özcan articulated it: "So, it is not only a simple understanding of religion, but its applicability, its practicability for the modern times and needs and then also appealing to and responding to the needs and the understanding of both believers and non-believers." Fully rooted in Islam, Özcan explains that Gülen also draws on wider sources and therefore: "While he is doing this he doesn't only benefit only from the Messenger of Islam only, Prophet Muhammad, but he uses all the Messengers of Islam, in a sense biblical Prophets in the past so that he can take this understanding to human beings properly." For the majority of those in Hizmet who have never personally met Gülen, it has been this kind of understanding and vision of Islam as found in his writings that came to have a formative influence on their lives. As AS1 testified, it was his reading of books by Gülen that first brought him into the movement:

No one gave me these books. I was in Istanbul staying in a dormitory, and I saw the books there. I just first read one book and I found many answers to the questions I had in my mind for many years and to which nobody had been able to give an answer to these questions. And I was shocked. This was a great motivation to me to finish. This was also how Mr. Gülen was doing his questions and answers in the mosque. It was also very attractive for me and gave me a very great motivation to finish one book in one day! – however many pages.

And, as AS1 went on to explain of this: "I read many books, sometimes one book per day. I finished nearly totally one hundred books. I was actually searching. I tried to improve myself and find my way. It was so educating for me. It took two years. And I found a chance to know the Hizmet followers closely."

It is the sense of this combination in Gülen's teaching—that, while he is deeply and properly in the tradition, he also takes seriously and addresses contemporary questions, which has proved so attractive to many over the years. At the same time, interestingly and significantly, and as already to some extent explained in Sect. 2.6, nearly all of those who spoke about the impact of Gülen's teaching also testified to what was actually a combined effect of his teaching together with their experience of some aspect of Hizmet. As AS3 elaborated this:

> The first stage I liked the people; I liked to talk with them; I liked many things with them. I said that for me, by myself, they are not bad people, they are good people. I can go easily with them. They don't hurt me or give any bad things because they are doing their job, they are working. In Turkey there are many different ways to learn religion, many movements. But some of them are not so easy to come into....But the Hizmet movement is easy to come in, and to know people is so easy, because it is everywhere in Turkey – in our classrooms, our friends: they are not so different from us.

It was only then, according to AS3, that he and his wife, AS4, went on to what he described as "the second stage." Through these and many other similar testimonies, it can be seen that alongside the specific impact of the Hizmet schools and other educational initiatives, the reception and impact of Gülen's teaching has been strongly shaped and impacted by its mediation also through individuals' wider experience of the Hizmet community and its activities. At the same time, alongside those who have remotely encountered and been shaped by Gülen's teaching via cassettes, printed publications, and more recently, digital media too, for those who have encountered him personally, it is also important to recognise the impact of the Fethullah Gülen himself, as what might be called an 'embodied teacher.'

This was underscored by CA1 (see Acknowledgements), an anonymous close associate of Gülen who explained in relation to the effect which the person of Gülen can have that "I keep telling my friends here, that they need to introduce him to whoever you they meet, because Hojaefendi is not just for Turks, you know, take people whoever you meet to him so at least in their lifetime they can see a person who prays." In support of this,

CA1 went on to recount his own "amazing first encounter" with Gülen, in the context of which:

> I could tell he was a very godly person. So, this is an unusual person. I mean you could tell it in the first experience, in the way he approached where he was to stand to prayer; the way he stood up long in prayer; the way he opened his hands, you know, I mean that was something I never saw, I had never witnessed in my life, a person in such a deep connection with God. That was amazing too, I mean you could see as he was doing this. I mean he was kind of lost, he was kind of not with us. We were standing behind him and I shouldn't have been looking to him, you know, I should be looking down, but I meant, what's going on? – this man is not with us. This doesn't mean he's intoxicated, no, but you could tell when he prays.

In expanding on this personal experience and perception, CA1 also cited a South African Muslim community leader known to him and to whom a friend had given a copy of Gülen's important four-volume work on Sufism, *Key Concepts in the Practice of Sufism: Emerald Hills of the Heart* (Gülen 2004a, 2004b, 2009, 2010). After reading this collection, that leader testified that "You cannot write these if you have not made that journey." Hakan Yeşilova, when reflecting on Gülen as a person, said:

> It's perhaps not possible for a person like me to fully comprehend Hojaefendi's depth of devotion to God. But for those who are there, who are having similar experience can make that appreciation much better because they are also taking a similar journey of devotion; of repentance; of asking for mercy; of asking for *ihsan*; that perfect bearing of witness to him.

Yeşilova also recounted what he referred to as another story that Gülen "repeats all the time, that *ihsan* Hadith," and of which he said that it "explains a lot about the kind of person Hojaefendi is":

> The Prophet was sitting with his friends and this man comes in and he's wearing white clothes. Nobody has ever met him before, but he doesn't look like a traveller because his clothes were just so white and clean. He comes close to the Prophet, sits in front of him, knee to knee, and then he starts asking questions and everyone is watching. He asks him what Islam is, and the Prophet says: you bear witness to him, you pray five times, you go to *hajj*, you give charity, and fast in Ramadan. And then the man says "you have said the truth," confirming him. Everyone is curious, "who's this guy confirming THE prophet?" And then he asks what is *iman*, what is faith? He

says it is belief in the uniqueness of God; to believe in angels; to believe in afterlife; to believe in destiny and six of those – and scriptures, not just the Qur'an that all are part of the faith too. And, again, he said you have said the truth. And then he asks what is *ihsan*, and the Prophet says *ihsan* is being conscious; to pray as if you are seeing God and being in the consciousness that even if you don't see him, that He is seeing you.

Yeşilova argues that the reason why Gülen refers to this story so frequently is because "Islamic scholars consider this as being the ultimate capacity of a human being in that awareness that we are in the presence of the divine and being in that consciousness twenty-four hours a day, all the time, not just when we go to mosque to pray."

In the light of the testimonies about the effect of Gülen as an embodied teacher and person of prayer, one of the particularly valuable and illuminating things for the author in conducting the research that informed this book and its companion volume was the opportunity to meet and interview Gülen in a context of participant observation of Gülen himself; of some of Gülen's close associates; and a number of his students and other visitors who were present at the same time as the author over a few days in December 2017 at the Golden Generation Retreat Centre in Saylorsburg, Pennsylvania, USA, where Gülen is now based.

On entering the room where the author was due to meet Gülen for the formal interview, there was at its end a large chair where one might at first have imagined Gülen would sit. However, the author found himself being ushered to that seat as the honoured guest, with Gülen sitting in another seat to the author's right-hand side. When thanking him for making the time and space to be interviewed; explaining the particular interest of this research as being concerned with how Gülen's engagement and understanding with the deep sources of Islam have interacted with his life in terms of people, in terms of places and in terms of periods through which he has lived; and expressing the hope that the research and any publications arising from it might make some small contribution to truth, Gülen replied "That's out of your humility."

Noting that the author had, according to custom, removed shoes, Gülen asked "Do your feet feel OK?", with the translator at the time adding the explanatory note that Gülen was concerned that the author's feet might feel cold. In addition, on discovering that the author was sleeping in one of the ordinary dormitory rooms of a guest house in the Centre's grounds, Gülen said that the author should rather have been allocated his own former bedroom. In relation the presentation of gifts taken by the author, which included the recitation (see Sect. 3.6 in this chapter) from the Beatitudes of Jesus, an anonymous translator for the interview with Özcan later reported of Gülen that, "He liked it, he expressed his appreciation of your kindness."

At the time of recitation, the author explained to Gülen, "That's my prayer as a person of faith" and that "I will do my best in my academic work in the service of truth," to which Gülen responded that: "We wish to reciprocate you in all these goodness and good intentions and services." Again, towards the end of the second interview, Gülen said: "I thank you out of your humility you see me as somebody deserving to be asked questions. I don't see myself as such but I thank you for making the effort to come here all the way." Finally, although clearly unwell, Gülen personally took the initiative to offer to take part in a second interview, this time conducted in the presence of a wider group of his students.

While in Saylorsburg, the author also had opportunity join in participant observation of Gülen leading the prayers and conducting his teaching circles with his students. This observation made very clear, in the proper sense of the word, the traditional character of Gülen's way of being and working with students, albeit that along with sitting on the floor and as well as getting out their hard copies of important texts, they also had their electronic devices. In many ways, author's experiences during this visit echoed those reported by Rabbi Dr. Alan Brill (2018) who wrote at greater length and detail about his own visit to, and meeting with, Gülen and his students. When asked by this author what he hoped for from his students in the future, Gülen responded:

> What we discuss and say throughout our discourse, it is what we expect our students here both to learn and exemplify – that is themselves first to internalise respect for all shared human values, and then to become people of heart and spirit, to have a very strong spiritual life, and also have a strong knowledge and foundation of religious disciplines, if they are students of religion, while at the same time be able to read the universe and have some level of knowledge and expertise and observation capabilities in the sciences.

In summarising this hope, and in echo of Said Nursi's overall approach, Gülen expressed his conviction that "The integration of these three dimensions – the positive sciences, the material sciences, life of the heart and the religious disciplines... will lead humanity into a Utopia-like atmosphere." At the same time, Gülen's clear conviction in this matter was balanced by a realistic assessment of human ambiguities, when he noted that, "But, of course, never in the life of humanity has a Utopia happened" since, as he put it:

> There has always been people who harmed people, there has been evil deeds, devilish people. But at some point in history this negativity can be localised, so at least part of the world can be safe from this negative force, and then the remainder of the world. especially with communications technology, recognising each other, they are not after destroying each other, that they have the capability to live in harmony this idea can be disseminated, if not to 100% of the world, much of the world.

3.3   SOURCES, PLACES, TIMES, AND REVELATORY DYNAMICS

The importance of context in relation to an understanding of the distinctiveness of Fethullah Gülen is not only something that is being argued by this book as an external interpretive framework for his life and teaching, but also links with Gülen's own particular approach to, and understanding of, revelation. The interplay between the teaching of this Turkish Muslim scholar and preacher, rooted in the Islamic sources noted above, and the development of the Hizmet inspired by his teaching and example as extended into diverse places and times, as can initially be seen in the original Turkish contexts of Erzerum, Edirne, and Izmir, as explored in Sects. 2.2, 2.3, and 2.4. As Ahmet Kurucan summarises, these contextual influences had significant substantive impact in the development of Gülen's thinking and teaching:

> When he moved to Edirne and Izmir, the very West of Turkey, where there is this extreme secularism and very little practice of Islam, he moves forward from orthodoxy to conservatism which is a progress, and he comes to a point where he makes this categorisation of 'norm' from 'form'. So, there are the essentials of faith and there are the secondary issues – there are the essentials of belief, but it might have different forms, which are the secondary issues. That's a huge progress.

Citing one example to do with gender relations of the influence of such contexts on the development of Gülen's understanding and teaching, Kurucan noted that:

As example of this progress from Istanbul after Izmir until 1992, you could see the way ladies in his family were dressing, you know. Back in Erzurum and before Hojaefendi came to Edine, and Izmir and Istanbul, they were wearing those full gowns, from top to toe, and usually they wouldn't show their faces, you know. They were previously stricter with men and women relationships when they used to stay in different quarters in the house. But they could now interact more easily after Hojaefendi's coming to Izmir and Istanbul.

Then, in terms of how this contextually impacted developmental change in Gülen's understanding had a further outworking in terms of new developments in Hizmet educational practice, Özcan explained that following the early 1990s:

Up to that time we had only student girls' houses and he convinced people to establish student hostels also for the girls. He also encouraged people include other people, not from our community, who would not send their students to other schools because of so-called moral concern – for their girls to attend he convinced people in the provinces to establish girls' schools, girls' colleges, so that not only those girls, but also the other people in the community's girls would also attend. So up to the 1990s the system is very well established: houses, boarding houses or hostels, schools for the boys and the girls, and schools to prepare the students for the university entrance exams. And this became a symbol almost for the community and this became almost, in a sense, what I mentioned as progenitor movement stated to set a good example for others to follow up with their own initiatives.

Thus, while Gülen's teaching does not depart from the basic sources of the Qu'ran, it also does not see the truth or revelation as being either historically 'isolated' or 'imprisoned' in the 'frozen' historical deposit of an ideal past. Rather, as Öztürk seeks to explain it, for Gülen, revelation is something vital and present:

Revelation is not something that was revealed fourteen hundred years ago, but is something that is being revealed to each and every one of us right now, right in this moment. And how we are going to understand that message in this time and space, and actualise it in our relations with nature, with the environment, and with the rest of the human beings.

As also within Islam more classically and broadly speaking, Öztürk additionally underlines that, of fundamental importance to Gülen's approach is the example of the Prophet Muhammad, in and through whose historical life, examples of how what is believed to be the divine revelation can be seen as having been actualised. And this not in the life only of an historical figure, but also as an exemplar for contemporary possibilities in the human reception of divine revelation. Thus:

> In addition to acknowledging that the divine message is being continuously revealed, constantly to each and every one of us, it is also important to recognize the Prophet Muhammad, peace be upon him, as the very first person who got that message and did his best to put it into practice in his society, in his time. If this is so, then how should we look into his role model so that we can understand the message today in our own conditions?

Öztürk also highlights the importance to Gülen of the early adopters of Islam, again both in terms of their historical examples, but also in terms of the methodological practice of arriving at *ijtihads* through which "Mr. Gülen now tries to interpret the time we are living in and define how we should formulate our interactions with the rest of the society, the human being as well as the environment" and this finds connection with, and purchase in, changing historical conditions:

> So, in Gülen the first thing was the Qur'an, the second is the Prophet's traditions and his role in understanding the message. And the third, Gülen considers the first three generations, the first three centuries after the revelation of the Qur'an, as a time where there was this very quick, rapid dynamic of reinterpreting the message and where they came up with new reasonings, *ijtihads*, to understand that message, which actually laid down a very strong foundation for us to go to refer to when we aim to understand that divine message, which period we call *salaf-e-saliheen*, the very first pious predecessors, that followed the Prophet and his Companions.

Alongside the importance of recognising the emergence of change out of the interplay between Islamic sources, contextual learning, and practice development, when reflecting on the relationship between continuity and change as manifested in Gülen's teaching, Tekalan noted that "If you compare his speeches in Turkey twenty-five years ago with his current speeches you will almost always hear the same things." Tekalan does not mean by this that Gülen has not changed. Rather the "same things" that Tekalan means are what might be called the 'main things.' So, although

Gülen has articulated various matters in different periods of his life with different voices and emphases, there is that which is constant, namely:

> To know, to understand the existence of God, Allah; and secondly, the here-after. If you can understand and explain to yourself very nicely the existence of Allah, of the God, the hereafter, and if you behave also very properly according to Holy books, the people would understand the main goal. Whether you are a doctor, or the President of the country, or the President of a University, or you are very rich, the poor are not so important. What is important is being human.

What therefore is constant for Gülen is that he brings to bear what is both a deeply religious and concurrently deeply human perspective on life in which the eternal connects with the temporal. But, along with this consistency, Tekalan says "That doesn't mean he's always the same. He was saying things at first, and he's saying things now. But, over time, he also makes statements based on new developments." Tekalan furthermore explained that by taking and building on the foundations of the four main sources of Sunni Islam—namely the Qur'an, the Hadith (Prophet's words), *ijma* (opinions of scholars), and *qiyas* (comparison to find out similar cases in history)—"He added two more things to them. The requirements of your location and the requirements of your time," which is reflected in the title of Albayrak's (2011) edited book on Gülen and his teaching called, *Mastering Knowledge in Modern Times.*

In other words, what is in important to recognise in all of this is that, not only is it a social fact that temporal and geographical contexts profoundly affect and shape Gülen's interpretation and application of Islamic sources, but it is also the case that Gülen *consciously* takes these contexts into account when working with these sources. Thus, Tekalan noted that, "if an engineer or social scientist was explaining something new, he listened very carefully. He was trying to understand new developments in the world of science. That's what he was doing, and that's what he's still doing now." As an example of this, Tekalan cited that when the internet was invented Gülen underlined its importance as a development that everyone needed to know about. And it was the same with solar energy, of which Tekalan said "He told us to install solar energy at Yamanlar High School."

As another concrete example of the significance of this kind of approach for obscurantist readings of Islamic legal manuals, Kurucan gives the example of the handling of water and cleanliness, which plays a significant role in Islamic ritual practice:

> Classical manuals for Islamic law and practice usually start with how clean is the water. Water certainly is very significant, especially in our practice, as we have to wash ourselves for our ablutions, for our prayers. So there have been volumes of discussions on the size of the well; if a rat falls into it, is it clean or not; how much water should we remove from the well; if the animal is swollen or not, you know there are pages and pages of these questions.

In contrast to such an approach, Kurucan says that when Gülen's disciples started reading these classical books, "Hojaefendi basically grinned and said, 'Look there were no devices to measure the Ph levels of the water in the past. Now, you check with that and then you're done, you don't have to consider all those measurements and spend this amount of scholarship for this'." But Kurucan acknowledges that, more broadly, despite this:

> Unfortunately, still even the latest printed books on that classical scholarship start with the same discussions on how much water should go from the well, and there are many groups still spending a lot of time for that, although they are not using wells anymore in their homes; such a huge waste of time.

Kurucan also highlighted some of the wider implications of such instances for Islam, Muslims, and the world when he summarised that: "So, you know, just imagine a world where a group is reading these classical textbooks and they come out as the Taliban." In contrast, he points to "Another group, which Hojaefendi is leading, is reading the same classical books and this Hizmet is coming out." In summary, Kurucan notes "So that's a huge contrast, and that's how we should perhaps appreciate the value of how Hojaefendi considers that scholarship to be dependent on time and space. So, the conditions that were developed fourteen hundred years ago in Mecca and Baghdad certainly doesn't work here."

When Kurucan was asked about what he perceived to be at the heart of Gülen's teaching, in common with the key things already underlined by Öztürk, Kurucan commented that, "The first thing that comes to my mind in relation to what I understand of Hojaefendi and Islam is his deep connection to the Qur'an, Prophets, *sunnah* and traditions and the tradition of oral Islamic scholarship." However, in relation to these sources, what Kurucan went on to highlight from his own experience as a student of Gülen, is an integrated and balanced approach:

> The way you presented the classes to him or he organised his teachings is a proof of the way he is following that tradition from the Ottoman scholarship of touching on every discipline under Islamic sciences. He made sure, that we are knowledgeable to a certain extent at least in all those disciplines, from Sufism to *Hadith* and jurisprudence.

On this, Kurucan cited Çapan's (2011) book chapter on "Gulen's Teaching Methodology in his Private Circle" in support of his own view, which Kurucan summarised as follows:

> Hojaefendi represents that old Ottoman scholarship tradition where scholars were considered not experts in a single specific field, but in all disciplines and in this regard Hojaefendi's scholarship follows in that route where we could consider him as a full expert on *tafsir* (Qur'anic exegesis), traditions, *kalam* (theology), *tasawwuf* (Sufism), in all those Islamic disciplines, not just an expert in one discipline.

In the year following the end of his classes with Gülen in 1988, Kurucan explained that Gülen was still "advising us to study not just one discipline or one area but all of them but like reading bit by bit every day, like three pages from *tafsir*, three pages from *kalam*, three pages from *hadith*." At the same time, Kurucan admits that "I was a preacher. I was also travelling and I was busy with other things. I was now in the world. So, I tried to do that, like, for six months but I said, look there's something wrong here, Hojaefendi thinks we are like him, which is impossible" and because Kurucan recognised that he was not *hafiz*, he explained that he opted to focus on jurisprudence.

Thus, although context and environment play a key role in the development and re-evaluation of interpretation that one sees across the periods of Gülen's teaching, such development and re-evaluation comes about because of his solid and, in many ways (properly) traditional (rather than 'traditionalist') bedrock. However, and of great importance, this needs to be understood in combination with what Kurucan highlights concerning Gülen's basic methodological approach which is that everything else should be open to question. As illustrated again from Kurucan's own experience of Gülen's pedagogical practice:

On October 23 1985, when we started our first circle with Hojaefendi, we picked up some of those classical books from the main literature of Islamic scholarship, like Bukhari, and others. He said before we started reading, I'm not asking you to adopt scepticism as a profession, but you should be sceptical with whatever deductions I may come with those readings. You should always ask the reason and the main ground for those arguments. So that's how we started off. But, certainly, we worked with the Qur'anic scripture and *hadith*; this literature has everything very clearly defined. With the exception of these sources, there is nothing else that you should not approach with scepticism.

Overall, then, Gülen's teaching would therefore very much appear to be an example of that of the tradition of a religion being reinvigorated by a questioning and contextualised encounter with what is at its heart. And it is this contextualised understanding which those inspired by Gülen translated into the concrete and historical manifestation of Hizmet initiatives. As Fidan explained it: "With Hojaefendi's teaching, we saw in Hoja an expansion of the real focus of the *Risale-i Nur* of Bediüzzaman which was focusing so much on the faith in God and that divine awareness and consciousness" and that:

In Hojaefendi's work we saw why we need to be aware of this divine, why we need to worship Him, why we need to engage in charity and good work. Without that capital, you know, quite a majority of us were very lacking before, although by name, nominally we were Muslims, was actually introduced by the teaching and example of Hoja.

Indeed, Fidan went on to emphasise how those who encountered this deeply religious awareness also developed a consciousness of the need for the actualisation of this in terms of its implications for practice, not only in ritual obligations, but also in social works. Thus, when asked about what he perceived to be at the heart of Gülen's teaching, Fidan responded from the perspective of a businessperson looking for practical expressions of genuine religion, in a way that bears repeating at some length for the insight that it gives into the impact of Gülen via the combination of both his teaching and his practice on those first inspired by him:

To make an analogy with running a business: to be able to run a business you really have to have some capital. In this case of Hizmet, the real capital for these good services is a true faith. Yes, we already knew the principles of

Islamic practice from our past. We knew how to pray, we knew how many and what sort of a ratio we should give out of our annual wealth, and we knew also that our religion was teaching this through the Prophet's words: "if your neighbour's hungry, you're not one of us"; "if you are leaving him or her hungry, you are not one of us." Yes, we knew this but who was really caring for their neighbours?

And, as Fidan continued:

> Well, I mean, we're a Muslim nation back in Turkey. We are Muslims, our fathers were Muslims, our grandparents were Muslims, so we lived in that traditional Muslim life. But we also thought, in a way, that we were fulfilling our religious duties: when it is time for us to give charity, when it is time for us to go on *hajj*, then we'll be done, we'll be finished with our responsibilities. But that was, more or less, a traditional way of understanding religion.

By contrast with this, because Gülen's teaching issues into social action, Fidan concluded that:

> As time passed, we saw the fruits of these services when our younger generations were really growing, living like the friends of the Prophet with their relationship with God, with the way they engaged in an honourable life with others, and we saw the fruits of it, so this is why we believed in this person.

As Gülen himself articulated it, his teaching and work has been seeking to address the problem of what he calls the "appearance of Muslimness"— in other words, that of being a Muslim in just appearance or form and not in substance, in relation to which Gülen said:

> Indeed, at this time this is widespread. The so-called 'Muslim world' is devoid of truly devout individuals. One of the famous columnists in Turkey who is not known to be a very, you know, devout Muslim – nevertheless he was a believer, so he expressed his view that many of the pilgrims, Muslim pilgrims, don't appear to be really sincere and devout, as if they are performing simply as an empty ritual. Indeed, that is the picture that is put forward by many Muslims, unfortunately.

Thus, as Fidan put it: "What I believe is the most influential thing in Gülen's thought is the fact that he lives up to that ideal forms of living that has been described in the scriptures. He lives the Qur'an that he's teaching. He lives that out. He acts the way he teaches." And as Öztürk noted, "If we take a look at where Mr. Gülen started in that remote part of Turkey, in that village in Erzurum, and compare it where he has arrived, we can see the results this interaction can produce" in relation to the questions of the time for Muslims as articulated by Öztürk in terms of: "1. How do we live under the conditions of this worldly life? 2. How can we aspire to become 'perfect human beings' within the conditions of the time and space in which we are living? 3. And how can we have influence on the rest of the world?"

It is in his willingness to go beyond the limitations imposed by inherited taboos as further explored in Sects. 3.4, 3.5, and 3.6) that makes Gülen such an interestingly creative Islamic figure who does not conform to expected stereotypes. By contrast, as Kurucan emphasises it, "I mean what you would expect from a normal *imam* or preacher in Turkey and in the rest of the 'Muslim world' is to curse Israel, to curse America, to curse Europe, that's what you would expect because of the Crusader mentality." However, not only does Gülen not conform to such stereotypes, but as Kurucan puts it: "the kind of the human being Gülen is idealising in his own way" is one who, "accepting his own natural physical capacity and weaknesses, yet has this trajectory that goes beyond that and who does not imprison himself within those boundaries." In the course of this overall biographical and pedagogical trajectory, Ergene underlines the importance of realising that:

Hojaefendi has taken a lot of risks. Yet, this has not been fully credited neither in the Islamic world nor in the West. Decades ago when he said that he cried for the children of Israel because of those suicide bombers, he was excommunicated and cursed by Muslims. But he was actually saying something from the very basis of religion: that Islam is not allowing you to kill people in that way. Islam does not deny the reality of war; it is a part of human condition, but it brought rules to war. What Gülen was saying, as an *imam*, as a preacher, was referring Muslims back to those essential principles of Islam that you don't have the right, whatever the conditions may be, to kill innocent people. But he was excommunicated.

Succinctly summarising the impact of Gülen's teaching and practice, as Keleş put it, Gülen "broke a lot of taboos, you've got to think about this" which Sects. 3.3, 3.4, and 3.5 of this chapter now seek to highlight and explore in relation to key secular-political, national-cultural, and religious boundary taboos.

3.4   OVERCOMING SECULAR-POLITICAL TABOOS

It is arguable that Gülen's particular understanding of Islam in engagement with both rich Islamic tradition and contemporary realities could probably only have originally emerged in a Turkish context. This is because one of the things that is contextually distinctive of Turkey as a majority Muslim context as outlined in the first section of this chapter is its inheritance of a particular form of secularism alongside deep and strong traditions of Islam, combined with a particular flavour arising from the Ottoman inheritance as enriched by a number of Sufi-related traditions.

By contrast with this, in most other parts of the majority 'Muslim World,' the broader contextual shaping of the engagement between the religious and secular was characterised by the importation of the latter along with colonialism and imperialism. This was not, however, the case in Turkish history where, if it would be in any way correct to speak of colonisation it would be in terms of what might be called 'partially indigenised secularism' and the political parties associated with it. At the same time, as briefly discussed in the second section of this chapter, some have taken a stance of advocating for what one might call an integral 'Islamist' alternative.

In the case of Gülen and of Hizmet as it emerged from his teaching, they have had to position themselves with reference to the secular, Ottoman and Sufi heritages of Turkish public life, and the related challenge of the secular-political, national-cultural, and religious diversity taboos in relation to which Ergene has said that "Gülen's nature was always to go beyond the limits." Within this, with regard to engagement with "Western Enlightenment thinking and the challenges of the secular," as Ergene notes:

> In *madrassah* when Hojaefendi was reading books from other disciplines, his own scholars, his own teachers, actually, they did not accept him reading them. "How come you go beyond the literature available here?" So, you see, on the one hand, he had that search; and on the other hand, there was this very deeply constrained understanding of the time. In the Middle East, if you are trained in a *madrassah* there is no pathway or gateway to anything like western literature. But you see this young man, Hojaefendi, going beyond, wherever he got them, wherever he found them, he was reading this western philosophy, literature, and classics, all of them, he finished them when he was very young.

But both Gülen and Hizmet engaged not only with western philosophical thinking, but also with the concrete impact of aspects of this as embodied in the powerful secular current created in Turkey as mediated also through the historic role of the military as guardians of the Kemalist secular order and also of political parties that were supportive of this. The outworking of such engagement can be seen clearly in the work of the Journalists and Writers' Foundation, established in 1994, of which Fethullah Gülen was the Honorary President and especially in the work of the work of its so-called Abant Platform (Weller 2022, Sect. 2.3).

The early meetings of the Platform, for example, dealt with such challenging topics as "Islam and Secularism" and "Pluralism and Social Reconciliation." From 2006 onwards, the Academic Co-Ordinator of the Abant Platform was Professor Dr. Mete Tuncay of Bilgi University—who referred to himself as, "a person who believes in agnosticism in religion." This approach to engaging with the secular also embodied a way of steering a course in relation to the political realm that was, on the one hand, different to that of the political 'Islamists' but also different to that of Nursi's broader identification of politics as ultimately being to do with the devil.

Giving a flavour of the times in which Gülen originally emerged as a preacher and leader living and working in Izmir, as Özcan put it from his perspective, Marxist-Leninists and other leftists "were rampant and were causing havoc at the universities and were preventing people from even attending the universities." In this context, Özcan explained in relation to Gülen's work with university students "Some people were criticising him that, you know, you cannot go much further with this bunch of students," but that:

He was consistent in all his efforts and when even these students and the other students were having this chaos and skirmishes at the universities, he always convinced people that this reactionary way of acting will not be the solution for Turkey and the students. So, he stood at the right place. He always preserved that status and standing, and he always convinced people that they should be constructive, constructively thinking and acting, rather than being reactionary. And he didn't, he was not against any group, any race, any ethnicity. He didn't make a fuss about all this, but he directed all his efforts and teachings and lectures and lectures and convincing arguments to the need for appropriate education.

Nevertheless, among the various criticisms of Gülen, a more politically inflected criticism is that, especially in his earlier life, he was aligned with the political right. Indeed, according to Nurettin Veren—who knew Gülen since his sermons in Kestanepazarı Mosque in Izmir in 1988 and was one of original 12 people who founded the Akyazılı Foundation—Gülen stands accused of working for the USA's Central Intelligence Agency in the Cold War struggle against Communism and in the interests of the USA. As noted in Sect. 1.3 where reference is made to Koç's identification of various tropes that have been deployed to criticise Gülen, at least in relation the matter of US interests this is, in many ways, a self-contradictory trope when used alongside that Gülen being an Islamist 'wolf in sheep's clothing.'

Overall, according to those who at that time were closely associated with Gülen and have remained so since, the reality was more complex. According to Özcan, in Izmir "At that time we said he was not against any ideological group or other things," although as a religious leader he was perhaps unsurprisingly critical of the philosophical, ontological, and epistemological stance of atheistic materialism. Thus, as Özcan recounted, while Gülen was in Erzurum "there was an anti-Communist newly established organization and he was invited there to give some kind of moral lectures over that, not political." In relation to this, a close associate of Gülen, Muhammad Çetin (see Acknowledgements), further elaborated, as follows:

I have asked him if he became a part of this thing, and he said, no they just asked me to give moral lectures, and I only lectured once or twice he said. This is clarification by himself, so this is directly from Gülen. He was not constantly part of them. Among their activities there is this moral teaching and in that one he talked about Rumi, and his love of God and how he deals with the people and embraces all people, that sort of all-embracing love – the issues – he didn't go into the political issues....Thus, Hojaefendi said at that time that the, in a sense struggle against Communism or such trends could be only through faith, along with reading the modern times properly so that faith and the requirements of the modern times, if they are given to people, then they will not need such ideologies to make any progress for themselves or their country. So, faith along with reading the realities of the modern times and coming with a synthesis in a sense – faith and modern remedies.

Gülen's apparent stances in relation to the role of the military in Turkish society have also been a focus of criticism. This has been particularly so on the part of leftists in Turkey who, despite the suffering also at various times of Islamists and Nationalists at the hands of the military, have arguably disproportionately experienced this. From an analysis of Gülen's writings and statements in the period concerned, it would seem not be inaccurate to see Gülen as having had a general tendency towards the right of politics than to the left, primarily on the basis of his being at odds with the ideological atheism of many Marxists, but also because of his strong sense of both Ottoman and national inheritance in which Sunni Islam has played such a strong role. This combination, in turn, made him not unsympathetic to the so-called "Turkish-Islamic Synthesis" that was propagated by the military rulers in the 1980s to counter both Islamism and leftist politics.

Nevertheless, it is also the case that Gülen also has a history of suffering at the hands of the military. Thus, in the context of the 12 March 1971 coup, when Gülen was in Izmir, he was arrested and held with a large group of other people at Bademli Military Prison and charged with belonging to the *Nurcu* group. A number of those imprisoned with him acknowledged this and defended their position with some being acquitted while others were given relatively short sentences. Gülen, however, did not admit to being a *Nurcu* but, on the basis of the allegation that he was involved in an attempt to change the secular nature of the State, on 20 September 1972, he was (without legal representation) sentenced by the İzmir Martial Law Military Court to three years imprisonment and disbarment from acting as a civil servant, which meant he could no longer act as an *imam*. In practice, the court sent him to one year's house arrest in Sinop, on the Black Sea and when the guilty verdict was later confirmed by the Military Court of Appeals (9th Division), although the original punishment was judged to have been too harsh. Thus, when in 1974, an amnesty was announced under Prime Minister Bülent Ecevit, Gülen was released.

As previously noted in Sect. 2.1, the English translation of the title of an early Turkish biographical source (Erdoğan 1995) for the biographical details of much of Gülen's early life is *My Small World*. Prison is, in many ways, the smallest world one can experience. Here, Gülen also encountered people of various backgrounds and had opportunity to evaluate at least some of his previous assumptions. As Öztürk explained, "Turkey has this history of military intervention that took place every ten years. When the military intervened they would arrest people both from the right and the left. Gülen was in jail for about five months, but he had the chance to live side by side with ....those who were from leftist groups." In commenting on this, one of the anonymous translators of the interview intervened to note that Gülen has a saying that "you know people better when you are travelling, when you are eating together," but also even more so that "you know people better when you are in prison." As a result of this experience, despite coming from a background that was far removed from an ideologically atheist Marxism, Gülen positively evaluated some leftists, although Öztürk also noted of Gülen at the time that:

> He also had the opportunity to observe what those extreme leftists would do if they really were to come to power in the country. So, he also sets his measures in his relationship with them. I remember that he repeatedly said that his experience with the leftists there, where Hojaefendi was critical of the ideology or an idea of Marx, but one of those leftists was offended and said, "do you want me to start with your God and with your Prophet?" And then he said he realised this was not the way to go. "I don't want anyone to curse my Prophet, so I'd better stay quiet."

At the same time, Gülen also had some closer experience with students of Nursi who were in prison too, in relation to which Öztürk summarised of Gülen that "He was able to see them much more closely and how they reacted to conditions more difficult than come in civil life" and that, as a consequence of this, "he saw from that spectrum or window how different some students of Nursi were than Nursi himself. Then he realises that's not a long-term relationship he was going to build on with them because they were differing in many ways from his ideals."

By the time of the next military coup on 12 September 1980, a seeming contradiction emerged. On the one hand, Gülen wrote referring to the anarchy and chaos of the times in terms of soldiers coming to the rescue. As Gülen later put it:

> Some people were trying to reach a goal by killing others. Everybody was a terrorist. The people on that side were terrorists; the people on this side were terrorists. But, everybody was labeling the same action differently. One person would say, "I am doing this in the name of Islam." Another would say, "I am doing it for my land and people." A third would say, "I am fighting against capitalism and exploitation." These all were just words. The Qur'an talks about such "labels." They are things of no value. But people

just kept on killing. Everyone was killing in the name of an ideal. (Gülen 2004c, 189)

At the same time, during this period posters also came out showing Gülen as a 'wanted person,' during which time he travelled around in Anatolia continuing his work and trying to evade arrest. On 12 January 1986, he was finally detained in Burdur, although after only one night in police custody, Prime Minister Turgut Özal—who was broadly sympathetic to Millis Görüş, but also to the ideas of Gülen—intervened and Gülen was taken to Izmir where he was released.

When it came to the 28 February 1997 postmodern coup, Gülen appeared on television and the following day, his words that "the government should go" made the headlines in all the newspapers. This was on the basis that they were taken as being supportive of the position taken by the National Security Council. However, in interpreting both this and his earlier references to soldiers coming to the rescue, it is important to bear in mind that for an Islamic scholar such as Gülen, the dangers and threats that come from an apparent state of anarchy are generally evaluated as being more problematic than those associated with authoritarian and military rule, however problematic the latter might be.

With regard to the relationship between Gülen's own personal predispositions and those of the movement, Keleş commented that it is clear that "This is a social movement. Gülen doesn't need to issue a memo to everyone you know. It becomes clear where affinities lie: in the movement people, it's clear that there is no force on people to vote in a certain way." With regard to individual political figures, Gülen actively connected at one time or another with leaders from across a wide spectrum, including Prime Ministers ranging through Tansu Çiller (True Path Party); Bülent Ecevit (Democratic Left Party); Necmettin Erbakan (Welfare Party); and Mesut Yılmaz (Motherland Party), and in relation to individual politicians, Keleş noted that:

It's also clear that Gülen was more amiable to one politician over another. For example, the leader of the left-wing party, Bulent Ecevit. Bulent Ecevit was actually very supportive of Gülen, and at an intellectual level there was a confluence between the two. And Demirel less so, perhaps, than the two people I have mentioned, Gülen was also in communication with him, and Demirel, I think, was also supportive of the schools in Central Asia and so on.

Until the rise of the AKP, Keleş argues that Gülen and the movement "took a more measured approach" to any alignment with other movements and/or political parties, albeit significantly, as added as a footnote from Keleş—"with the exception of an antagonism towards the political Islam project." With the rise of the AKP, however, according to Muhammad Çetin who, in 2017, counted and checked photos of the meetings that took place in the Golden Generation Retreat Centre with Turkish politicians, as many as "Twenty-nine Ministers including Tayyip Erdoğan and the President Gul, and ninety-two Members of Parliament from the AKP alone came over to this country and visited Hojaefendi," although it was also noted that Erdoğan's visit was made before he became Prime Minister.

Nevertheless, Keleş underlined that the existence of such visits should carefully be distinguished from the question, as Keleş put it, of "supporting a political party in the way the movement subsequently did," when many within Hizmet did move into a much closer alignment with the AKP (Weller 2022, Sects. 4.1 and 4.2). With regard to the later and more direct relationship that developed between Gülen and Recep Tayip Erdoğan, and which some have presented as originally having been of the nature of a close personal alliance, Keleş recounts that by 2010, when he was getting ready in a UK seminar to say that Hizmet and the AKP are not ideologically aligned, someone from the UK Foreign and Commonwealth Office's Turkey desk said to him "We believe that Erdoğan sees Gülen as a challenge and threat." Keleş furthermore suggests that, even at this time, Gülen's view of this was much more nuanced than many have suggested, explaining that "I believe that Gülen's view of this was: 'Is this long-lasting? Is this sincere?' And I think he had his doubts from the very beginning." In connection with how Fethuallah Gülen's doubts grew, Keleş refers to a letter sent, in 2006, by Gülen to Erdoğan, of which Keleş says:

Gülen mulled over it for a long time. One of Gülen's close students showed me a copy of the letter. Gülen is obviously aware of the ongoing profiling in the state, against all category of people, including those sympathetic to the movement. This continues during the time of the early Erdoğan government as well. I suspect Gülen was writing to him about this, although he doesn't specifically say in his letter. In that letter, respectful though he is, he says something along the lines of, if they are forcing you to do this, either leave it or remain true to yourself, do not allow them to force you to change. But then he relates this dream that two different Hizmet people had allegedly seen – they had the same dream apparently. And it's a derogatory dream, in the sense that they see Erdoğan entering a building with a group of others. Among them, Erdoğan is the only 'ordinary' looking one. The others have scary and somewhat 'abnormal' features. On exit however, Erdoğan has morphed to look like them. This letter was delivered to Erdoğan in 2006.

Overall, then, as with many Sufi figures in Islamic history, Gülen's relationships with the governing 'powers-that-be' have been varied, with him experiencing at various times in his life being in the public eye and celebrated, while at other times needing to be 'on the run' and/or being locked away in prison.

3.5   OVERCOMING NATIONAL-CULTURAL TABOOS

Sunier (2014) argues that what has been produced by Gülen in interaction with those inspired by him is what he calls, in his article of that title, a "Cosmopolitan Theology." If Sunier's evaluation is correct, then one should not underestimate how substantial a development this is. This is not least because, for example, as interviewee Termijón Termizoda (normally known as Temir) Naziri (see Acknowledgements) from Spain and a Tadjik by origin highlighted, "I can say that every Turk is very nationalistic by default, I can say that. And this is the product of, I think, if it is before I don't know, but at least it is the product of the Republic of Turkey." In this, Naziri was alluding to the foundational ideology of Turkey as a nationalistic unity—one religion, one language, one ethnicity, and of which Naziri says "They have managed to put it in every piece of the society, no matter which background, they really do have this, OK." Indeed, in important ways such identity also played a historically significant role in the emergence and spread of Hizmet itself, not least into the culturally resonant Turkic regions of the former Soviet Union.

Importantly, if there is at least some truth in Naziri's evaluation in relation to the nationalistic tendencies of Turkish people in general then such an evaluation at the least implicitly raises the question of how far this might also have applied and/or still applies to Gülen himself. And, indeed, such a question was anticipated by Naziri who, after making his clear statement about the widespread influence of nationalism on Turks, went on to say of Gülen's engagement with his own Turkish heritage "And by the way, I suppose that Fethullah Gülen used this positively, positively" because "It was Turkish reality, the reality of Turkey, you know, the inter-locutor, so you have to use some code, some expressions etc."

Indeed, and especially but not exclusively in his early teaching, Gülen used a lot of both Turkish and Ottoman referents alongside those of Anatolian Sufism. Of course, a love of a country and of its heritage which Gülen clearly demonstrates should be carefully distinguished from a more populist or ideological form of nationalism, and Gülen's role as a national-cultural taboo-breaker can perhaps be illustrated by reference to his stances in relation to Turkish membership of the European Union; the positions that he took in relation to the MV Mavi Marmara incident with Israel; and finally the positions he has increasingly been taking in relation to matters of Turkish and Armenian history and present-day relations, with each of these being explored in the remaining section of this chapter.

It was in relation to the debate around Turkey's possible future full membership of the European Union that Gülen revealed himself more strongly and clearly as a breaker of national/cultural boundary taboos. In the early years of the AKP government, the debate about Turkish mem-bership of the EU became stronger and more insistent, both inside Turkey itself and within the EU itself. Such debates have tended to act as a micro-cosm for a wider range of key issues, both within Turkey and beyond, concerning the nature of the appropriate relationships between economics and politics, religions and cultures, and states and societies. While some EU member states have supported eventual Turkish accession, others have argued that the cultural and religious differences mean that full accession is not appropriate, including on religio-cultural grounds. In Turkey itself, some supporters of EU membership have seen it as a major economic opportunity for Turkey: while others have seen it as a means through which to further development and entrench human rights and civil society over and against the continued shadow cast by Turkey's history of military coups; and still others have opposed membership on either nationalist and/or religious grounds.

Overall, the country's predominantly Muslim population; coupled with the strongly secular heritage of its public life over the past century; its geopolitical location at the crossroads between the predominantly 'Christendom' Europe, the Eurasian landmass of newly independent countries of the former Soviet Union, and the predominantly 'Islamic' Arab world means that the issues clustered around this debate are of great importance for the future of both Turkey itself and of the EU and, in many ways, Gülen contributed to a climate in which Turkish membership of the EU could become more thinkable, both among Turkish Muslims and in the wider Europe.

Indeed, as already explored in relation to the taboo of the secular, Gülen's more general teaching and perspectives had arguably effected a shift in some of the debate's preconceived frameworks, suggesting that Hizmet might have been able to play a helpful role in the internal and external civil society dialogue that would be a necessary part of any EU enlargement to include Turkey. In contrast to the 'clash of civilizations' approach espoused either by secular or Christian new 'cold warriors' or by contemporary Islamists, Gülen has argued the positive case that Turkey could be a bridge across Europe, the Middle East, and the Far East and, specifically, supported the aim of Turkey's accession to the EU (Gülen 1994; Weller 2013). However, as time went on, the AKP began to pivot away from EU and towards the idea of Turkey re-establishing a strategic regional focus and role, and Hizmet's ability to act in the way that it had previously done within such debates, came to an abrupt end with July 2016 and its aftermath. This resulted, on the one hand, in the complete dismantling of Hizmet's infrastructure and capacity within the country and, on the other, while formally remaining a member of NATO, in the Turkish government's new foreign policy orientation towards cultivating relationships with Iran and the Russian Federation.

Another major indicator of Gülen's readiness to be a national-cultural taboo-breaker—as well as of how Erdoğan and the AKP were increasingly pivoting into directions divergent from those of Hizmet—was the so-called MV Mavi Marmara incident (Weller 2022, Sect. 4.3), and of which İsmail Sezgin (2014) said that:

> In my opinion, this incident provides one of the most important pieces of evidence that show the difference between the 'political Islamist perspective' in Turkey and the 'civil Islam' that the Hizmet movement seems to represent. Political Islamism strongly advocated a military response, while the civil Islam representatives were a bit more cautious before they reacted. Gülen prefers to stay away from politics, while political Islamism willingly champions a political cause even in the guise of charity.

In many ways Sezgin's analysis of the situation is also reflected in the opening chapter—"Responsibility in Practice: Testing the Blockade"—of Simon Robinson's (2017) book that discusses Gülen's approach to ethical responsibility within the wider context of Islamic thought and which says of Gülen in relation to this that:

> Here was a Muslim thinker who seemed to be supporting Israel, and certainly wasn't supporting that were perceived by many to be the liberating efforts of a largely Muslim non-governmental organisation (NGO). This meant that for others, inside and outside the Hizmet movement, his message was surprising or even shocking. The case serves to introduce a person who is hard to categorize. (pp. 10–11).

To support his argument, Sezgin identifies a series of what he calls "some of the principles that Gülen and the Hizmet movement follow." First of all, integrity: Gülen situated his response in the same advice he had been giving on methods to the Hizmet-inspired relief organisation, Kimse Yok Mu (Weller 2022, Sect. 2.4), which was also delivering aid to people in Gaza as well as other parts of the world. Second, the "positive contribution" (*musbet hareket*) principle: in Gülen's evaluation, the Gaza flotilla operation seemed to be aimed more at creating awareness of the blockade and getting it lifted would not "lead to fruitful matters." And, indeed, instead of aid, it actually resulted in nine additional direct victims, injuries to many indirect victims, as well as new hostility between Turkey and Israel. In relation to this, Gülen argued that nobody has a right to perform an act of "heroism" (*kahramanlik*) at the expense of creating further troubles for others. Fourth, non-political activism: Gülen believes that virtuous actions should be, ideally, carried out for the right reasons using the right methods.

Fifth, the law of the land: that people should try to be respectful of the law of the land and, when they do not agree with the law and are pursuing their rights, they should use democratic, peaceful, and non-violent methods to change it without oppressing other people. Sixth, respect for the 'other': responsible people should be looking for ways to achieve our aims that do not impose force on another but instead show respect for all people, their identity, and their beliefs, especially when dealing with people with whom we do not agree. Seventh, balance of action and outcomes: and within that the importance, in our moral responsibility, of distinguishing struggle and achievement, in the sense that our main responsibility is for the way in which we work to achieve moral goals rather than for the outcomes. Eighth, legitimate goals with legitimate means: there is an important inter-relationship between these. Ninth, responsibility of action and outcomes: Gülen argues that the moral accountability of a person may even include unintended outcomes of their actions, quoting an *ayah* in the Qur'an (*Surah Az-Zumar*, 39: 47), which states that people will be confronted with things that they had not taken into account.

On the basis of having examined the applicability to the MV Mavi Marmara incident of these identified principles, Sezgin argues that this shows how, if Gülen's response to the incident had been any different than it was then it "would have contradicted the main principles of Hizmet." Therefore, in taking the stance that he did, "Although these comments were not welcomed by the political authority," and despite the fact that Gülen may "have gained some public support in the short term," in the longer term, "He would have dismissed his own principles and would lose his ethical standards."

A final example of national-cultural taboo-breaking on the part of Gülen, but also one that underlines how the wider experience of Hizmet has itself contributed to change and development in Gülen's own thinking and previous stances, concerns the place of the Armenians in Turkey's self-understanding. In relation to what happened to the Armenian people in the former Ottoman Empire during 1915–1916 and also during the 1920 war between the then new Turkish Republic and Armenia, the Turkish state, and the vast majority of Turkish people have, over many decades, been in a state of denial of the nature and degree of what occurred. As summarised by Keleş, also Gülen's original view was of what happened was that "it wasn't necessarily a genocide."

However, following a challenge based on historicity coming from Hizmet intellectuals involved in the media and in academia who, as recounted by Keleş, said "Hojaefendi, you know, it wasn't that, you are mistaken, your reading on such and such is historically flawed," Gülen wrote an article for publication within which not only did he acknowledge the historic Armenian experience, but he also argued that "Armenians should be paid…reparations, and they should be apologised to." In relation to this, Keleş recounts that "Unfortunately *The Financial Times* at the time didn't publish it" because, apparently, and somewhat extraordinarily, it felt that "it was not newsworthy, although it was newsworthy in a Turkish context." Nevertheless, as Keleş notes, this remains an important example of how, when challenged, Gülen can and does change his views, even when such views might be deeply embedded in his culturally inherited perspective "especially if it relates to the movement which is so important to him" that "you have to be able to go at it and tell him that."

Especially through this example, one can discern an interactivity of development between Gülen and many in Hizmet, and in relation to this there are an increasing number of reports and examples of how the experiences of Hizmet people in terms of their own persecution and exile has been feeding into a re-evaluation of how to understand and describe such profoundly difficult and sensitive issues. Having themselves reflectively learned from Hizmet's own experience of itself having become a persecuted, shocked, and traumatised group, increasing numbers of Hizmet people are now able to see how such things could have happened to others in a way that they had not previously perceived, nor even have had a readiness to consider the extent to which an exclusive and defensive form of learned Turkish nationalism might have clouded the necessary historical honesty, analytical clarity, and human empathy required for the development of sufficient civic courage to question and challenge otherwise socially dominant perspectives.

For example, on the other side of the events of July 2016, Tekelan reflected on how much he had learned in this regard from his own experience of becoming 'de-centred' from Turkey: "Of course, it's a book in itself" and "I've learned a lot from this process" explaining that this is because "When I was in Turkey, the way Syrian people were crossing the Mediterranean made me cry. I'm in the same situation now. I'd also like to say that in the process, I've learned that it's very important to be human. Regardless of colour, tongue, thinking."

In fact, one of the remarkable things that has come out of the movement of Hizmet and other asylum-seekers from Turkey is, as Tekalan says, "When they crossed into Greece, the Greeks asked them, 'Welcome, what do you need?' There are a lot of examples of that. Not only the Greeks but also the Armenians behaved the same way. They treated those who had to leave Turkey just like their relatives." Further illustrating the revised thinking that this trauma has brought about for many Hizmet people, Tekalan says "We were always told that Greek and Armenian people were enemies of Turkey and that those countries were very dangerous countries." However, significantly, even with reference to the relatively distant past, Tekalan testifies that "I remember Fethullah Gülen said about twenty-five years ago: 'Why are we made enemies with each other? We're from the same geography. Maybe we come from the same background'."

3.6   Overcoming Religious Boundary Taboos

In relation to religious boundary taboos, it is the case that those which exist within a broad religious tradition and related groups can sometimes be stronger and deeper than those which concern people of completely different religious traditions. In this connection, it is important to understand that Gülen has also been a taboo-breaker within Islam and the Muslim community itself. With reference to the Muslim community itself, Keleş says of Gülen that "He is actually telling us, as Nursi did, he is saying to us, don't be defined by religious form and religious ritual and these types of outward symbols. Rather, focus on what the meaning is." As examples of this, Keleş highlighted not only that "Gülen broke the taboo of mosques" but also that on shaking hands with people from the opposite sex. Furthermore, Keleş highlighted that:

> He does a sermon in the 1980s about the musical sound of the Qur'an and, you know, he does it by going up into the pulpit and playing the Qur'an audio from a tape player, and putting his microphone next to it, and stopping it and rewinding it, and talking to the congregation about the musical melodies of the Qur'anic recitation- I mean even the word music and Qur'an side by side is a problem! I mean, ten years later Turkey would debate whether the *Azhan*, which is not the Qur'an, could be read from a microphone – ten years later!

As noted in the previous section on Gülen's relationship with national-cultural taboos, in relation to religious traditions other than the predominant Sunni Islam, Turkey has historically been a context in which the reality of the social diversity of religion has usually been suppressed in the context of the Turkish state's promotion of "One religion, one language and one people" that can be found in both religious and secular nationalist forms.

Where this came from historically can be understood, as explained in Sect. 3.1 of this chapter, in terms of an historical context of the founding of the Turkish Republic most of the rest of the so-called 'Muslim World' had been subjected to external military colonisation. But Turkey is in reality much more ethnically, religiously, and linguistically diverse than allowed for by either secular or religious nationalisms. Such diversity was already a part of the Ottoman inheritance in which ethnic, national, and religious diversity as was only allowed to exist within a framework of acknowledging the military, political, and religious hegemony of the Ottomans. But overall, it has not been uncommon for traditional Turkish Muslim leaders to point out and appeal to the relative tolerance of Islam, especially in its Ottoman forms as compared with many other historical configurations for the relationships between religion(s), state, and society. Indeed, some of Gülen's earlier contributions in relation to matters of religious diversity might be seen as unexceptionally similar. However, while there are many other Islamic scholars who speak about religious diversity, with regard to Gülen, one needs to look at what Gülen says in combination with his contextualised *actions* and, as Bekim Agai (2003) pointedly explained it:

> Although many Islamic leaders may talk of tolerance in Islam, it may be problematic to put it into practice. Gülen himself has shown that he has no fears of meeting leaders of other religions, including the Pope and the representative of the Jewish community in Istanbul. He also crossed the borders of Islamic discourse to meet with important people in Turkish society who are atheists. These activities were not easy from a religious perspective because Islamic discourse in Turkey has definite boundaries that do not appreciate close ties to the leaders of other religions and nonreligious persons. Also, his support for the Alevis was not very popular among most Sunni-Islamic groups. (p. 65)

When generally discussing how Gülen's views and perspectives have changed over the years, Kurucan cites the example of wider inter-religious relations and dialogue as illustrative suggests that, as with other things, for a rounded understanding of this one needs to set Gülen's changing positions in the context of the ongoing interaction between sources, places, and revelatory dynamic:

> The way he understood the Qur'an and the way he preached in late 1960s and 70s was not much different than the classical approach, which was like the classical approach. An example is in the very first chapter of the Qur'an where there is a reference to those who have diverted from the main path. And this has usually been interpreted by almost all the scholars as Jews and Christians who have left the main path of belief, of true belief in God, and that we should not be following that route. So, you could hear Hojaefendi speaking in those early years repeating almost the same thing because he later actually confessed that I might have misunderstood the Qur'an and, secondly, I basically repeated the way classical scholars understood those passages. There are other verses in the Qur'an about the people of the Book in which they are being censured, but the classical approach considers these

censures as if they were for those Jews and Christians. But Hojaefendi is now saying I understand that the Qur'an is speaking to the Muslims and that the censure is not to a certain people, but to the attributes and if Muslims adopt such attributes they are also an addressee to that criticism. So, if I did that, in that sense, I was wrong, in that classical approach.

As Kurucan says, "Back in those classical, early years, Hojaefendi was within four walls, filled with books, and he was basically studying with his students, but he was not really with the world. So, things have changed when he stepped out of those four walls." But "especially since 1994 with the establishment of the Journalists and Writers Foundation and the start of his initiative for inter-faith dialogue you see this huge, much broader approach to the Qur'anic scripture where he is probably moving forward from the classical approach."

In many ways, indeed, it was Gülen's emergent ability as a traditional Muslim scholar to recognise and at least to begin to deal with religious diversity, linked with his ability to encourage and enable Hizmet people also to begin to do some of this, which has been one of the most distinctive and important markers of the contribution of his teaching and practice in engaging with what is one of the greatest challenges of the contemporary world. This challenge is so important because even when one lives in a relatively homogenous geographical environment, as the British historian Arnold Toynbee put it, we are living in a world on the other side of "the annihilation of distance" that has come about through the means of modern transport, even though the recent Covid-19 pandemic has underlined the fragility of these interconnections, while at the same time making clear that through the emergence and spread of the internet and of social media we increasingly live in a practically unbounded digital universe that is even more diverse than the world to which one can have more immediate physical access. Since one cannot escape such diversity even if one wished and tried to do so, the question for all, including for Muslims, is that of how one relates to that diversity and deals with it. As well as being the expression of Gülen's understanding of the centrality in Islam of the love of God, Gülen (2004c) also warns against the illusion that the uncomfortable plurality of the modern world can be wished away—whether by believers or by non-believers:

The desire for all humanity to be similar to one another is nothing more than wishing for the impossible. For this reason, the peace of this (global) village lies in ensuring that people appreciate these differences. Otherwise it is understandable that the world will devour itself in a web of conflicts, disputes, fights and bloodiest of wars, thus preparing the way for its own end. (p. 249–250).

Indeed, the Qu'ran itself teaches that, if God had willed it, God could have made all peoples one, but in fact made them different in order to compete with each other—but as Yeşilova reflects, many traditional Muslims nevertheless prefer to remain within their 'comfort zones.' Sharing an example of a more traditional perspective from within his own family which underlined why "they did not understand what Hizmet was about" Yeşilova cited one of his traditional relatives as asking: "Why do you go and meet other people? Why do you visit their churches? Why do you engage with them? Why do you spend time with them?" With regard to this, Yeşilova commented that:

I did not understand them, why they were asking me these questions. I thought many times that I was wasting my time in Turkey trying to deal with this mindset which was not able really to read the world. They are just are happy with their own comfort zone, and they don't want to move beyond it.

By contrast, as Yeşilova explained it: "What Hojaefendi brought to us was that the world is, as he kept saying, a global village now, you have to go anywhere you can to interact with the world; give whatever you may; but also learn from them. And this is the true nature of our times." Of course, if something has been part of one's background environment, unless a life experience such as migration brings an inevitable disruption, one does not particularly have to think about it or need to articulate why one does this or does that. Rather, it is only in interaction with 'the other' that generally speaking, that one is forced to face the question of whether that particular form of one's religious practice is ultimately of the 'essence' of what one is doing, or whether it is merely 'cultural.' Rather, it is in interaction with others that one has to face these things.

Of course, such questions are far from simple because, in the end, once one starts to distinguish between an essence and a cultural form, it can be a bit like an onion: and the question arises as to whether one ends up peeling all the bits of the onion away and then finds that there is nothing left! Therefore, while there is a good argument to distinguish between primary and secondary things, and between form and substance, it is important to understand that, for things to exist at all in this world, form is necessary. The 'secondary' things are therefore also a fact of life since primary things cannot be transmitted without cultural forms. Therefore, as Yeşilova explained it:

> It's a risk and you have to answer when you go out there, people ask you questions, and you don't want to answer those questions if you are not confident enough. That's one thing I liked a lot about Hojaefendi, why shouldn't we be engaged in dialogue with others? If you're not willing to do so, this means you're not confident enough about your faith.

How this works itself in practice can be seen in Yeşilova's observation that:

> What lies in the heart of all those things if I am going to call this Hizmet, as someone who grew up in a very secularist setting I could see in the example of these people (my encounter with Hojaefendi was much later) was that what these people are telling me is that I can, yes, be a good Muslim but still relate with the rest of my family who are not practising Muslims. That is possible. I don't have to separate myself from the rest of the society. I can still be a proud Muslim, but I don't have to push myself away from the rest of my environment. So, I think that was a great thing, that was a great confidence that came with me because, you know, we are living in modern times and people question faith. They want to believe in things they can reason with. They want to visualise. They want to see and touch things, and when you talk about faith you're talking about responsibilities; you're talking about accountability; that there is this God who is out there, and whose watching over and who is aware of what you're doing, yet He is also very compassionate, that He is also very understanding. So, the way I looked into religion, the way I am understanding faith and the world around me has certainly changed a lot and it brought me confidence with my encounter with Hizmet.

Consistent with Yeşilova's observations, in many ways it was indeed also through Gülen's travel beyond the geographical boundaries of Turkey, and as he increasingly encountered the wider non-Muslim world, that he developed some of the themes that are now quite characteristic of Hizmet. As Tekalan recounted: "I wasn't there when he first visited America. But on their second and third visit, I was with him as a doctor. He talked about the necessity and importance of visiting people through dialogue, invitations. He was always motivating people to do these things." Tekalan gave the example that:

> In the early days in New Jersey, he was asking everyone what they were doing to dialogue with others. No one showed up for the second week. Because they couldn't. Because they couldn't do anything to tell you. In the third week, friends started coming. Yes, one of them was saying that "I invited my neighbour." The other one was saying that "I visited the church." It motivated the younger generation.

In terms of the Hizmet vision of dialogue through *hoşguru* (or, hospitality) which, over time, developed so strongly in terms of the organisation of groups of international visitors to Turkey, Tekalan reports that Gülen advised that "You should not only invite people to Turkey, but also to your home." Tekalan also explained that through this "especially our young friends from America" but also "businessmen, journalists, congressmen, academicians," and so on "were brought together." And when they visited other countries where Hizmet schools had been founded, "After these trips, those people visited our homes and learned about Islamic culture, Turkish culture, Turkish tradition, and then they invited us." As a result of these kinds of exchanges, Tekalan concluded that "We, as the Turkish people, have learned about their religion, traditions and cultures, not only in the United States, but also in other countries. Through these contacts, we have improved our perspectives on Christians, Jews, Buddhists, other Muslims and so on."

When meeting Gülen in Saylorsburg, and bearing especially in mind his health and the experiences being faced by many in Hizmet, the present author felt moved to recite the Beatitudes of Jesus from the Christian New Testament Gospels (Matthew 5 v. 3–10). As the recitation of the Beatitudes took place, the Muslim call to prayer was broadcast into the room such that the two mingled and, in relation to that, Özcan later explained that:

> After the Beatitudes, Hojaefendi asked for the translation and we checked on the internet and the Turkish Christian sites, and he says that Jesus (peace be upon him) didn't limit to any person. He mentions that such people then and there and in the future will be those people. So exactly the same way.

This was, in principle, an example of very good New Testament exegesis. In addition, Çetin also explained in relation to the reading that:

Hojaefendi liked it and he said that I either I have been writing on this issue most probably will use that one again, so this reminds him of something. He was writing a series for a new monthly journal in Turkish and he's writing the editorials, and he comes with a series and you know, about the, in a sense, the weaknesses and the, what do you call it, the negativities of the modern human beings and how we could overcome this. And he said that he would write from the Sufi Masters some of the things, but knowing that Prophets (peace be upon them all) are the true teachers and the examples of this, so I should stop writing about this from the Sufi tradition and I start it from the Prophet history. So that just comes on time and timely.

And indeed, in relation to the place of Jesus of Nazareth and his teaching, Ergene explained that in Sufi tradition:

We mentioned about the Perfect Man [*insan al-kamil*] when we started discussion this morning. In that tradition you make your journey to the Perfect Man by stopping at stations where they are spiritually nourished by a different Prophet. Without benefiting from them they cannot make the journey. Without visiting these Prophets, their journey to the Prophet cannot happen. In a way, visiting them they witness all the divine revelation and *sunnatullah* (to the tradition of God) that came down to Adam, to Prophet Muhammad, and all those in between.

With regard to the Sermon on the Mount in particular, which had been recited by the author at the end of the first interview with Gülen, Ergene says:

It's the same thing, it's the same divine message that has come through all the Prophets. It's no different than what we would have been taught. In a Qur'anic verse the Prophet is told to say "I'm not bringing you anything new. I'm just reminding to you, that's the tradition that I'm reminding you of."

When interviewing Gülen, the author asked if a person of another than Muslim religion—for example, a Christian—came to him and asked for advice about how to be a better lover of God, what his advice would be, Gülen said that:

> Indeed, different religious traditions they do have their differences. But when we consider the pillars of faith, we see the essences of these pillars of faith are so similar. So. the way we talk about the roads, the paths that take a servant to the path of the love of God, to become a lover of God and the beloved of God, I believe those paths are essentially very similar. So, I would say the same thing. I would encourage them to strengthen their belief in the pillars of their faith in the existence and the attributes of God, in the concepts of the Prophets of God, the Messengers and in the formulas, the methodology that they bring in order to uplift humanity to an angelic life from an animal level of life – their belief in the resurrection and the blissful eternal life.

In relation to this, Muhammad Çetin noted that he knew a couple of adults who visited Gülen to say that they would like to be Muslims and they would like to give up Christianity. And he reported that Gülen's response to them was "That there is nothing wrong with Christianity, there is nothing wrong with Jesus (peace be upon him). If you have such a thing you shouldn't give up anything from your own culture and belief, otherwise these are the same things." Therefore, because of this, in relation to the possibility of changing religion from Christianity to Islam, Gülen says that "You shouldn't – this could be changing of a room in the house, but it couldn't be change of the house in a sense."

Özcan added to this the following observation that, "Changing the faith community, or from atheism to even Christianity or Islam or whatever, it should be a personal choice and should be through freewill and not be by compulsion. Even we Muslims we become happy when an atheist become even a Christian" and that "With any compulsion or force if anyone changes their religion they do not become Muslim, they become hypocrites." When Gülen was later questioned by the author of this book about the possibility of those which are not part of the historic or sociological community of Muslims being able appropriately to respond to the love of God, which is the heart of Gülen's teaching, he responded:

> Of course, what as Muslims or just humans, what we expect from others depends on how well we are representing the things that are our core beliefs and values. There cannot be an expectation without exemplifying what you claim to believe in. If we are representing through our life what we believe

in, then we can expect others to embrace shared values and beliefs. So, when we consider the life stories of the Prophets, we see that, yes they convey God's message to people and they emphasise the importance of God's words, but their life was equally impressive upon their communities, and in their lives we see our examples and we see that this same message of love and caring for others, we can see this same message in the lives of all these prophets.

In illustrating this, Gülen went on to cite an example from the life of Muhammad:

When Prophet Muhammad (peace be upon him) was hurt, was wounded in the Battle of Uhud, rather than praying for himself or other things, he was caring about other people, he was worried about other people, and he was relating the story of a former, previous prophet. He was relating that this former, previous prophet when subjected to this the level of animosity and enmity, he said: "Oh God, please forgive my people because they don't know; they don't recognise me, my role, my relationship and this religion. And we can see the same story in the life of Noah, in the life of Abraham, in the life of Moses.

And addition, Gülen also cited Jesus himself, as follows:

When we look at the life of prophet Jesus, peace be upon him (peace be upon him). In the Qur'an when God questions him about his people, he says if you forgive them that is so suiting to you. If you decide to punish them, those are your servants. But you can see his sadness at the possibility of his people being punished, and his seeking God's forgiveness, compassion. Properly translated in the Qur'anic narration of Jesus' dialogue with God, "If you chose to punish them you punish them, those are your servants; but if you choose to forgive them you are indeed most forgiving, most wise."

Thus, in relation certainly to the Abrahamic faiths, Gülen said that "When you consider the Abrahamic faiths, their scriptures, yes you will see that they disagree on some details, but they agree on these pillars of faith." Or, as Ergene put it, expanding on his understanding of Gülen's teaching in this matter:

All the time, of course, people adhere to slightly different ideologies, but referring to one *ayah* in the Qur'an, the book invites people to "come to a common word between us, which is God." It doesn't mention Christianity, or any other religion, or Judaism or Islam, but our common word is God. It is not an invitation to leave one's Prophet or faith. The essence of all religions are the same, that's what Gülen is emphasizing. It is not a possibility to bring all religions together and make a 'soup'. No religions, even man-made belief systems, would not accept such a thing. This is against nature.

Interestingly, however, despite this clear evaluation, Gülen is not one of the signatories of the call drafted by Prince Ghazi and issued by a large number of Muslim leaders to Christian leaders, under the title of *A Common Word Between Us and You* (Royal Aal al-Bayt Institute for Islamic Thought, The 2007). At the same time, while there are quite a number of other Muslim scholars who will affirm a spiritual kinship in relation to Christians and Jesus, Gülen has gone even further than this to say that:

> You can even argue that in the Uphanishads and Vedas, or the Buddhist tradition, and even the similar other traditions, they have their own rituals and forms of worship that prepare their soul and a person for eternal life. So, the essence of this path is to leave behind the corporeality of human life and to go into the life of the heart and spirit, and to reach this integration of the heart and mind, and to live in the angelic qualities as much as is possible in the human domain. So, the elements of the path and the discipline will not differ that much for those other traditions.

At the same time, although this might seem to represent a relatively new development in Muslim thinking being extended beyond the Abrahamic family of religions, one of the faults to which 'Western' thinking can be prone is an emphasis on the 'new' being likely to be most authentic and helpful. This, of course, contrasts with the general starting point of many classical civilisations in which the 'old' is more likely to be elevated. When approaching the topic of dialogue in the teaching and practice of Gülen and of the movement inspired by his teaching, in many ways it is important not to fall into what could ultimately be a false dichotomy in looking for either 'newness' or 'oldness' as a criterion for authenticity. As Ergene explained:

> When you have in philosophy new ideas, you have new theories, they have come to oppose other ideas that came before me. But this religion doesn't say that, it says I come instead to complete the religions that came before. It's talking about process here, an ongoing tradition.

> If you come with something as a new movement, as a new idea in philosophy or politics, you try first to show how different you are from the previous ones, so you surface the differences between people, push your ideology or your religion or your faith forward, so that you can be more visible and construct your identity. But Islam doesn't say that. Yes, it does bring in many new things. But the last revealed verse is warning in a way: "do not take this to a wrong direction; this is not something new."

Thus, in many ways, although this extension of Gülen's understanding of the love of God as going beyond the Abrahamic religions could be seen to represent a new development in Muslim teaching and practice, it is not an 'innovation' in the sense that it departs from Islamic norms and values. Rather, it is something that arises because it is thoroughly contextualised in current socio-cultural conditions while also being firmly rooted in an Islamic inheritance. Indeed, the power and effect arising among Muslims of Gülen's teaching about Muslim relations with people of other religions and the important of inter-religious dialogue is effective precisely because it is clearly rooted in Islam or, as Naziri articulates:

> The perspective is from that of a Muslim scholar who advocates and also promotes inter-faith co-operation, and then also explaining that this also has to do with, the origins in the traditional Islamic teachings. It is convincing, I mean. It is very important that very many Muslims throughout the world, come to know and have to listen at least and then they will accept it or not accept it, I don't care. At least explain this approximation into welcoming the difference, welcoming the diversity, and celebrating it.

And, as Naziri added:

> And this is my comment, and being very sincere in it, not using it like a tactic, be sincere, really sincere, because there is a Qur'anic *ayah* that everyone could be one nation. If He (God Almighty) wanted so, it could be homogenous. If He didn't want it to be all homogenous, who are you to make it, to try to make it homogenous. Its good to be heterogenous. The diversity, I look at the diversity through this glass. It's very important.

Thus, one can say that Gülen's inter-religious dialogue connects with the times. And indeed, unlike a number of other Muslim emphases on dialogue which have developed reactively to events such as 9/11 in the USA, and the Madrid and London bombings, it is important to understand that Gülen's efforts on behalf of dialogue already pre-dated the impetus to dialogue that came about as a result of these terrible events. Therefore, even in his earlier period within Turkey, one can see Gülen's commitment to dialogical engagement and learning through concrete praxis when, for example, Özcan noted of Gülen that "When he was in Edirne as a young nineteen-year-old *imam*, he was the only *imam* going to the synagogue to listen to the Psalms of the Jewish people, even though the Jewish people were very few and concealing themselves. At that time, he was the only *imam* going to the synagogue and listening to the Psalms and how they recite even from their tune and their Hebrew language, tried to benefit." This biographically and contextually rooted point is well made because, although it can certainly be argued (as noted earlier by Kurucan) that Gülen's view on dialogue have developed, there are critics who see Gülen's statements about dialogue, either as something merely reactive to events such as 9/11 and/or as purely 'instrumental' in the sense of them being deployed to gain a sympathetic hearing on the 'Western' and Christian facing side of a two-faced strategy in which Muslim and Islamic dominance remains the main aim. Özcan, however, argues that: "This understanding was not conjunctural and is not in a sense strategic in that sense .... of, you know, being close to other communities and to interact and benefit from them." And Tekalan testified of Gülen that "He was perhaps the first person in Turkey to visit other religious leaders. He invited them to where he lived, and they came. After these invitations, the visits became traditional. Then they invited Muslim people." Tekalan explains that these local beginnings were then taken to another level in that "In the continuation of this process, Gülen visited Pope John Paul II in Rome from Turkey; he was perhaps the first religious figure in Turkey to do so. Many people in Turkey said it was completely wrong. They said a Muslim could not go to Rome to visit the Pope."

Tekalan says of Gülen that, basically, overall, "He motivated Muslim people to engage in dialogue with Christians and Jews...and we learned about these behaviours by communicating with people who are Christian, Buddhist, atheist, Jews. What they have in common is being human." Therefore, while being rooted in a traditional and Turkish-inflected Islam, Gülen is a 'border transgressor' who advocates the primacy of the human over national, ethnic, or even religious identity, including Muslim identity. Thus, as Ergene summarised the approach of Gülen:

Since the 1970s he's trying to inculcate in us not to look at the world from that same prism – from around twenty years ago, when he met the Pope, that picture is still being used by those extremists in very embarrassing forms – secret Cardinal. That was one of the best things he did in his life. That's what our Prophet did. When the Christians came from Najran, the Prophet did not just meet with them, but he also gave his mosque for them on Sunday to pray when they asked to go outside the city, he said this is my mosque for you.

In terms of Muslim antecedents, like the thirteenth century Muslim poet and theologian, Mevlana Jalal al-Din al Rumi, Gülen's approach is richly theological and spiritual. Indeed, Gülen (2004c) cites Rumi's famous saying that "One of my feet is in the centre and the other is in seventy-two realms (i.e. in the realm of all nations) like a compass" or a "broad circle that embraces all believers" (p. 199). While nowadays it might be relatively more commonplace to say that engagement in dialogue requires a confident rooting in one's own religious heritage, Gülen's teaching goes beyond that. This is because, as with Rumi, the fixed point of pose is ultimately not one's religion, shaped, informed, and limited as that is by historical circumstance, accident, and accretion but, rather, that to which one's religion points. In this, Gülen invites those who are inspired by his teaching to focus on seeking out those whom both Rumi and Gülen call "the people of love" and to follow the example of those who understand Islam as a message of love. In making this invitation, Gülen cited Rumi who said:

Come, come and join us, as we are the people of love devoted to God! Come, come through the door of love and join us and sit with us. Come, let us speak one to another through our hearts. Let us speak secretly, without ears and eyes. Let us laugh together without lips or sound, let us laugh like the roses. Like thought, let us see each other without any words or sound. Since we are all the same, let us call each other from our hearts, we won't use our lips or tongue. As our hands are clasped together, let us talk about it. (Gülen 2004c, 6)

Summing up the risk-taking nature of Gülen's border-transgressing and taboo-breaking are a series of observances made on this by Enes Ergene when he was interviewed and which, although extensive, seem to this author to be worth quoting in full:

Perhaps there is no other intellectual in our lifetime that has taken this much risk, which has put him in many big dangers up to the point of perhaps never having the possibility to return back home anyway. And when he said "Muslims cannot be terrorists; terrorists cannot be Muslims" after 9/11 he was excommunicated again by Muslims. The risks were not understood by the West either. This is perhaps because they do not know the inner dynamics of Islam and Muslim community; or perhaps the Muslim world is not open to be discovered.

When he says "dialogue" he is opening himself, his hard disk, up to others, and he asks others to open themselves too, so they can be discovered as well. Because of his dialogue efforts, he has been accused to represent "moderate Islam" (not real Islam). Because he lives here in the US, many people think he is under the protection of FBI and CIA, living a luxurious life, and that we are all American spies, first and foremost for Hojaefendi himself, in the eyes of the rest of our Turkish people. This thesis is getting stronger.

So, he always took very huge risks to the point of being refused by our own nation. But, all right, our fellow Muslims cannot see this. But what is so disappointing is that the western world is also almost blind to this reality, to the role he can play in the world. They see not enough appreciation of the risks that is taking. One cannot count too many examples from the among intellectuals in the West who took this much risk in their lives. Take the example of Heidegger, the great philosopher; he sided with Hitler, you know, so he didn't take the risk. But now, Gülen's risk is a very fatal one. He's facing charges where the threat is his execution. If he believed all the problems would go away, he would be ready to go and face death there, because he is already waiting for the day for that reunion with the divine. He is in love with God, and he doesn't really fear death at all. So, it's not the danger, but that is the risk that he is taking, that risk of an intellectual, the risk of a human being who is facing death.

I mean for us to be able to measure the importance of the risk he is taking, I remember when I came here, probably it was 2000 and I was in New York, and the time for prayer was about to finish, I threw myself into a church and asked the priest to allow him to pray there. You know, imagine this happening in Turkey, or in the rest of the Islamic world, a Christian going into a mosque and asking the imam to pray there – this is a reason for a revolution, this a reason for a coup, you know. And now think of what Gülen is saying when he meets with the Pope and he does other inter-faith initiatives in such a context. That means much more than a normal time, you know. The themes that he brought up are untouchable things, they are reasons for huge danger, that's a big risk to take on.

REFERENCES

Agai, Bekim (2003). The Gülen Movement's Islamic Ethic of Education. In Hakan Yavuz, and John Esposito (Eds) (2003). *Turkish Islam and the Secular State. The Gülen Movement* (pp. 48–68). New York, Syracuse University Press

Albayrak, İsmail (Ed.). *Mastering Knowledge in Modern Times: Fethullah Gülen as an Islamic Scholar* (pp. 127–156). New York: Blue Dome.

Brill, Alan (2018). The Book of Doctrines and Opinions: Notes on Jewish Theology and Spirituality. "My meeting with Hocaefendi Fethullah Gülen" 10.7.2018. https://kavvanah.wordpress.com/2018/07/10/my-meeting-with-hocaefendi-fethullah-gulen/.

Çapan, Ergün (2011). Gülen's Teaching Methodology in His Private Circle. In İsmail Albayrak (Ed.) *Mastering Knowledge in Modern Times: Fethullah Gülen as an Islamic Scholar* (pp. 127–156). New York: Blue Dome.

Doumont, Paul (1986), Disciples of the Light: The Nurju Movement in Turkey. *Central Asian Survey*, 5 (2), pp. 33–60. https://doi.org/10.1080/02634938608400542

Erdoğan, Latif (1995). *Fethullah Gülen Hocaefendi: Küçük Dünyam.* Istanbul: AD Yayıncılık.

Gülen, Fethullah (1994). *Gülen's message to the European Union.* December 17, 1994.

Gülen, Muhammad Fethullah (2004a). *Key Concepts in the Practice of Sufism: Emerald Hills of the Heart. Volume 1.* (revised edition). New Rutherford, New Jersey: The Fountain.

Gülen, Muhammad Fethullah (2004b). *Key Concepts in the Practice of Sufism: Emerald Hills of the Heart. Volume 2.* (revised edition). Somerset, New Jersey: The Light.

Gülen, Muhammad Fethullah (2004c). *Towards a Global Civilization of Love and Tolerance.* Somerset, New Jersey: The Light.

Gülen, Muhammad Fethullah (2009). *Key Concepts in the Practice of Sufism: Emerald Hills of the Heart. Volume 3.* Somerset, New Jersey: Tughra Books.

Gülen, Muhammad Fethullah (2010). *Key Concepts in the Practice of Sufism: Emerald Hills of the Heart. Volume 4.* Somerset, New Jersey: The Light.

Karasipahi, Sena (2000). *Muslims in Modern Turkey: Kemalism, Modernism and the Revolt of the Islamic Intellectuals.* London: I. B. Tauris.

Mardin, Şerif (1989). *Religion and Social Change in Modern Turkey. The Case of Bediüzzaman Said Nursi.* New York: New York State Press.

Robinson, Simon (2017). *The Spirituality of Responsibility: Fethullah Gülen and Islamic Thought.* London: Bloomsbury.

Royal Aal al-Bayt Institute for Islamic Thought, The (2007). *A Common Word Between Us and You.* Amman: The Royal Aal al-Bayt Institute for Islamic Thought.

Sezgin, İsmail (2014). Mavi Marmara and Gülen's Critics: Politics and Principles. *Today's Zaman*, 16.1.2014 in *Hizmet Movement News Archive* (https://hizmetnews.com/9499/mavi-marmara-gulens-critics-politics-principles/#.Xhmm3m52s2x).

Sunier, Thijl (2014). Cosmopolitan Theology: Fethullah Gülen and the Making of a 'Golden Generation'. *Ethnic and Racial Studies*, *37* (12), 2193–2208. https://doi.org/10.1080/01419870.2014.934259

Toynbee, Arnold (1948). *Civilization on Trial.* Oxford: Oxford University Press.

Turner, Colin and Hurkuç, Hasan (2008). *Said Nursi: Makers of Islamic Civilization.* London: I.B. Tauris.

Weissman, Itzchak (2007). *The Naqshbandiyya: Orthodoxy and Activism in a Worldwide Sufi Tradition.* Abingdon: Routledge.

Weller, Paul (2013). Fethullah Gülen, Turkey and the European Union. In Greg Barton, Paul Weller and İhsan Yılmaz (Eds.), *The Muslim World and Politics in Transition: Creative Contributions of the Gülen Movement* (pp. 108–125). London: Bloomsbury.

Weller, Paul (2022). *Hizmet in Transitions: European Developments of a Turkish Muslim-Inspired Movement.* London: Palgrave Macmillan.

Yavuz, Hakan and Esposito, John (Eds) (2003). *Turkish Islam and the Secular State. The Gülen Movement.* New York, Syracuse University Press

CHAPTER 4

Islamic Spirituality and Social Processing

4.1 MUSLIM INSECURITY, THE 'HEROIC' TRADITION, AND ALTERNATIVE HERMENEUTICS

Perhaps ironically, given the confidence of faith to which the Abrahamic religions call those who affirm them, among contemporary Muslims there is, in reality, a lot of insecurity. This is partly historically and sociologically rooted and is to that extent understandable in the light of the impact of colonialism and imperialism and their aftermaths upon the majority 'Muslim world.' As Öztürk explained this with reference to Gülen's understanding of 'Western' civilization: "In 1991, when I was his student, Hojaefendi said 'I'm really concerned that the Muslim civilization will reject this because of their religious fervour.'"

That such historical and sociological insecurity can be manifested in a strident and combative form of Islam was clearly identified by Gülen (in Ünal and Williams, Eds. 2000) in his following articulation of the problem:

> When those who have adopted Islam as a political ideology, rather than a religion in its true sense and function, review their self-proclaimed Islamic activities and attitudes, especially their political ones, they will discover that the driving force is usually personal or national anger, hostility or similar motives. If this is the case, we must accept Islam and adopt an Islamic attitude as the fundamental starting-point for action, rather than the existing oppressive situation. (p. 248)

However, such social and political insecurity seems often also to have seeped through into what might be called a 'theological insecurity' to the extent that when Muslim crowds (usually of men) shout "God is great!" it might be that what they are, in fact, thereby doing is giving expression to the underlying feeling that "We are poor and weak!" and projecting onto the divine an inverse version of their theological insecurity of a kind that is far removed from the kind of theological confidence in the ultimacy of the divine to which Islam calls humanity. In commenting on this perspective, interviewee CA1 said, "Yeah, yeah. You put it so nicely" and went on himself to describe this in the following quite graphic terms:

> This is just like what fans do in football stadiums to satisfy themselves. You're not doing it to please God, you're just doing it to let out whatever you're keeping inside. So, this is why I didn't like them and I am so glad I met with Hizmet people and so I really thought there is some divine element in the way we live, and in the way we are, and a human being's mission is to explore that truth and to look and search for perfection and bearing witness to that reality in whatever form it may be. But I learned that, I had that motivation. I cannot claim I have achieved anything. I am just an ordinary fellow human being who calls himself a Muslim. But I always have this link to Hizmet which made life meaningful to me. Hizmet is what makes life meaningful to me.

In contrast to this kind of combative historical, sociological, and theological insecurity, this chapter explores the alternative hermeneutics offered by Fethullah Gülen that leads to a proper Islamic confidence of the kind that, at its best, Anwar Alam (2019) argues is exhibited within a Hizmet that facilitates those involved within it to confidently, but also humbly, engage with the wider world of modernity, including those who are of different religions and beliefs. But in the first instance, the chapter will trace something of how the historical, sociological, and theological insecurity that was flagged above is, in many ways, rooted in what could be called a 'heroic' heritage in Islam.

This heritage, at least in its Sunni form (recognising that in the Shi'a tradition of Islam there is more of a tradition of the suffering and apparent 'defeat' of key figures) is linked with a tendency to expect that what is right should always ultimately win in this world. Keleş sees this as intimately being linked with the much bigger theological challenge that he believes observant Muslims in general can have with loss and defeat, the self-awareness of which he believes has been "crystallised in the face of common challenges and in conversation with other Hizmet participants, demonstrating that this is a widely shared sentiment." And out of this, he says:

> It is not that there is no sense of 'loss' or 'defeat' in early Islamic history or theology but that it has been whitewashed or interpreted in a way that the event in question is no longer perceived as a loss in any sense of the word, which in turn has robs us of the ability to learn from it. The Battle of Uhud, the burial of the Prophet in the dead of night without a communal funeral prayer, the civil wars that followed wherein tens of thousands of Muslims (the Prophet's Companions) killed one another, the beheading of Hussain, and possibly the murder of his brother Hasan, at the hands of Muslims... there is a lot there that pertains to loss but it has been whitewashed.

By contrast with this more 'hidden' history of loss, as articulated and explained by Haylamaz in relation to many Muslims: "We are imagining this heroic Prophet with his sword at the battlefield at the front line and engaging with the enemy. But the reality is he never killed anyone." In relation to the tendency towards what might be called a 'universalising interpretation' (by non-Muslims as well as by Muslims) of such violent incidents that are described in the Qu'ran, Haylamaz points out that, in fact "The duration of battles or fights the Prophet had to engage were much less than what has been envisioned and preached to us. It only lasted a couple of hours perhaps, and the number of casualties are all catalogued and identified already. So, the numbers are pretty small. But this has been shown as if this was how he lived." However, Haylamaz also notes that the "The first twenty books written on Islamic history were books of military expeditions (*maghazi*). So, the first literature that developed on Islamic history actually developed around those battle stories" but this was "a very wrong place to start." As a consequence of this, "The heroism that was shown in the battlefield was praised more than any other thing. Virtues like compassion, mercy and gentleness exist in the literature, too, but compared to war heroism, they are minimal." By contrast, in relation to Muhammad himself as Haylamaz explained it, "One can see that, although he was undergoing violence and persecution, he continued to teach no retaliation, with no way of responding in the same kind. But you can see a life of achievement in that manner with no violence" and that in:

That fifteen years in Mecca under severe pressure and torture and violence and persecution, you see a very successful form of preaching with non-violence, with mercy and compassion, but which are being undermined at the expense of losing those values perhaps, but praising the other values like heroism which actually were a part of the Age of Ignorance.

And Ergene has underlined how influential these 'heroic' stories have become as a prism through which to understand both the Prophet and Islam, noting that "Many people grew hearing these heroic stories found in this literature. This was a kind of romanticism, heroism, which actually exist in all nations. As Haylamaz commented, "They used to say, 'are we going to leave our wealth to the ones who cannot ride a horse, who cannot use a sword?',", while as Ergene noted, that was "Simply because they could not be heroic. All the people, the children and women, who were useless in the battlefield, had no right/entitlement to inheritance." In relation to a realistic assessment of human experience and history, Ergene says that, on the one hand:

War and conflict exist in human nature; we cannot get rid of this completely. We cannot get rid of the sword, too. It exists even on flags, and it gives a symbolic message. But what can be done is how to keep that in its sheath. This is what Islam brings, to teach people how to keep their sword in its sheath, so they learn how to engage with others in different ways.

But also, while recognising the reality of this, Ergene says that what Islam brought was also "to draw ethical boundaries to war" and went on to note that:

Especially after the third century Islamic era, there have been many discussions in Islamic law on what constituted the basis of human relations: war or peace. Scholars referred to the main sources of information to find answers to this question. The Qur'an clearly says "Peace is good," and this normally defines the basis. However, what determined international relations for a long time was the opposite: war is essential.

Indeed, to some extent it was the case that, through engaging in war was how the nations developed their international relations and, because of this "Jurists in the past formulated their rulings accordingly. And even today many scholars, even in the schools of Theology even today in the Muslim world, including Turkey, still read the legal systems based on the systems that were developed in the Middle Ages which was based on or centred around war." Such perspectives have also informed much of Turkish popular culture through the many television 'soap operas' of the heroic Ottoman times and in nearly every street and neighbourhood in Turkey one can also see this heroic sentiment still at work, and which is something on which Islamist groups, including the AKP, feed on in their narratives. Thus, as Ergene explains, "They are generating this macho culture that challenges the world" and that "there is this new narrative developing around how Erdoğan is the new Caliph, how he is the Mahdi, the Saviour that is being awaited. Indeed, Ergene highlights of Edoğan that:

He sees himself even more than Suleiman. He considers himself as the protector of all Muslims and their Caliph. Type in Erdoğan, *Caliph, Mahdi* on your computer and you would see tons of videos. They are in a state of paranoia. He believes in this. In the past, others were trying to make him believe in this; now it is him who tries to indoctrinate others. He is always trying to keep this agenda of *Caliphate* and *Mahdi* in trend.

On a global level, Yeşilova says that "This conflictual perspective is, for me, very problematic and doesn't take us anywhere, and goes against the spirit of the time." In contrast, Yeşilova gives expression to a very different and proper form of Islamic confidence that he has found in and through the teaching of Gülen that informs Hizmet:

I have to confess, as Muslims, we have lagged behind centuries from the rest of the developed world. And there is this inferiority complex in many Muslim nations and that's a part of it. But with Hizmet, with this willingness to engage with the world, and do it with confidence, I think that's a very empowering reality that came with Hizmet philosophy, that it comes with the confidence of me in my faith, it comes from the way Hizmet understands religion and identity.

Although one can find some echoes of the 'heroic' in some of Gülen's early sermons, by far the main focus in his preaching was focused on Muhammad himself and on his Companions. As Ergene pointed out in a way that, for its significance in the way that Gülen used a re-reading of the life of the Prophet to challenge this 'heroic' heritage, is worth quoting at some length:

In this context it is important to remember a series of sermons that Hojaefendi gave at the beginning of the 1990s. I believe they started in 1989. For more than a year, like 60 weeks, he delivered these sermons in the biggest mosques and, actually, what he did was to read the life of the Prophet again. And he spent a lot of time on how he engaged war too. You could see him trying to re-read his life in a way to make an emphasis on the other aspects of his life and how he was so compassionate even in the battlefield towards the enemies. He even portrayed those scenes as he wept, which for me was an effort to show the humane side of the situation. But, unfortunately, we rarely see a scholar at such a level to follow a similar path in the Islamic world; perhaps a few, but none came out especially from community leaders. Many of them have been unfortunately very silent, and some even provoked their congregations and endorsed violence. But Gülen spent a lot of time on trying to understand the Prophet and his mission and message, not from the perspective of the battles, but from perhaps the 99% of his entire message and lifetime, the amount of time he spent on the battlefield and in conflict and in violence were much more minor than the rest of his life.

Many other Muslim scholars said. 'Look this guy Gülen is obsessed with the friends of the Prophet.' Probably they were obsessed with the heroic aspects of Islamic history. But Hojaefendi was trying to portray a true reflection of the message which was lived in the best way possible in the lifetime of the Prophet.

Other Muslims was critical of Gülen for his emphasis on the examples of the Prophet's friends, rather than focusing on the current problems of the Muslim world today. He did not only give the examples of the friends of the Prophet, but he also gave the apostles of Jesus as a good example, the way they were so pious, the way they behaved so leniently with others, he gave their example on many occasions too.

The distinctiveness of Gülen's approach derives from the fact that, in engaging with the Qu'ranic narratives that deal with conflict, Gülen has a very different starting-point and therefore also a very different overall approach that flows from that. Not only does Gülen transform the narrative of the 'heroic' in relation to a re-reading of the life of Muhammad and his first Companions, which he then foregrounds and elevates above the triumphalist readings of early Muslim history, as Haylamaz pointed out:

What we see in Gülen's example is that he tries to look at things as a whole, rather than partially. Partial approach would miss many things from our sight. Verses in the Qur'an that relate to fight and war have two purposes: 1. To provide rulings about the battlefield – when we carry the rulings reserved for the battlefield to outside, then the problems emerge. 2. To give guidance in the battlefield that it is an arena where your enemies have come to kill you; so you have to do what you have to do right there; your leniency and mercy are not welcome by your enemies. If killing others was a divine order to the Prophet, he would not have left this world without killing even one person. Also, there are at least seven rules to be observed even during warfare. But some people pick the ones they want to move forward with and ignore the rest. God reprimands Muslims in so many verses of the Qur'an, but some Muslims choose to act upon those where others are reprimanded.

Basically, what Gülen is doing is reading the Qur'an and Muslim tradition with a different and alternative kind of hermeneutical key and that is to emphasise the ultimate aim and goals and ends, which are concerned with the doing of peace and the whole trajectory of Islamic and of human development, rather than taking the conflicts that have occurred as the hermeneutical key to understanding the Qu'ran and Islam. As Haylamaz explains it:

There is also this selective reading from scripture. Some choose these verses that related to the battlefield to be used elsewhere. They select those verses which refer to the battlefield and they come to an understanding of a global Islam, playing on those in a way similar to what they do to the engagement with the People of the Book, for instance. There are, yes, some verses which are critical of them, which are critical of the People of the Book, and this is actually why many Muslims are accusing us to be as if complicit with what the People of the Book are doing to Muslims. But they never see how critical God is on Muslims themselves. It is as if God is only critical of non-Muslims and they deserve all the wrath and curse, and it as if God is saying nothing to the Muslims. So, they are using God as a stick.

Therefore, in contrast to such a combative form of religion rooted in theological insecurity, Gülen's teaching arguably promotes the kind of practice in which authentic Islam can itself become a resource for Muslims to engage with the issues and challenges of the world as it is, while also being capable of communicating in a serious way with people of other religious traditions, as well as those of secular perspectives because it is arguably only through common engagement in that task that it might be possible to find a way through it. It is thus Fethullah Gülen's consistency of focus on key and central things that leads to an emphasis on Islam that, in contrast to what might be called an 'Islamist Islam' which is a form of Islam that is constructed and lived out in a way that is rooted in reactivity to a sense of external threat. Rather, it is an Islam that engenders a proper sense of self-confidence which is fully contextualised and engaged in a way of individual integrity and collective proactive action.

Recognising the dangers of reactivity, Gülen warns that the transformations which have occurred in our social, historical, institutional, and theological realities may provoke in those who are theologically insecure, a temptation to retreat into or to seek to create, idealised patterns of life which are, in fact, illusory. Thus, for example, for Gülen the notion that plurality can be abolished is not only illusory it is also dangerous and, against such dangerous illusions, Gülen (2004) warns that:

> ...different beliefs, races, customs and traditions will continue to cohabit in this village. Each individual is like a unique realm unto themselves; therefore the desire for all humanity to be similar to one another is nothing more than wishing for the impossible. For this reason, the peace of this (global) village lies in respecting all these differences, considering these differences to be part of our nature and in ensuring that people appreciate these differences. Otherwise, it is unavoidable that the world will devour itself in a web of conflicts, disputes, fights, and the bloodiest of wars, thus preparing the way for its own end. (pp. 249–250)

Gülen's teaching and the Hizmet associated with it can positively contribute to the development of a 'style' of Islam in the modern world within which Muslims can be open to being informed by the strengths that exist in countries and regions beyond the so-called 'Muslim World' while also themselves being confident enough to continue to make a distinctively Islamic contribution that is characterised by both robustness and civility. And this is highly significant because it is the difference between a confident and empowered identity and one that defines itself in defensive, fearful, and reactionary terms. Reflecting on his own life, Yeşilova says:

> You know if I were to again remain in my neighbourhood and interact with those other mosque oriented community leaders, or just locals, I probably would again define myself in opposition to the west; in opposition to the Crusader philosophy; in opposition to this animosity that is always there, that will always be there. And it's as if there a struggle needs to be won; it's as if we need to be stronger so that we can become victorious.

As AS1 explained it: "So, finding an answer to questions was a big motivation for me and everything started like this. I think the youngest people, they look for an aim in their lives, can I say. When they find a goal it is of course motivating them." But that can lead into various directions: "Because I remember very well that some other youngsters they got themselves with MHP – it is the Nationalist Party of Turkey, and that party was also rising." So. it is often the combination of thinking and of a concrete movement that is important, "And I found my way in this movement, because people I saw was very sincere, and that attracted me because people in Turkey don't trust too much in other people. But these people came over to me at that time as very sincere." In relation to all of this, interviewee Alper Alasag (see Acknowledgements), from the Netherlands, said:

> Why Gülen? Gülen is for me that, because we are kind of traumatised, full of fear etc and not being able to trust other people, and kind of in a survival mode in Turkey (and this is more than thirty years ago) he opened us up and made us believe in dialogue helping people, etc.

> And I know for myself I grew up in Turkey from leftist parents who have lost friends who got executed after the coup in 1971. So, I was also kind of filled with hatred towards the society, towards Government. And now thanks to Gulen and this Hizmet I have been engaged in dialogue and trying to help people also in dialogue to come together. In Turkey in the 1970s the society was so polarized that people were even killing each other.

> All this experience, everything I learned I tried to put into practice. Thanks to Hizmet I am changed, from being a kind of traumatised and fearful person who didn't trust, to being someone who tries to bring those people into dialogue with each other, and learn to trust each other, learn to lose their fear and gain trust. So, in that I see he has fulfilled his promise, whatever I hoped to gain from him, or to learn from him.

In summary, Haylamaz arrives at an overall evaluation of Gülen's teaching relative to the 'heroic' heritage in Islam that is, in contemporary reality, so often an expression of weakness and insecurity that:

> So, if there is success, or we are going to speak of distinction of Hojaefendi's message, it is that has been very skilful and able really to reach out to access the essential message of the Qur'an and the Prophet's example and to separate out the other later added bits of values like heroism.

4.2   Spirituality, the True Human, Love, and Service

Thijl Sunier and Nico Landman (2015) argue that "Gülen's message is primarily spiritual. It is not a political-ideological program, nor a philosophy that deals with Islamic law" (p. 90). It is also not a form of escapist mysticism but what, they argue, can be called an "activist pietism" (p. 91). The depth and richness of this is something that more traditionally sociological studies of Hizmet can fail properly to understand and communicate, which is to say the fundamentally *religious* impulse that is at work at the heart of Hizmet. As Fidan expressed it:

> But what we saw in the example of Hojaefendi the first thing I was exposed to in Hojaefendi's career was the way he was teaching about God. I mean he reminded us the fact that we are Muslims because we believe in God and that there is this reality of God we have to be aware of. He brought into our attention that, first and foremost, we have to be in this consciousness of the divine. And how has this happened? Yes, through his teaching, but also through his personal devotion to his worship, and his encounter with the divine reality.

In addition, the anonymous interviewee publicly associated with Hizmet in Europe, HE1, observed that:

> One of the biggest motivations in Hizmet comes from spirituality. So, we do this voluntarily, in altruism, because we are believing in God, and by doing things voluntarily and doing good things in life, we are seeking the love of God. This is a very strong motivation, and it was actually the first motivation that Hizmet had.

At the same time, along with this rooting in spirituality, it is because of Gülen's insistence that a living Islam equipped to engage with scientific and political challenges is an Islam that should be reflexively engaged with its times, that the primacy of the idea and practice of education became so foundational in the teaching and example of Gülen and the practice of Hizmet. As Özcan put it, because of this "Doing this education is the solution and it should be done through proper education along with, you know, all these contemporary issues, positive sciences, but Islam also should be studied in a modern way along with all these modern developments." In taking this approach, Gülen and those who were early inspired by his teaching, could be said to have been trying to meet the challenge expressed in the vivid phrase found in Daniel Lerner's (1958) influential study of the transformation of Turkish peasant life, *The Passing of Traditional Society*, and to demonstrate that Lerner's dichotomous identification of "Mecca or mechanization" (p. 405) is a false dichotomy. But it was against this kind of broad background in which a relatively unexamined Islam was under challenge from, on the one hand, epistemologically scientific and technological advances and, on the other hand, politically, from Communism that, as Özcan contextually explained it:

> When Hojaefendi came to Izmir in 1965, I attended his school there, and I was then at the age of 15. Since then I have been with him and I tried to benefit from all his teachings and I hope, you know, benefited fully. But from that day on he always directed us to the true authentic Islamic resources and the text. If you consider the time we were with Hojaefendi as young students it was the time of 1968: this was what, you know, was called the '68 generation. During that time the atheistic Communism or disbelief was rampant and the believers in the Muslim lands, or the intellectual people were in shock in two senses: one the defeat against, or in the face of, western technology and development and being unable to do anything to develop their countries; and the second is the atheistic communism's influence. So they were, in a sense, shocked, paralysed and unable to do anything and they were unable to produce anything intelligently and appealingly to the younger generations.

Within this context, Gülen did not respond by developing and teaching what might be called a 'modernist Islam.' Rather, he taught, preached, wrote about, and, in many ways also modelled, key aspects of traditional Islamic piety, rooted in a Sufi inheritance that is deeply concerned with the interiority of Islam but that also gives expression to this in service. As Özcan expressed it in relation to the relationship between ritual practice and service:

> Hocaefendi at that time came forward to believe to understand to practise Islam in such a way that it shouldn't be concerning itself with traditions, customs or only the, you know, visibility. He said that Islam should be learned and studied and practised according to the true text and the resources and it should be not only theoretical but practical.

Ergene says that in discerning what is important for understanding Gülen and his teaching, it is centrally important to realise that "He's a man of belief, concerns of ethics, morality," although he also went on to add that, "If we really have to pick one out of all of these equally diverse expertise of Hojaefendi, I would pick *tasawwuf* (Sufism) as the number one scholarship that we should relate him to." And Gülen himself, when asked about the central place that he gives to love in religion, and asked about which individuals had most demonstrated and exemplified that love which he identified as being at the heart of Islam and of God's call to humanity, Gülen himself responded by citing especially the Sufis and, in particular, Yunus Emre:

> Among the people of religion, people of faith, scholars, *alims*, there can be many, but especially the Sufi lodges in a sense specialised on this aspect of Islam, the love centre. And you can see this very clearly in the verses of Yunus Emre when he says when someone attempts to slap you, or someone actually slaps you, you remain, you act as if you don't have hands, and when somebody slurs you, you act as if you don't have a tongue, which is so similar to Jesus saying you should turn the other cheek to the person who slaps you.

As Ergene explains:

> It was a very powerful curiosity he had, deep ingrained down there in his heart and his mind. So, I mean he was deeply pious from early youth. So, for a very pious Muslim the most ideal people are the Prophet and his Companions. So, he has shaped his ideal personal qualities with the examples he understood from the stories of the Prophet and his friends. So, he also studied in a very classical *madrassah* school in the east. Also, a place where many Sufi groups are very influential, and it's a part of the social life. He certainly had relations with those Sufi circles, he perhaps visited and had some influence perhaps, but he was more involved with the *madrassah*, otherwise we don't know him as somehow connected to any certain Sufi group.

In Chap. 3, Sect. 3.2 of this book, it has already been noted that Yeşilova drew attention to the place of Sufism in Gülen's teachings—in particular, within collections of Gülen's works on this. Specifically, Yeşilova drew attention to two articles in the second volume. These, on the one hand, highlight *ghurba*—separation, but also *ightirab*—double separation, and which Yeşilova says "beautifully connects his internal separation from the divine, from the rest of us, from the rest of the world, while still keeping his faith alive." As Gezen explains it, there is also:

A concept in *tassawuf*, in Sufism, which is *riza*, and this chapter in Gülen's book about *tassawuf* is the longest chapter in the book. *riza* – getting God's appreciation is the longest chapter, whereas the others are three to four pages, this one is fifteen pages. I think everyone is seeking that *riza*, and that *riza* has been defined by so many scholars. And Gülen has explained one way, but there are many ways in history.

It is in this overall Sufi perspective that, as Kurucan puts it:

The ontological domain of the drop is the ocean. We come from that presence and we aspire to go back. So that perfection is this magnetism which draws you and us and all of us to this. Yunus Emre, the Sufi Turkish poet, he said, 'we have been dressed with flesh and bones, and we have appeared as Yunus.' By this he tries to say this is not who we are, you know. We are coming from a much bigger, much loftier, nature.

But also, importantly, Kurucan sees this emphasis on the permeative presence of divine love as not being free-floating, so to speak, but as closely linked with and rooted in Gülen's emphasis on, and expertise in the "chain of narration that is an important discipline on the *hadith* studies" in relation to which he explained that:

Hadith scholarship is divided into the text and the chain of narrations which is considered an important element of how we could rely on the text based on the trust on those people who narrated the *Hadith* or the text. So that discipline – today – is almost like dead. But we could consider Hojaefendi as certainly, perhaps, one of those few persons in the world who are an expert on this chain of narrations.

However, Gülen's piety and teaching is also distinctive in comparison with the more 'inwardly oriented' traditions of some of the traditional Turkish Sufi orders. Therefore, the Jesuit Christian theologian Thomas Michel (2010) has emphasised Gülen's role as "the role spiritual director and teacher of an internalised Islamic virtue" (p. 57) but also the connection between spirituality and service in which Michel notes that Gülen says that "God rewards the small act done with purity of intention more highly than many ostentatious deeds done without the sincere desire to serve

God alone." (p. 68). Thus, as Michel also puts it, for Gülen "spirituality must always be oriented towards the service of God and others" (p. 64). Therefore, Gülen's teaching has always engaged and inspired pious businesspeople and ordinary Muslim believers in the development of civil society organisations, including those concerned with the education, dialogue, and the relief of poverty. Because of this balance in Gülen's teaching and life, Ergene says:

> I liken him more to Imam Ghazzali than any other person...Imam Ghazzali had these two wings, if that's the right way to put it, he had these embers of fire, you know, burning that spiritual search deep down in his heart. But he first took the path of scholarly research and studied and completed all possible religious and philosophical disciplines in that era... But he, then, after fulfilling, completing that entire studies in those disciplines he then turned back to that spiritual search which is that Irfan tradition, the search for the divine knowledge. So, he probably was not fully satisfied with those disciplines. He took the other path as well after he's done. When a person chooses one path over the others, his or her aspirations may die away in time...You know, Gülen's soft, velvety Islamic view that is all-welcoming, all-embracing, open to plurality that focuses on the human being, ethics, and spirituality, I believe, comes from that similarity with the Ghazzali's case where the spiritual dynamics in his heart have not died away. This has the greatest influence on him when he tries to understand Islam in the twenty-first century, where he is trying to welcome anyone to his circle. This is why he gives much more emphasis to the human being rather than to things like state, government, Caliphate, Sultanate etc. He rarely points to these issues – his main emphasis is on the human himself.

According to Gülen, when they move away from what he calls "the centre of Islam, the heart of Islam" and when people "develop a distance with God and the Prophet and his philosophy on life, then you see them actually losing the love-based relationships themselves as well and then going into conflicts, and sometimes violent conflicts." Gülen underlined this by reference to the classical Muslim theologian Al-Ghazzali, of whom he says that:

> Imam Ghazzali reminded us that, within human nature we have certain tendencies that are not necessarily angelic or human, but which are a kind of lower levels forms of life, some animal tendencies. So sometimes these other tendencies dominate our behaviour, that's when we see human beings straying away from the centre of love.

It is because of this kind of balance that Selma Ablak from the Netherlands (see Acknowledgements) explains that, through Hizmet and her learning from the teaching of Gülen "I have learned to love God. Before it was a frightening person. Now I have completely other view of Islam and religion. And then also that we can co-exist with all human beings – that's the most important thing that I have learned in Hizmet" and, when asked about what is at the centre of Gülen's teaching she answered "Doing good for others. And that's for me, personally, in the centre. For myself, being a good Muslim, and in society being a good person, and looking each day, each hour, how can I better my life by helping others? So that's in the centre."

In explaining this and making the linkage again with the centrality in Gülen's teaching of the theme of divine love and love of the divine, when asked about what he saw as being at the heart of Gülen's teaching, Ergene said that:

If you need to express it in one word, it's the human. It's a matter of religion, I know, but if you really need to boil it down to something, it's the human. Certainly, it transcends that, it goes beyond the matter because God is a transcendent being, but religion is for the human being. I would consider the human being is the centre of his thought. So, I would consider the human being as the centre of his thought.

Both Ergene and Öztürk also argued that this human-centric focus of Gülen's teaching is closely related to a key concept in Sufism which, as Ergene explained it, is "this concept of *insan-ı kâmil*, 'the perfect' human being or the 'perfected' human being is in the very centre of Islamic thought. Because the 'perfect human being' is the very centre, it's the very reason why the universe has been created in the first place." As Kurucan explains it:

Well, again from Islamic mystical thought the human being, yes is the steward, is the viceregent of God on earth, but is also the most perfect mirror of that divine, regardless of him being a believer or not. The human being as the human being per se, regardless of his other affiliations with regard to race, identity, however you may name it.... If that human being is that brightest mirror of the divine, if he is that honourable being of being the brightest mirror of God, then regardless again, isolated from his other identities or affiliations, he or she deserves that respect. So that respect holds the very centre.

Of course, the focus on the human can be found elsewhere than in the teaching of Gülen or Islam alone:

> Many humanistic philosophies also have this understanding also of respect to the human being, but in the case of Hojaefendi, where we see this man who is a believer of God and who sees the human being as that brightest mirror of God who, again from our divine scriptures we learn that we are also coming from Him – from that divine element, where he says he 'blew from his spirit into us'. We carry a knowledge, an essence that are from Him, that belong to Him. So, again, in Gülen's understanding, the human being is that piece that has come out of that divine element that eventually deserves again respect and honour.

Thus, as Öztürk expanded on this from his perspective, such a person is one who can, while remaining within the overall constraints of the physical world, become "a person who not only changes himself, but also transforms his environment. *Insan-ı kâmil* has that empowering, or perhaps civilising power, to change, make changes, make reforms around him in the nature, in his interactions with other individuals, and the rest of the society."

For Fidan, the particular genius of Hizmet is that through Gülen's teaching and challenges, he was able to move beyond the temptation for such an understanding to become a kind of pietistic cul-de-sac. Rather, his challenge to businessmen like Fidan, was that they should integrate their Islam and their business.

> So, we did our best as a businessman, as a business owner I was in Ankara. But in the footsteps of Hojaefendi. And Hojaefendi was advising us to make trips to other cities and to meet with new people, with new businessmen and to share Hizmet with them. So, I was one of the co-ordinators of those trips, and meeting with new people, introducing to the idea of Hizmet. Hojaefendi was there, we were being nourished by him, but we were in the field perhaps spending more time than on our own businesses and trying to meet with new people and teaching them about this philosophy (if it's a philosophy) of Hizmet, making things possible for people to have better access to a virtuous life, because simply the Qur'anic message is not only for us, it's a universal message and belongs to everyone. Hocaefendi challenged us to move forward on claiming, reclaiming our Muslimness by giving even more, by meeting with people, by speaking with them, by hosting them, by being generous.

Therefore, the practical engagement of Gülen's vision has deep roots in spirituality and, although a 'secular' understanding of issues of social capital, social cohesion also contribute to a holistic understanding of Fethullah Gülen and Hizmet, without understanding something of this profoundly religious dimension of Hizmet, one will not understand what lies at the heart of those who are inspired by Gülen's teaching. In this, one sees illustrated what Thomas Michel (2010) means when he says that, "Gülen has not written a systematic theology textbook," but "Upon the twin pillars of sincerity and worship, Gülen has built a practical theology orientated towards the life of worship and service" (p. 81). As articulated by Yeşilova:

> It's in the philosophy of Nursi there's this understanding that being in the world with your hands but not with your heart. When you are fully connected with your heart the world will fail you. Certainly, either you or the world will leave you behind. Eventually, you will certainly be separated. So always keep your heart reserved for the divine love, for that eternal love. This doesn't mean we shouldn't love the world or reform it, again that's something else; it is another duty and responsibility, but being there with your hands is something different to devoting your entire soul and spirit and heart to the world.

As Gülen sought further to explain this in terms of what he himself sees as being at the heart of religion:

> The essence of religion – Islam or any other religion – the essence of religion is connection, and this connection should be so strong that it finds a way to express itself, and it colours the actions and life of the individual. So, if it is not colouring the life of the individual that means there is no substance there. So, at this time in the majority Muslim world we are living through this concept known as *Kaht* or scarcity, which is the absence of true – literally translated it means – the absence of people, the lack of true individuals. You might have seen this expressed by the Greek philosopher Diogenes, I believe, you know he looks around the streets saying that, 'I'm looking for a person, individual.' There are many people. But who are the true devout. Their connection is expressed through their life, through their actions. If that is not happening, then of course that picture does not attract anybody, it does not look appealing to anybody, it does not lead anybody to ask questions. People say, doesn't interest me. There's nothing of value there.

4.3   FOR HUMAN FREEDOM

In the twenty-first century, the importance of human freedom in general and, within that, of religion and belief diversity in our globalising and pluralising world is critical for the internal peace and stability of states and societies; for international relations; and for the future of the religions themselves. As the Christian theologian Hans Küng and Kuschel (1993) put it in his famous dictum: "There will be no peace among the nations without peace among the religions. There will be no peace among the religions without dialogue among the religions."

Within this, the issue of freedom, and within it that of freedom of religion or belief, is one that poses challenges both to people of all religions and to many traditional religious approaches and practices, as well as to aspects of modern 'secular' ideologies and constitutions. In order properly to be able to understand the place of religious freedom within Gülen's articulation of Islam it is important to appreciate that, what are today articulated as 'human rights' in relation to matters of freedom of religion and belief are, within a religious vision such as that of Gülen's, understood to have roots that are also profoundly theological. Thus, if the reality of religious freedom is to be both deepened and extended, it is important that this is done not only 'externally' to the religious traditions of the world deploying 'secular' reasoning and the instruments of international law, but also that the importance and significance of such freedom is developed in articulation with the 'logic' and the 'grammar' of the religions concerned.

In highlighting the centrality of love in his religious and theological vision, and the damage done to humans and humanity as a whole from the loss of love, Gülen underlines how closely love is allied to the importance of freedom in response (or otherwise) to the call of divine love, and to mutual respect and dialogue in diverse human relations. Thus, Gülen says that:

> When Islam was described by early adopters they were describing it is as a collection of systems or disciplines that guide a person to worldly and eternal happiness through his own will. The emphasis on his own will is important which means that any kind of pressure, any kind of force has no place in the heart of Islam. If Islam is understood in its original nature, I think in conjunction, in combination with other systems, it has a potential to make a great contribution to humanity.

In this it is interesting and significant that Gülen uses the phrase "in combination with other systems" rather than seeing Islam in isolation. As an example of this, Kurucan suggested: "For instance, Hojaefendi, when he came to the West, when he saw Muslims freely practising their faith in a non-Muslim environment that was a huge influence on his worldview too. That has made a lot of change on that." According to Kurucan, one of the major ways in which Gülen has changed his theological perspectives over the years is in relation to that of the understandings of apostasy, which has substantial significance in relation to matters of freedom of religion or belief. Apostasy was the topic on which Kurucan did his doctorate and on which he says that:

> The classical approach to it was if someone steps out of Islam when he was Muslim he is executed. That was the classical approach. But Hojaefendi said, actually in one of his books, which had made headlines in one of the most secular newspapers in Turkey back then, Hojaefendi said this is not a religious issue, it is a political issue. It is in the penal code of the country. As someone is free to enter Islam he is as free to leave Islam because faith, for that matter, is all about freedom of conscience, one has to be able to make that choice without any oppression, without any caution – that's when faith really manifests itself.

The argument here, which was a revolutionary one when Gülen first made it, was that while acknowledging that there were rules and agreements during the times of the Prophet and after him, and that those were interpretations for certain times and conditions, the times and environments have changed in the light of which there also has to be change in the rules. Significantly, Kurucan cites Gülen's approach to freedom in a wider sense as an example of Gülen's theological creativity, noting in relation to classical ideas of the purposes of Islam:

> As it has been again I think formulated from the time of Imam Ghazzali and Imam Shatibi, I believe, the five purposes of Islam which are related to the protection of one's faith, life, family, property, mind, (some add "honour" as the sixth). But Hojaefendi considers very significant to add a sixth one which is freedom.

What Kurucan hints at here is something that might be called an 'expansive development' of the core purposes of Islam. This is because, as Kurucan says:

Whereas freedom in the classical scholarship was understood as in opposition to slavery. It was praised, for that matter, as a rewarding act to free someone. So, it is something that was praised, but it has not been included in that paradigm of five essentials that need to be protected and are purposes to be achieved as Islam envisions it in human social life.

Giving this as an example of how contextual emphases can develop according to the needs of the times, Kurucan went on to say that "But maybe later on, a decade later, when freedoms will already be ensured or be a part of that protection of family, religious thought, freedom of conscience will be a part of those other five essentials, then we may no longer be needing to consider freedom as a sixth principle." While this might then well be an example of what this author is calling an 'expansive development,' in Kurucan's understanding what Gülen is doing is still in line with the Qu'ran on the basis that:

A Qur'anic verse says whoever will so believe, will believe, but whoever does not will to believe does not believe. So, God is allowing us, giving us the freedom to deny His existence. So how much wider can we really formulate the concept of freedom? This is as wide as it could be. But human beings are actually narrowing down that huge expansive liberty that God is giving us by birth.

Kurucan goes on to underline the importance of this because, although Islamic history is sometimes cited as an example of relative religious tolerance it is clear that, today, the 'Islamic world' has a number of problems with the freedom of religion when considering, among others, the position of the Bahá'ís in Iran; the Ahmahdis in Pakistan; the Coptic Christians in Egypt; and the Jehovah's Witnesses in Turkey. Therefore, as Kurucan comments:

In Islam those purposes of religion as they were formulated a millennium ago, it was considered as – like, you know, the Vatican's teaching and it's absolute, that's the teaching – that was so firmly established that no one has ever thought that they could add a sixth to the purposes of faith. So, this is what Hojaefendi is actually doing, which is going beyond those parameters of considering those teachings as already done, and introducing a new one. This doesn't mean that he puts freedom as sixth or the first – he's not ranking those issues. Each of them are as equally required as the other.

In relation to the kind of challenge that Muslims might put to this in terms of inappropriate innovation, Kurucan explains that:

I mean there is the classical Islamic discourse, where there are these other formulations still: there are these five things where you have to testify…So why not six, why not seven? Why are we not including the unlawfulness of theft or robbery or being bribed? They are also all being used in the same imperative language as the Qur'an is using the prescriptions on prayer. Those are equally imperative in the Qur'anic teachings. These are only formulations and the numbers do not really matter there, but the *Shariah*, or the purposes of the religion or the law were formulated a thousand years ago and that has been the way it was based on a certain *hadith* perhaps. This doesn't mean we need to ignore the rest of the Prophet's teaching and the Qur'anic message which is emphasising good character, virtues etc.

Understanding that the basics still remain, when asked why freedom is being particularly emphasised in this context, in this time, Kurucan opined:

Well I mean the way he put it, I believe when he emphasises freedom I think that has a lot to do with the sixth period in his life since 2013 when this persecution (in Turkey) started. And then, you know, new mothers are being imprisoned. People are being put behind bars for no reason. And they are still there having seen no judge at all for the last fifteen months. And you see you are putting people behind the bars for no reason. And the right of freedom to be able to move, to be able to travel, to be able to be outside of the bars, I think that is what he really is referring to in that specific case.

In other words, this is in many ways a stronger development of Gülen's related, although different, notion of 'tolerance' in relation to which Gülen he says: "First of all, I would like to indicate that tolerance is not something that was invented by us" (Gülen 2004, p. 37) and that "Tolerance was first introduced on this Earth by the prophets whose teacher was God." Thus, Gülen sees tolerance as something that has roots that are much deeper and more constant than a product of historical development alone. Indeed, it is arguable that, in many ways, the word "tolerance" which appears in English translations of Gülen's Turkish originals, does not do proper justice to the strength of the translated Turkish word *hoşgörü*, of which Pahl (2019) says:

My understanding of *hoşgörü* is something like 'principled pluralism.' A person committed to *hoşgörü* lives with integrity in one's own tradition (hence "principled") but also lets others live out their deepest commitments that might differ dramatically from one's own (hence "pluralism"). But principled pluralism or *hoşgörü* as preached by Gülen and lived out in Hizmet was not mere relativism, where every opinion was equally likely to be as true as any other. Instead, principled pluralism or *hoşgörü* in Hizmet wagered that Islam provided a foundation from which differences could be engaged and turned to productive co-operation through dialogue. (p. 190).

Within such a vision, it is possible even for committed believers in one religion to benefit not only from the cognate ideas of others, but even from opposing ideas. As Gülen (2004) expresses it, "We should have so much tolerance that we can benefit from opposing ideas in that they force us to keep our heart, spirit, and conscience active and aware, even if these ideas do not directly or indirectly teach us anything." (p. 33). As expressed by Gülen (2004) himself, what he means by tolerance is set out clearly, as follows:

Tolerance does not mean being influenced by others or joining them; it means accepting others as they are and knowing how to get along with them. No one has the right to say anything about this kind of tolerance; everyone in this country has his or her own point of view. People with different ideas and thoughts are either going to seek ways of getting along by means of reconciliation or they will constantly fight with one another. There have always been people who thought differently to one another and there always will be. (p. 42).

Therefore, in contrast with those whose lives are at the mercy of shifting intellectual or other fashions, the perspectives found in what Gülen's vision of Islam seeks to promote are rooted in a conviction about received revelatory truth which is believed to reflect the nature of reality as it is, and to which those who respond to it are called to bear witness. On the basis of the implementation of an authentic Islamic vision, Gülen's (2004) hope is that a "new man and woman" can be developed in which, as he says:

These new people will be individuals of integrity who, free from external influences, can manage independently of others. No worldly force will be able to bind them, and no fashionable -ism will cause them to deviate from their path. Truly independent of any worldly power, they will think and act freely, for their freedom will be in proportion to their servanthood to God. Rather than imitating others, they will rely on their original dynamics rooted in the depths of history and try to equip their faculties of judgment with authentic values that are their own. (p. 81)

Of this "Golden Generation," Gülen (2004) has argued that: "The generation that will become responsible for bringing justice and happiness to the world should be able to think freely and respect freedom of thought. Freedom is a significant dimension of human free will and a key to the mysteries of human identity" (p. 99).

Thus, neither Gulen's own Islamic vision of the affirmation of religious freedom, nor the promotion of the practice of social and political tolerance that is associated with this, is to be understood in terms of a 'liberal' or 'modern' adaptation to a plural world consequent upon the loss of the power or influence of religion. Rather, they are rooted in a view of religious truth that, ultimately, has confidence in the inherent power of the reality to which truth claims point. In terms of lifestyle, this leads to an approach to religious plurality in which dialogue and tolerance are key.

Applying this more particularly to freedom of religion, while other Islamic teachers can be found who refer to the Qur'an's negatively expressed injunction that there is "no compulsion in religion" Gülen expresses an authentically Muslim commitment to a positive position on religious freedom with an unusual clarity and consistency of emphasis. And extending this to the relationships between religion, state, and society, based on the evidence of history about attempts, on the one hand, to enforce religious conformity of various kinds and, on the other, to enforce atheistic and/or anti-religious stances, Gülen (2004) has pointed out that, "Efforts to suppress ideas via pressure or brute force have never been truly successful. History shows that no idea was removed by suppressing it. Many great empires and states were destroyed, but an idea or thought whose essence is sound continues to survive" (pp. 151–152). What has always been true of history in this regard is also argued by Gülen to be even more the case in our modern globalised world and of relevance to this discussion of contemporary forms of governance, as Ergene (in Gülen 2004) notes:

Gülen has stated that in the modern world the only way to get others to accept your ideas is by persuasion. He describes those who resort to force as being intellectually bankrupt; people will always demand freedom of choice in the way they run their affairs and in their expression of their spiritual and religious values. (p. 12)

What is particularly significant about the clarity and consistency with which the Gülen's vision of Islam supports and upholds religious freedom is that this is not the voice of only an individual teacher. Rather, it resonates within Hizmet as a global movement and has influence beyond it. Furthermore, this theological commitment has been given expression in the activities of the civil society initiatives that are inspired by his teaching, such as the work of the Journalists and Writers Foundation in Turkey, and that of dialogue societies and initiatives inspired by Gülen's teaching. So, in this context, Gülen offers religiously authentic, creative, and corrective resources that can help contemporary Muslims to live in faithful, committed, and peaceful ways in a religiously diverse world.

Islam is a global religion with billions of adherents worldwide and has an enormous influence that stretches far beyond its committed faithful followers into the cultures, societies, and states that have been shaped by its values. Thus, in face of the challenges of living together posed by our globalising and pluralising world, how Muslims understand and put into practice issues related to religious freedom is of critical importance. In interviewing Gülen himself, when drawing his attention to the fact that another interviewee had put a big emphasis on his understanding of freedom as something given by God to human beings, Gülen responded as follows, which is worth quoting extensively:

> In Islam according to many scholars there are five principal values that are meant to be protected. These are, of course, the life of a person, private property, progeny, religion, and mental health or intellect. And some scholars, with whom I agree, add a sixth element, which is the freedom of the person. So, I see this as the sixth essential element that needs to be protected by any system of governance or by any social system. Bediüzzaman Said Nursi, in expressing the same view, he says I can live without water, without food, but I cannot live without my freedom.

> It can be argued that without freedom can a person be called a true human being? A human being without true freedom is, in a sense, a slave. Sometimes in the past, in history, it was openly a slavery system. But today we don't have open slavery in most of the world but we are seeing people in different parts of the world who surrender their freedoms in exchange for a possession, in exchange for money, or out of fear and therefore they come under

dominance by some force, some entity or group and therefore they cease to have this essential element of humanity.

Unfortunately, in the so-called 'Islamic world' we are seeing this phenomenon very often. Many rulers, ruling classes or groups or individuals bring masses under their domination by threatening them, or offering money or positions and other things, so people are surrendering their freedom into the hands of these authoritarian rulers. And so in a sense they are becoming modern slaves. Can they be called truly human? There is a question mark there.

In the Islamic world, this was about freedom in general. In Islamic tradition, the freedom of choice is an essential value, is an essential principle. We see, if we look at it, in an unbiased way, we can see the examples of this value, this principle, expressed in so many instances and cases. For example, when we consider the example of the Christians of Najaran from the southern Arabian peninsula, they visited Medina. And the Prophet's mosque, which is considered haram – forbidden for others – the Prophet not only welcomed them, they actually were permitted to practice their religion inside the mosque for days.

So just like you were observing the prayers today, they were also observing the prayers, and they were observing the behaviour and lives of Muslims. Of course they were not completely free because they were under pressure from the Romans or Byzantines as they were called at the time. So at that point they had some dialogue with the Prophet and other Muslims. At some point they also argued a little bit, but ultimately they said, 'let's sign an armistice and then we go back to our land and then we don't attack each other'. So they did that. But later on, others, they wilfully embraced Islam, but that was completely out of their free choice. So this free choice is very essential.

So, in the time periods where Muslims were true to the spirit of their religion you see them valuing and ensuring the expression, the living of this freedom. Then you go a little bit further and consider the Muslims taking over the area of the Masjid al-Aqsa, Jerusalem. When they were governing that area, you can see Christians, Muslims and Jews practising their religion freely in the Masjid Al-Aqsa area. You can see the same practice during the time of Salahuddin. Salahuddin also valued religious freedom, so he did not enforce any kind of pressure or oppression on the members of other religions and let them practice their religions freely.

When Hazrat Umar, the second Caliph, when he arrived at the Masjid al-Aqsa in Jerusalem, he was sharing his camel with his servant, so sometimes he was riding it and sometimes his servant was riding it, and although he was second Caliph his dress had some patches on it. The observing Christians and Jews at the time when they saw this humble state of the Caliph, they said this is the person we have been waiting for, this is the person predicted in our books and therefore they brought the key to the city to him. When he needed to pray, they invited him to pray in what was a church at the time. But he said that if I do my prayer here Muslims will turn this into a sacred Muslim place and then all the members of the other religions will lose their rights to pray, so I'm not going to pray here. So he chose to pray in an undeveloped place.

None of this, of course, should be misunderstood in terms of this being a 'modernist' approach in which, in Islam or in other religions, there is a tendency, perhaps for pragmatic reasons, to downplay the truth-claims made by what are both, at their root, universalistic religious traditions which have an understanding of what they have received as being something not only for themselves as a particular cultural, ethnic, or religious group, but rather as something that is held in trust by them for the whole human community.

Within Islam, the teaching of Gülen and the practice of the movement that looks for inspiration to his teaching has emerged out of a clash within Turkish history between a radical and often anti-religious form of 'secularism' and obscurantist and/or oppositionalist forms of being Muslim. It draws on the best elements of the Ottoman Turkish inheritance with regard to toleration. But it has also issued into a global vision of Islamic integrity in its commitment to religious freedom that is deeply rooted in the Qur'an and the Sunnah, while being fully and dialogically engaged with the plurality of the contemporary world. Superficially considered, it may seem that a commitment to uphold religious freedom might be fundamentally incompatible with a desire to present the particular claims of a religion and to invite others to consider their validity for themselves. However, what enables this to remain a 'creative tension' rather than an 'impossible contradiction' in the "Gülenian" approach to trying to live faithfully as committed believers, is the prior and theologically informed affirmation of religious freedom. It is this that facilitates the possibility of an ethical practice in which truth claims can be advocated, but where the freedom of the other to accept these claims or not is seen as being rooted in the nature of humanity. In Gülen's vision of Islam, the revelation received in the Qur'an is one to which people of all cultures are invited to respond. But not only people of all cultures: also people of all religions, since revelation is not be confused with the 'property' of any group of human beings. Within this, testimony to what has been received within each religion is believed to take place before God, and in dialogue with others whose integrity is affirmed and respected, rather than being an activity that is directed at others in a threatening or manipulative way. Reflecting on the global network of schools founded by Hizmet, Özcan says that "There is no missionary understanding" and were it not so, then "these people, the people non-Turkish people in these one hundred and seventy countries would never ever accept any idea with compulsion, with a missionary mentality. So, you should appeal to the free will and sense and intellect and when you show that you are sincere they will pick it up."

Coming back again to the image of Rumi cited by Gülen and which promotes a dialogical way of being in the world like that of a compass that has one of its feet firmly planted (in his case, in Islam), while its other foot 'en-compasses' the world's diversity. Gülen argues that it is therefore important both to live out of an inner freedom, but also that freedom of conscience, conviction, and religion is both an Islamic and a human necessity.

4.4   AGAINST THEOCRACY AND FOR DEMOCRACY

As traced in both great detail and also panorama by the English historian, Arnold Toynbee in his epic 12-volume series of books, *A Study of History* (Toynbee and Somervelle, Abridgements 1947, 1958), questions arising from the relationship between religion(s), state(s), and societ(ies) have, in many ways, shaped much of the history of the world. On the other side of the philosophical challenge of the Enlightenment and the political challenge of Marxism-Leninism concerning various forms of 'secularisation,' these questions have once again emerged with the 'return of religion.' At the same time, in the predominantly Muslim world, the fractured history of societies shaped by Islam that came about through the interruptive traumas caused by imperialism and colonialism, have led to reactive attempts to reassert a different vision, including more theocratic models, whether of the Sunni 'mullahs' of the Taliban in Afghanistan or the Shi'a revolutionary guards and Ayatollahs in Iran.

Presented with a choice between the privatisation of Islam, and the enthusiasm followed by corruption and eventual disillusion that can accompany the assumption of modern state power by Islamically-informed ideological movements, Gülen's teaching offers an alternative approach that might provide the possibility of transcending the externally configured dichotomies Islam and political pluralism and Islam and democracy. If so, this can perhaps be accomplished through offering a way of engaging with both ideological 'secularism' and political 'Islamism' via a critique of the political instrumentalisation of Islam alongside the advancement of an argument for a more active Muslim engagement with the wider (religious and secular) society based on a distinctive Islamic vision characterised by what this author elsewhere calls a combination of "robustness and civility" (Weller 2022).

As already noted in Sects. 3.1 and 3.2, fully to appreciate the significance of Gülen's vision, one needs also to understand something about the crucible of modern Turkish history and society out of which it has emerged. Yavuz and Esposito (Eds. 2003) point out that in Kemalist ideology "modernity and democracy require secularism" (p. xxiii). Indeed, the version of secularism that has been dominant in Turkey is what these authors call a "radical Jacobin liaicism" in which secularism is treated "as above and outside politics" and in which therefore, "secularism draws the boundaries of public reasoning" (p. 16). But Kemalism was established against the background of a traditional Islam that never disappeared from Turkish society and, in more recent times, it has been opposed by an 'Islamist' form of Islam. Thus, the Gülen's vision of Islam is one that that has had both to distinguish itself from obscurantist and oppositionalist forms of Islam, while also needing to engage with the secular.

Therefore, as also discussed in Sect. 3.4, even before the dismantling of Hizmet in Turkey from 2016 onwards, Gülen's vision has remained distinct from an 'Islamist' vision that seeks to capture the ruling machinery of government through its variants of either electoral or violent means. As argued in the first section of this chapter, to understand both Gülen and Hizmet one must understand them religiously—not in the narrow sense of religion, but in the sense of the spirit of religion which Gülen advocates. It is this vision and understanding that contrasts strongly with that of those Muslims who would wish either to establish an Islamic theocracy in a particular country, such as Iran under the Ayatollahs, or Afghanistan under the Taliban, or seek the re-establishment of a universal Califate either by peaceful democratic means or in the way that ISIS attempted to create this through violent action.

A different way was advocated by many Sufis. However, given the way in which in modern Turkish history, religion was systematically excluded not only from the political sphere, but also from education and other key sectors of civil society, one of the consequences of such alternatives was sometimes that of a withdrawal from society. In relation to such issues, in interview, Gülen noted:

> Bediüzzaman Said Nursi at some point in his life, he said, I seek refuge from Satan the outcast and from politics. So, he distanced himself from active politics. But at the same time, he said I am more Republican than any one of you – that means I value the Republican form of governance which is participatory, which does not give a special status to any particular group or individual.

And the vision that Gülen inspired is not dissimilar, in that at least until the mid-point of AKP rule in Turkey, Hizmet was not aligned with a particular political party but was actively engaged with society. It is this vision has that has inspired the engagement of pious businessmen and ordinary Muslim believers in the development of civil society organisations and initiatives that give expression to the notion and practice of Hizmet. And this vision and understanding is the reason why Gülen could lay down the challenge that seems so radical to many Muslim individuals and movements and majority societies, as quoted by Yavuz (2003) that "Islam does not need the state to survive, but rather needs educated and financially rich communities to flourish. In a way, not the state but rather community is needed under a full democratic system" (p. 45).

This is, in many ways, an unusual message within the Muslim world. It offers a radical understanding of how to be present as a faithful Muslim, in the world, contributing to it, and transforming it. Gülen critiques theocratic models of government; challenges contemporary 'Islamist' visions of Islam; and advocates democracy. Thus, while noting that "Supposedly there are Islamic regimes in Iran and Saudi Arabia," Gülen (2004) goes on to say that these "are state-determined and limited to sectarian approval" (p. 151).

While medieval scholars and contemporary 'Islamist' Muslims highlight a tension, if not outright incompatibility, between what is identified as *dar al-harb* (territory that lays outside the sway of Islam) and what is called *dar al-Islam* (those lands within which Islam has taken root). Gülen's teaching informs and facilitates the taking of another path, and the development of another understanding. Thus, Ihsan Yilmaz (2003) sees the community associated with Gülen's teaching, whether they are in the world as either a majority or a minority as being concerned with what he identifies as *dar al-hizmet* (country of service). Because of this, despite the charges of the current Turkish authorities, the author of this book would concur with Bulent Aras' and Omer Caha's (2000) summarisation of the relevance of Gülen's teaching to matters of religion, state, and society:

> Gülen's movement seems to have no aspiration to evolve into a political party or seek political power. On the contrary, Gülen continues a long Sufi tradition of seeking to address the spiritual needs of people, to educate the masses, and to provide some stability in times of turmoil. Like many previous Sufi figures (including the towering thirteenth-century figure, Jalal al-Din Rumi), he is wrongly suspected of seeking political power. However, any change from this apolitical stance would very much harm the reputation of his community. (p. 30)

Such an approach offers an alternative to the instrumentalisation of religion in the service of politics or politics in the service of religion, and emphasises instead an understanding of the contribution to public life which service based on religious motivations can make. As the Indian political scientist Achin Vanaik (1992) articulated this in his journal article on "Reflections on Communalism and Nationalism in India":

> To say that politics and religion should be kept separate is understandable, especially at a time like ours. But what it really should mean is that politicians should not use religions for short-term political ends and religious leaders should not use politicians for narrowly communal gains. But surely every religion has a social and public dimension. To say that religions should be a private affair is to misunderstand both religion and politics. (p. 56)

In this regard, Gülen's vision challenges any form of religion and state relationship in which either religion or state are instrumentalised in the service of the other, or in which temporal structures are held to approximate to a Divine blueprint. As Gülen (in Ünal and Williams 2000) himself expresses it:

Politicizing religion would be more dangerous for religion than for the regime, for such people want to make politics a means for all their ends. Religion would grow dark within them, and they would say: "We are the representatives of religion." This is a dangerous matter. Religion is the name of the relationship between humanity and God, which everyone can respect. (p. 166)

Overall, one of the strengths especially of the so-called prophetic religious traditions of Judaism, Christianity, and Islam is that at least, in principle, they have self-critique built into them a kind of 'hard-wired way' due to their absolute differentiation between the divine and the religious communities that are called to bear witness to it. In the exercise of that critique comes a clarity and realisation that none of the religions as a historical community embodies the absolute. While one or another community may feel that it can point to the absolute better than another and/or that they have the last or most complete revelation, none of them can—if they are historically, sociologically, and theologically honest to their central beliefs and values—truly believe that, in practice, their community fully embodies the absolute.

Against the background of a Turkish system in which military coups have several times cut across the democratic process, Ergene (in Gülen 2004) has pointed out that Gülen has come to a position in relation to which he argues that:

Democracy .... in spite of its many shortcomings, is now the only viable political system, and people should strive to modernize and consolidate democratic institutions in order to build a society where individual rights and freedoms are respected and protected, where equal opportunity for all is more than a dream. (p. 12).

As Gülen (2004) says, "Democracy is a system of freedoms. However, because we have to live together with our different positions and views, our freedom is limited where that of another begins" (p. 151). When interviewed, Gülen was reminded of what he had written stating that "Islam does not need the state to survive" and he was asked to explain how he understands the relationship between personal piety, social responsibility, and the state, in response to which, he explained that:

When we consider the way the first righteous Caliphs, the four Righteous Caliphs came to rule, came to become rulers, we see that they came to rule through some form of democratic process. Ibn Arabi expresses opinion and praises this process. And in his book, *The Eternal Message of Muhammad,* Abd Al-Rahman Azzam, former Secretary General of the Arab League also expresses praise for those processes, for the four Caliphs.

In relation to the various possible forms of democracy, Gülen said that: "In today's world and in the recent past there have been so many forms of democracy, many governments claim to be democracies, and there are so many variations. I believe that among these variations, some of those variations are perfectly aligned with Islamic values." At the same time, Gülen does not have an idealistic or unrealistic view of democracy, as can be seen when he pointed out that, "In the past we have been deceived by many promises by politicians" and "people will vote for, or elect, politicians whom they view as respectful of the beliefs and values of their electors." In summary, Gülen says that:

> So, ultimately the real matter from a religious perspective is that the society should have its formation, its ideas, its values at the right place and they will elect their rulers. Yes, there is some portion, the government structure, the governance form, does have some value. But ultimately what is most important is the electorate, if they are enlightened, if they are embracing each other, if they are actually living the democratic values, their governance will reflect those values.

4.5   ISLAM, TERROR, AND DERADICALISATION BY DEFAULT

When evaluated historically and/or sociologically, but also when measured against theological standards, the historical and sociological actualisations of religion can be very ambiguous. Indeed religion can, when it is bad religion, be very dangerous. Because it is concerned with ultimate things, ultimate convictions, and ultimate commitments when things connected with it go wrong, they can tend to go very wrong indeed.

The kind of association that exists in the thinking and feelings of many other than Muslim people in the world with regard to the relationship between Islam and terror can be exemplified in the Danish so-called 'Cartoon Controversy' (Kublitz 2010) in which the Prophet Muhammad was portrayed with a bomb in his turban. That picture also highlights the challenges faced by contemporary Islam and Muslims if they are to overcome such a view because it underlines the widespread nature of non-Muslim perceptions that transmit and reproduce such a view, in which Islam is associated with fear, in relation to which it is therefore no accident that the term 'Islamophobia' has been coined (Runnymede Trust 1997). Gülen recognises the extent of this challenge and warns that "The present distorted image of Islam that has resulted from its misuse, by both Muslims, and non-Muslims for their own goals, scares both Muslims and non-Muslims" (in Ünal and Williams, Eds. 2000, p. 248). Indeed, a large part of the challenge for Muslims is that the issues around this are not limited to perceptions alone. Rather, there is also the reality that there have been those who, in the name of both of Muslims and of Islam have indeed, used terror in order to advance their cause. This included *The Satanic Verses* controversy; the murder of the artist Theo Van Gogh on 2nd November 2004; Charlie Ebdo killings and a range of other terror attacks since then. Therefore, condemnation and critique, while important, are not sufficient. Looking for an antidote to 'radicalism' and for preventing 'violent extremism' in the sense that these words and phrases are often used in Western political and security discussions, many state authorities seek to identify and promote what are seen as 'moderate' or 'liberal' in contrast to 'Jihadi' and 'Islamist' versions of Islam.

In this connection, some commentators have deployed the terminology of religious 'liberalism' in relation to Gülen and the Hizmet movement. However, while this author does want to affirm that Gülen's teaching has a very important contribution to make in relation to challenging the deployment of terror in the name of Islam, his teaching does not fit the paradigms of the secular powers-that-be in this regard and Gülen cannot appropriately be called an exponent of 'liberalism.' Indeed, what is particularly important about Gülen and his teaching, as well as the practice of the movement associated with it, is that the constructive impulses which they offer are based on an authentic Islam that is deeply and recognisably rooted in the Qur'an and in the Sunnah of the Prophet. This is important because, in the face of the terror by Jihadi and similar groups, the cultivation and promotion of a 'liberal Islam' or a 'modernist Islam,' while understandable, is likely to be self-defeating. Rather, in tackling what has taken hold among some Muslims, it is necessary for those from within Islam who wish to counter this to identify resources which, precisely on *Islamic* grounds can both authentically connect with the Muslim community in ways that will resonate with them, while also contributing to a transformation of the wider public imaginary.

Gülen is, in many ways, a traditional Muslim without being 'traditionalist.' What he offers is an Islamic contextualisation that is ethically authentic without loss of integrity in terms of both its rootedness in Islam and its
readiness to engage with the wider world. In this one finds a dynamic and
holistic theologising which can only be properly understood in relation to
its formation at the nexus of interaction between Gülen's knowledge of,
and proficiency with, Islamic sources, and the contexts, questions, and
issues of his geographical, social, political, and religious life and times,
including with those engaged in by Hizmet around the world. Because of
this it is important to understand that the position that Gülen has clearly
articulated in relation to such matters that should not be seen as simply
reactive to the enormity of that event and the challenge that it posed to
Muslim leaders to differentiate themselves from what was, through it,
done in the name of Islam.

Indeed, basing his argument on the sayings of the Prophet and the
Qur'an, Gülen goes so far as to say that if one commits such an act it
results in such a loss of faith and that if one dies in such a state, one dies
outside the fold of Islam. Although it was the case that Gülen came into
both wider Muslim and wider public view in the context of his clear statements of condemnation of the 9/11 terror attacks on the USA, he did, in
fact, have a longer and more rooted history in condemning terrorism in
the name of Islam:

> In Islam, killing a human being is an act that is equal in gravity to unbelief.
> No person can kill a human being. No one can touch an innocent person,
> even in time of war. No one can give a fatwa (a legal pronouncement in
> Islam) in this matter. No one can be a suicide bomber. No one can rush into
> crowds, that is not religiously permissible. Even in the event of war – during
> which it is difficult to maintain balance – this is not permitted in Islam.
> (Gülen, in Çapan 2004, p. 1).

In fact, one can find equally clear and forthright condemnations by
Gülen of violent terror from periods before Gülen became more globally
known. Thus, while explaining the impact of 9/11 upon himself, the
asylum-seeker AS2 recounted a story in relation to the person of Gülen
and the question of violence and his underlying attitude to the question of
violence:

Because my background, from my childhood to now I never learned something rude or, for example, in Hizmet you couldn't even kill an ant. It is a very big fault, it is not good. How can you kill an ant?! Fethullah Gülen, for example, I respect him because of that. There are a lot of books, and I have read them, but his humanity, his love, his tolerance is very high. For example, years and years ago I read them and I heard about the people that they were making a camp in a forest. And about one hundred came together to make worship, read books, read the Qur'an, and they spiritually get well in the forest. Thirty or forty years ago, they were doing that kind of things. When they were building a camping place they had to dig some places to make a toilet or something. And they were digging some places and there was a very big ant nest, and they had worked for about five or six hours then. They had organised many things. But when Fethullah Gülen saw the ants and he said, OK but these places had a lot of ants and we couldn't harm them or unrelax them. So we have to move from here. So they got all the things and moved to other places.

That story, in itself, also had a contextual rooting in terms of the role of terror violence in Turkish political and religious history and in which, during the period of near civil war in the Turkish Republic. And, just as historically, a number of Christian movements have identified and used theological resources to challenge the European Wars of Religion, including the religious logics within them so, arguably, Muslims have a responsibility to address those matters related to Muslim interpretations of Islam that religiously undergird and/or justify the use of terror. And what Gülen offers in relation to all this is a way forward for Muslims that both recognises issues that need tackling and also promotes a particular vision of how to do this. Both in Gülen's own teaching and in what is socially produced by Hizmet out of interaction with it, he is active within the wider community in creating alternative positive and challenging Islamic visions of a proper *jihad* that can inspire the idealism, especially of young people.

Thus, what Gülen offers in the struggle against terror and also injustice and unfair treatment, is not a wishy-washy modernist version of Islam, evacuated of its content merely to adapt to the prevailing social, political, and economic norms. Such an approach cannot, even on pragmatic grounds, connect with Muslims of traditionalist orientation. Rather, Gülen offers a robust renewal of Islam, based on deep knowledge of authentically Islamic sources. Only a resource of this kind can, at the level of values and worldview, find resonance with the broad sweep of traditional Muslims. In doing so, it can at least in principle be capable of effectively challenging and marginalising the influence of those who have turned Islam into an instrumentalist political ideology and who see themselves as the revolutionary vanguard of a theocratic world order. Indeed, more than one interviewee testified personally that they would likely have followed a very different path had it not been for their encounter with Gülen and/or his teaching and the Hizmet practice inspired by that. But only to cite two examples of this, as Haylamaz put it—referring to Gülen's foreword in the award-winning book, *The Sacred Trust* (Aydin 2005):

> Without Hojaefendi we all could have become radicals, radical extremists. For, this is what the 'neighbourhood' breeds. It was a shocking experience when I read a piece by Hojaefendi where he wrote about the Prophet's sword that it was "never stained by human blood, a sword which never hurt any person."

As HE3 expressed it, "I know Gülen and I have met him several times for my projects and for some visits in the US. I write about him." Out of this knowledge, HE3's evaluation is that "He is an inspirational person, and I am very happy that I know him and his books and ideas" not least because "Maybe I would be another person from my religious or Turkish origin, maybe a radical or a nationalistic person. I am thankful to him that I know Islam in that moderate/peaceful way, with his ideas."

References

Alam, Anwar (2019). *For the Sake of Allah: The Origin, Development and Discourse of the Gülen Movement*. New Jersey: Blue Dome Press.

Aras, Bulent and Caha, Omer (2000). Fethullah Gülen and his Liberal "Turkish Islam" Movement. *Middle Eastern Review of International Affairs Journal*. 4 (4) pp. 31–42.

Aydin, Hilmi (2005). *The Sacred Trusts: Pavilion of the Sacred Relics, Topkap Palace Museum, Istanbul: Pavilion of the Sacred Relics (Topkapi Palace Museum, Istanbul)*. New Jersey: Tughra Books.

Gülen, M. Fethullah (2004). *Towards a Global Civilization of Love and Tolerance*. New Jersey, The Light.

Kublitz, Anja (2010). The Cartoon Controversy: Creating Muslims in a Danish Setting. *Social Analysis*. 54 (3) pp. 107–125. DOI: https://doi.org/10.3167/sa.2010.540307

Küng, Hans and Karl-Josef Kuschel. (Eds.) (1993). *A Global Ethic: The Declaration of the Parliament of the World Religions*. New York: Continuum

Lerner, David (1958). *The Passing of Traditional Society: Modernizing the Middle East*. Glencoe, Illinois: Free Press.

Michel, Thomas (2010). The Theological Dimensions of the Thought of M. Fethullah Gülen. In Gürkan Çelik and Martien Brinkmann (Eds.), *Mapping the Gülen Movement: A Multidimensional Approach, Conference Papers from Felix Meritis, Amsterdam, The Netherlands, October 7th 2010* (pp. 56–80). Amsterdam: Dialog Academie and VISOR Institute for the Study of Religion, Culture and Society.

Pahl, Jon (2019). *Fethullah Gülen: A Life of Hizmet*. New York: Blue Dome Press.

Runnymede Trust (1997). *Islamophobia: A Challenge for us All*. London: Islamophobia.

Sunier, Thijl and Landman, Nico (2015). Gülen-Movement (Hizmet). In: *Transnational Turkish Islam: Shifting Geographies of Religious Activism and Community Building in Turkey and Europe*. (81–94). London: Palgrave Pivot.

Toynbee, Arnold/D.C. Somervell (1947). *A Study of History/Abridgement of Volumes I–VI*. Oxford: Oxford University Press.

Toynbee, Arnold/D.C. Somervell (1958). *A Study of History/Abridgement of Volumes VII–X*. Oxford: Oxford University Press.

Ünal, Ali and Williams, Alphonse (Ed.) (2000). *Advocate of Dialogue*. Fairfax, Virginia: The Fountain.

Vanaik, Achin (1992). Reflections on Communalism and Nationalism in India. *New Left Review*, *196*, 43–62. https://newleftreview.org/issues/i196/articles/achin-vanaik-reflections-on-communalism-and-nationalism-in-india

Weller, Paul (2022). *Hizmet in Transitions: European Developments of a Turkish Muslim-Inspired Movement*. London: Palgrave Macmillan.

Yavuz, Hakan (2003). The Gülen Movement: The Turkish Puritans. In HakanYavuz and John Esposito (Eds.) (2003). *Turkish Islam and the Secular State: The Gülen Movement* (pp. 19–47). New York: Syracuse University.

Yavuz, Hakan and Esposito, John (Eds.) (2003). *Turkish Islam and the Secular State: The Gülen Movement*. New York: Syracuse University.

Yilmaz, İhsan (2003). *Ijtihad* and *Tajdid* by Conduct: The Gülen Movement. In: HakanYavuz and John Esposito (Eds.) (2003). *Turkish Islam and the Secular State: The Gülen Movement* (pp. 208–237). New York: Syracuse University.

PART III

Islamic Heroism, Hizmet Loss, and a Future Beyond Gülen?

CHAPTER 5

Learning from Loss?

5.1 Wounded Exile

With regard to Gülen's relationship with the USA where he now lives, Öztürk very succinctly summarised this as being: "His first visit to the US was in 1992; then in 1997; in 1999 third time which was the last one, never to go back again." Gülen is today in the USA as what might be described as a 'wounded exile.' In terms of the iterative impact of Gülen's time in the USA on his life and teaching, Kurucan divides Gülen's life in the USA into two parts. The first part, he says, was "from 1999 to 2013 when things really started going bad in Turkey." As Haylamaz explained those first years: "Eighteen years ago (1999): those are the times when Hojaefendi had to come to the US because of this extreme persecution and possible prosecution he was going to have by the regime of the time in Turkey. Again, similar charges of treason and toppling down the regime were being brought against him." In terms of Gülen's response at that time:

He wrote in one of his articles at that time (in *Sukutun Cigliklari*), that God did not give us the claws of a beast or the teeth of a lion so that we can bite. So, we really don't have that. In the same book in which this article appears, he says, "In spite of so many lies, fabrications, and devilish schemes, I turn to myself and say, 'You have assumed trouble as your healing from the beginning; then what is this protest for? The one with teeth will certainly bite, and the one with claws will rip through; no one can change this as long

© The Author(s) 2022
P. Weller, *Fethullah Gülen's Teaching and Practice*,
https://Doi.org/10.1007/978-3-030-97363-6_5

155

as those who consider the truth to be with the powerful continue to exist. Be tolerant to everyone.' I bury my cries inside and pronounce my feelings with silent woes."

Overall, as Haylamaz put it of Gülen: "He preferred to keep quiet and silent, not to widen the rift between us and other people." With regard to the broader ways in which Gülen's time in the USA has interacted with the development of his thinking and teaching, Ergene explained that: "I believe it has given him a much wider perspective. Even us, we probably travelled more than he did and I know how much we have changed, and I am sure that his vision, his perspective has become much wider since he moved to the west, to the US." Indeed, as Gülen himself put it during a 2000 interview with Hakan Yavuz (2003):

> We all change, don't we? …By visiting the States and many other European countries, I realized the virtues and the role of religion in these societies. Islam flourishes in Europe and Islam flourishes in Europe and America much better than in many Muslim countries. This means freedom and the rule of law are necessary for personal Islam. (p. 45).

And Ergene summarised it, "His experience here, I believe, has widened his perspective on the way he understands the human and the nature." Kurucan pointed that this contrasts with "the way 'Islamists' in Turkey, and in the rest of the Muslim world, understand the United States. It is important to understand this, for Gülen is coming from such a conservative environment." As Ergene explained this, "The United States, for those, you know 'Islamist' Muslims, who are scholars in the schools of theology, who are being raised in those Imam Hatip high schools, or from those *madrassahs*, America, US, is always, the 'ultimate other'." Of course, there are sensitive political and international issues in the Middle East, especially with regard to Israel and the Palestinians about which all Muslims feel strongly, but:

> A lot of people are ignorant of what America stands for, what America is – they don't know it.…You can't understand America while staying in the Middle East. And when you look into the streets of the Muslim lands, there's still that very extremist element of understanding the world because this is how they define it: 'us' and the 'other' concept. It's a part of that Muslim identity, unfortunately, that radical extremist elements are there always. It's a huge change when they go back to their Muslim countries, where this rhetoric is so dominant and alive. It's almost impossible not to be

a part of that rhetoric: those radical elements of discourse, in the neighbourhood, in the streets of the Muslim countries are really alive.

In summary, Ergene notes that "Religion is a dominant part of the
Muslim society, and when this form of radicalism comes in the dress of
Islamic practice it is hard to escape from it." But, in line with Gülen's
taboo-breaking discourse and actions as discussed in Sect. 3.6, as
Ergene noted:

> Even before he moved to the West, Gülen never had this ideology of 'us'
> versus 'them' understanding, he never had that philosophy, even before he
> came to the US. But still, living here, being a part of this country, living here
> for almost twenty years now, I am pretty much sure, meant that he certainly
> had expanded his visions.

Of course, in the light of what happened to Hizmet in Turkey and
across the world since July 2016, it could in principle be possible that
either now or in the future, Gülen and/or Hizmet could, through reaction to the negative impact of their experiences, find themselves being
drawn into the absolute 'othering' of the ruling authorities in Turkey. As
Tekalan summarised the general situation and how it impinged on a wide
range of people in Turkey:

> They confiscated properties of the people, banned going to other countries.
> Those people, academicians, businessmen, prosecutors, judges, doctors,
> who are outside the country (Turkey) try to find out some works such as
> Uber, pizza delivery. During this situation, of course, we try to develop
> ourselves in front of the difficulties of life, and also, we develop our beliefs
> in terms of the Qur'an, in terms of Islam, international human values also.
> There are so many dramatic cases, in jails, in the country, outside the coun-
> try. Everybody tries to deal with these difficulties sometimes alone, some-
> times all together.

Ergene provides some personal texture to this broader picture from his
own individual experience which he explained in the following way:

> After like ten months after the coup, I had to hide out in Turkey and in one
> apartment building where I was staying, the police raided the apartment.
> Thankfully they did not enter the flat I was in. But two storeys above they
> actually pushed a friend of ours out of the balcony to fall and die. I saw it

with my own eyes. And I had to flee through the river, through walking in the forest into Greece, where I had to stay in the jail with PKK terrorists who said, 'You guys are suffering a lot, but you are not doing anything about it. We cannot be any more patient in the face of what you are facing. This is too much; we will do something on your behalf.' The PKK terrorists, their main ideology, you know, is violent Marxism. They are very fond of marching in the street, protesting and chanting, you know, and they say 'Why are you not doing this?' and I said 'Hojaefendi is not allowing us to do this, that's not in our nature anymore. We cannot do it, it's not because we want it, we just cannot do it. It's not with us anymore.'

And the following series of testimonies from anonymous asylum-seekers give some insight into the sudden and profound nature of the shock experienced in relation to their previously 'normal' daily lives. As AS3 explained it:

We were fired from our jobs. My wife was working in the state hospital, she was a nurse. But one week after the coup they fired my wife and our school was closed. And we couldn't find any work to do in Turkey. Before that coup, we had a good life, you know. I have daughters, they were going to school, I was going to school, we were living normally. I was not a very rich man, but not a poor man also. We had some savings. I had a flat and a car. I could go to my job and come home. It was a good life for us, but suddenly everything was finished and we were shocked. We couldn't find any job, we couldn't earn any money.

In the light of such experiences, as for some many others, AS3 and his wife AS4 had to weigh up the options still available to them, and:

We waited for two years after the army putch. Our life changed a lot and two years we waited and nothing changed and it went worse and worse. So for us, and especially for our children, we came here. It was difficult to make this decision because we had to take very dangerous ways. Our passports had been confiscated so we could not go in legal ways, in illegal ways we came here, through Greece and in a boat.

There were eight people in their boat, and AS4 said "It was dangerous, and this decision was very hard for our families because it is very hard to send us like this – because of the grandchildren, they thought, it's very dangerous." But in summary she said "So we are here now" and he said "We have a new life. We will see how it goes." Another asylum-seeker,

AS2, said of Hizmet asylum-seekers in Switzerland that there were "approximately one hundred and thirty families." Of his own situation, he went on to explain that "In Turkey I was a teacher. I was a Deputy Manager in a Hizmet high school. I had been working there for about fourteen or fifteen years in a Hizmet school," but that now, he and "A lot of friends here like me, and they are in a dramatic position now," going on to explain that, "Psychologically they are not in a very good position, and economically, and you know they haven't got any status here. Most of them came here as a refugee and they are new in a refugee camp." AS2 elaborated that, after the events of July 2016:

I had been in prison for seven months. I was a teacher and my wife was a nurse. And she had been in jail, fortunately not prison. And if we couldn't come here, my wife and I would have been put into a prison again. But what could I have made for a coup?! I am only a teacher. I was doing my job and my wife was doing her job. Suddenly, something happened in Turkey – I don't know what it was, I think it was planned by some powers – maybe made by Erdoğan or the government, or by other things or powers I don't know. But we were, as a Hizmet people, we were very shocked about that and we have suffered a lot from it.

As AS2 succinctly summarised it: "You are an officer of the state and teaching and everything is normal, and one day later you become a terrorist!"

Before that, most people in Turkey loved us: OK you are doing good, you are educating all of the people, and you are educating my son. We were integrating the people. We always visited the parents, families, we were always in touch with the others. So, they know us. We were communicating with the people. They know our inner life. They know we are innocent. I am sure that they know we are innocent. But they are affected by power – who has power and money and who is politically very powerful.

I know that when the police come, they come at five o'clock in the morning, when my daughters were sleeping, when my wife was sleeping. They came with the guns and there are a lot of, six or seven police, and the kids get shocked. When they came, I said, "Please, sit down and drink my tea. Do you want to have breakfast. You are a citizen of Turkey. We are brothers, what is happening? I am not a terrorist?! Don't search for terrorists in my home?" I couldn't be a terrorist, I couldn't be, even if I wanted to be. How could I do that?!

AS2 also referred to the demonisation in the media that they suffered, explaining that, "All the newspapers were always saying bad things about you. When you open the pages, all the pages are about you" and that through this, "the people in Turkey also began to hate us" and that therefore "We didn't have a safe life. We had to protect our life, our children, our house also. There was a lot of abuse that someone would come to our home and burn our home." In the media "They say, you know, 'Let's take their children and kill them…We have to hang them on the trees in the streets, all the members of the Hizmet, we have to hang them, we have to kill them!'" As a result of this overall atmosphere, AS2 said:

> So, we had no chance but to leave the country. But some of our friends couldn't leave the country. They had to stay there because coming here means some money. You couldn't come here by the legal way, because they don't allow you to go abroad. They take your passport and you can't go anywhere. So, you have to pay some money to human traffickers. You have to find them, how you can find them. So, it was very difficult because we were never accustomed to that kind of life.

Again, the degree of shock experienced by many is expressed by AS2: "In my life I have never been questioned before by the police. I haven't done anything like that. I haven't even had a traffic punishment" but now "My colleagues, most of them are in prison now. I am very lucky, because after about seven months having been imprisoned they take me and charge me and said, 'You are a terrorist' and your punishment is to be imprisoned six years and three months." AS2 was then allowed out of prison pending the decision of a higher court "But by that time, I fled from Turkey," and since that time "They are looking for me in Turkey. Many times there went to my mother's home and my brother's home asking where I am – and my wife:"

> But I believe one day it will be OK because everyone understands our innocence. But now, psychologically, the Hizmet movement people are not good because of that position in Turkey. Also, in Europe it is like that. For example, here in Switzerland there is not much pressure from the fans of Erdoğan, I don't know exactly. But in Belgium, for example, in Germany, there are a lot of fans of Erdoğan and they are doing a lot of bad things. For example, they wanted to try to burn the buildings of Hizmet people in Belgium. So, in Europe also, Hizmet members are also under pressure. So, their psychology is not very good nowadays.

Of what has been both an individual and a collective trauma, AS2 says "We are living in shock now. It is not very easy to deal with the shock. So, our job here, my friends and other friends is to motivate, to tolerate each other, to make each other happy."

5.2   Gülen, Hizmet, and Dealing with Trauma

Gülen himself, when interviewed, and looking back at both his previous experience during military coups, and the period in Turkey immediately before he became a 'wounded exile' in the USA, says of himself that "now when I tell about those times I tell them like stories from history. I don't feel any grudges or hard feelings." And Ergene underlined that: "Gülen has never cursed any person because of any persecution to which he has been subjected." Indeed, with regard to any breach of his personal rights, Ergene reports that Gülen says "Those who persecuted me or did wrong to me or hurt me should know that I forgive them for what they have done," while in relation to the rights of the wider public, Gülen takes the position that these "will be dealt with by God." This is because, as Gülen himself elaborated:

> This last time was a little different because this time they did not simply target me, they targeted in a very ruthless way, they are targeting thousands of people including women and children – and, you know, they may have sympathy toward me, but I don't know one in a thousand of those people. They are people who are gathered around this movement, this idea, because they found it reasonable, something worthy – just because of that they are sometimes spending time in jail, sometimes facing torture. Our idea was to bring people other people of all colours, of all backgrounds, all ethnicities, of religions, and the international festival of language and culture demon- strated this idea brilliantly, but even this was considered a crime and people have been put into jail and punished.

Indeed, the process of interviewing anonymous asylum-seekers in Switzerland brought the author of this book to tears, which resonates with what interviewee Abdulkerim (normally known as Kerim) Balcı (see Acknowledgements) from the UK recounted when he told the story that he arranged for a young journalist from UK to go to Greece to do a docu- mentary with Hizmet asylum-seekers there. Very early on, she realised she could not carry it through and came back to the UK and "for about six months she continued dreaming nightmares and so on about the stories she heard from other people, you know, it is not always easy to listen to the trauma."

For those who directly experience it, trauma can paralyse individuals and groups and overcoming it is by no means straightforward which Balcı acknowledged from his personal experience as a journalist of longstanding when he said that, "I can see that for me it is much more difficult to write now, and I'm not able to write in Turkish at all....I am unable to write in Turkish because when I write Turkish it brings all kinds of those memories." Therefore, Balcı acknowledges that the reality is "That trauma is there, it most probably will stay there."

But Balcı is also aware of the danger of such trauma also continuing beyond those whom it directly affected in the instance in that "It might also be inherited. There have been genetic studies that say it really is genetically inherited not only by means of experience and memories and so on, by the third generation." Indeed, this potential for inter-generational trauma is a matter of clearly emerging and deep concern that came up in a number of interviews. As Naziri put it "it's easier for the adults, but imagine the children, and mostly the psychology of the kids, the children" and also that, "It is a challenge for all of them, for all of us, I mean, like we have, I think, we have to try to transform it into an opportunity. There is a challenge, there are some issues, but there is an opportunity if one thinks about it, and then hopefully it works." Arising from it, Balcı developed the idea that despite Hizmet's long involvement in education in Europe, until now it has not been involved in educating children in Islam as such and noting that in future this might be a necessity.

As Balcı recognised, this is a very complex, multi-layered and by no means straightforward matter, posing the question that: "Whether speaking about trauma in a 'communitarian' environment is good or bad – whether it helps overcome the trauma, or whether it revives the trauma again and again." With regard to this, Balcı had spoken with a British academic expert in post-traumatic syndrome disorder (PTSD) who explained that relevant academic literature indicates that "relating to your trauma together with other people who are also passing through a trauma, it only repeats it and relives it. It is not relief-ing, it is re-living the trauma again and again." Because of this, Balcı explains that Hizmet has organised a group of young psychotherapists who are "giving a service on Skype to people who are in, particularly, Greece."

However, when set alongside not only now externally located asylum-seekers, Balcı estimated there were also "some forty thousand people behind bars" in Turkey and therefore the overall available help that is not enough since, as Balcı comments, for these forty thousand, their "trauma is going to be unthinkable when they come out" and therefore "It's going to be a huge test of us." Of the people who passed through trauma in Turkey between 2011 and 2017, Balcı said "We are bringing our trauma with us into Europe, into new countries and if the established Hizmet here manages to drag us back to our Hizmet energy, activism and so on, fine. But if we drag them back to our traumatic mindset, we might be doomed, it is a possibility." And in a particularly sensitive comparison, he said:

> I have observed, particularly in the Armenian diaspora something that the third generation is becoming even more nationalistic. So, I am fearful. Do I hate Erdoğan? Yes, I fight him. And I hope the world is going to get rid of him soon, but I don't want my daughter to continue hating Erdoğan and Erdoğan's offsprings and so on, and I don't want the next generation to be stuck with that hatred. I don't know how to stop it, but in the Armenian population, I have friends who were exiled from Turkey in 1915, elderly people, you know, and they suffered and the suffering was there, but we were quite good friends. But their sons and daughters, they didn't want to speak with me. So, if we manage to overcome that, manage to overcome this inheritance, then it is going to be a role model for the rest of humanity, you know. But it needs a lot of courage, it needs a lot of self-restraint, what we are speaking to our younger generation.

Partly because of this, Balcı says that "You know, I am advising people to go and listen to the traumas of non-Hizmet people, but really helps in the sense that you realise that what you have passed through, it's actually nothing, it's actually nothing." In relation to this, he cites Syria, Yemen, Kashmir "and I'm saying OK, we passed through difficult times, we didn't deserve this maybe. Yes, but our cities were not bombarded. We have had a few cases of rape, or threats of rape and so on, but it was never a mass rape, or a mass torture, never." Overall, Balcı says it is right to acknowledge that "OK, we are passing through difficult times, but if we exaggerate, if we only think this is the whole of it, this is the whole picture, it becomes the largest thing in life, and overcoming it becomes even more difficult" and therefore "I always advise people to read about the Holocaust, to watch a few movies or documentaries about what the Jews passed through." Consistent with this, Balcı also organised Hizmet young-sters to go and visit Holocaust survivors and following such a visit, he explained that they realised that, while the experience of Hizmet had been bad, it was not of genocide and therefore that, learning from the inter-generational trauma of Jews after the Holocaust, "If they have, to a certain extent, overcome the memory of genocide, we can certainly over-come this."

It is, however, important to note that the trauma does not only affect the asylum-seekers directly. As HE1, an anonymous interviewee publicly associated with Hizmet in Europe put it: "One of my friends told me, it was, I think, a nice quote, that if you lose someone, in that case you mourn for someone and you have to. But for our case, that trauma, if it continues it affects all the body, and the whole body cannot act in a healthy manner." It is against this overall background of the impact of the events of July 2016 on the whole of Hizmet, that Gülen is both himself dealing with trauma and also trying to assist Hizmet as a whole in dealing with it. As Haylamaz then summarised the time since the events of 2016, in which "You know, billions of dollars of assets have been confiscated. Two hun-dred thousand people dismissed from their jobs. Many have to flee from the country with boats and some of them drowning in the sea":

Looking at what has been happening for the last four years: all this foul language used against him, being called a terrorist, and this entire govern-ment mobilizing all its resources, as well as their political diplomatic power to declare as number one enemy. And even bribing, you know, there is this Michael Flynn case here, millions of dollars to kidnap him and portray him as the cruellest person living on earth. And having lost his forty or fifty years of work and still trying to be destroyed not in Turkey only, but especially in Africa, unfortunately.

In relation to all of this Haylamaz says that Gülen is "one of the most sensitive, most fragile and delicate person I've ever known" but that "Despite that nature that he has, he also has a very strong willpower that balances that nature and uses it in the favour of forgiveness." Therefore:

You know, normally, a person as sensitive as Hojaefendi should have exploded by now, but he has a huge willpower and he stands as he does where the Qur'an and the Prophet's example is teaching us to stand. It is the reason why while this guy is putting us in jails, dismissing us from our jobs, but no violent retaliation has ever happened in these last four years. In the most sorrowful occasions in the life of the Prophet, when his most beloved Companions and family died you can see he was very sorrowful, but he balanced it with his faith in the mercy and compassion of God Almighty. So, he was always able to strike that balance, not to go extreme in his emotions, and balancing them with reason and faith.

And, therefore, Haylamaz says:

And in the last four years, perhaps he has been reserving three fourths of his sermons to inculcate in our hearts to learn to forgive. It was the same thing with the Prophet. The Prophet did his best to eliminate all the conflicts in his time, so they are not carried further to be burden onto the next generations. He buried so many things in his own soul, so that grudge and hatred were not inherited to turn into something like blood feud.

Ergene also emphasises that post-July 2016, Gülen now even more frequently underlines that if one is a Muslim, one should be merciful, fair, and forgiving, or at least be able to reach a conclusion in a dispute without violence. But not only avoiding such things, but also emphasising the positive possibilities:

If God ever gives us a chance again to engage peacefully with these people, we have to learn how to forgive as well. Hojaefendi follows this example of the Prophet, for, there are many who cannot digest all this persecution and who may be tempted to transgress what is permissible.

In such a context and taking seriously the degree of its overall impact, Balçi poses the sharp question, of which he says, "We have to ask this question, maybe we have to revoke biblical orders not to forget and maybe we should forget." Elaborating on this and picking up on the general stance being taken by Gülen, Balcı noted that:

I assume Hojaefendi has been preparing us for that for the last three years. He has been speaking about that forgiveness, which does not exist in our books. He says you will forgive and you will even deny when the repenters come and say, forgive us for we have done this, you will say, no you didn't do that – it never happened. It's not easy, I am not ready for that. But, in order to save, I think, the future generation from that burden, we have to make a certain kind of, we have to give up.

In summary, Haylamaz refers to the prototypical *Treaty of Hudabiyyah* with regard to which a majority of the friends of the Prophet were angry with him because he did not insist on his previously recognised rights to enter Mecca for a minor pilgrimage and that,

> Following the footsteps of the Prophet, Hojaefendi is not asking for any blood feud. If you need to be enemy against something, be enemy to the feeling of animosity; this is what he is saying. He doesn't want the conflicts of this generation to be transported to the next generations. This is in fact why he is emphasising on this forgiveness issue. That's what the Prophet did.

Thus overall: "Hojaefendi is trying to diminish the tension between Hizmet and other people, because the other side is not ready to listen. He once said, 'Sometimes taking one step back enables you to take ten steps forward the next day.' " And with regard to the example of the Treaty, Haylamaz underlines that:

> Although they resisted for twenty-one years, once they become friends of the Prophet, he treats them as if they had always been friends from the beginning. Spiritually he takes them as if they had been together from the beginning. And they do not become friends at the surface; they embraced him wholeheartedly and did many sacrifices on his path.

Thus in this situation, the stance being taken by Gülen is of great significance. Tekalan says that "He recommends patience to us. He advises against any illegal retaliation." At the same time, as Yeşilova makes clear of Gülen, that in taking such a stance "He's not saying do not pursue your legal rights, that something else."

Nevertheless, in terms of what has happened following July 2016, the challenges involved have reached a new level both for Hizmet and for Gülen himself. Indeed, when meeting with Gülen for interview, the author of this book could clearly see how the present situation was weighing very heavily upon him because thousands of people who have been suffering injustice because of their connection in one way or another to him, whether real or imagined, conscious or accidental. In relation to this, Naziri from Spain commented "It's difficult, it's difficult, feeling that responsibility, yeah of course, yeah of course, God help him, I don't know," while Ablak said "It is very hard for him to see and know that all those people suffering because of just being part of the Hizmet movement. He doesn't see himself as being, like the founder or the leader of the Hizmet movement. But it is painful." Coming from his background as a medical doctor, Gülen's close associate Tekalan further explained the inter-relationship between Gülen's physical and emotional state:

> Fethullah Gülen now has some problems from his intestines. They don't work properly because he eats really minimally and some physicians come and visit him and explain that 'if you eat only a little, they won't work properly and then you will have some problems. He says, "Yes, I know very well. But unfortunately, there are so many people in Turkey, they cannot find out anything to eat, so I don't eat to understand their situation doing empathy. Yes, I know, if I don't eat, I will have a problem but I am conscious of these things." As a medical doctor, I try frequently to explain things – and one time I said, "I understand that you to do the empathy really deeply, very deeply, on behalf of those who are in jail, who are outside of Turkey, who need so many things. As a Hizmet Movement, we need that you have your morale and your health. And we learned to believe in destiny from you. For these reasons, please keep your morale and keep your health." He said to me "Yes, Mister Doctor, I understand. I believe in the destiny of course, but it is very difficult for me, very difficult, but I will try."

In summary, with reference to the post-July 2016 events, when questioned about this in interview, Gülen himself said that "this last time has taken a real toll on me. I sometimes say it took a toll of twenty years within two years on me." Nevertheless, as a person of faith, he could still affirm that "I never fell into desperation" and that "I still preserve and keep my hope, but I cannot say I am not affected." Despite this, as Tekalan says of Gülen: "He always gives us morale and motivation. He's advising us to keep our psychology intact." With reference to an image used by Rumi and often cited by Gülen, AS1 says of his own asylum-seeker experience that:

> And this actually was against the famous word of Rumi to keep a space in your chest for the whole of humanity. Now I can open my arms just totally. For instance, we are now staying in collective accommodation centers in camps and there are too many people coming around the world. It is like a dream, I can say. Some come from Tibet, some come from Ethiopia, African part, and we are coming from the other Asian parts. And we can live together. And it is also so educating for me. I hope this education will, at the end, reach a good point and that I will be able to model or sample for my

children at least, and at the most for all those who know me, and this voluntary movement can go further, and get better.

5.3   The *Hijrah* Interpretation and Post-Fact Religious Causality

In addition to the direct effects of the events of July 2016 and their aftermath upon him and upon many people in Hizmet, Gülen has also had the challenging task of trying to advise Hizmet people on how best to navigate an understanding of their often radically changed circumstances. One of the ways in which a number of people in Hizmet have tried to conceptualise and interpret their situation has been by reference to the Islamically important—and often invoked in Hizmet—leitmotif of *hijrah*, building upon Muhammad's importantly constitutive of the Muslim *Ummah* journey from Mecca to Madina. It is because of sharing such a perspective that, in speaking of those Hizmet people who have had to flee Turkey, Naziri from Spain explained that "We never want to use, *multeci* (*multaji* derives from *iltija*)" which, in terms of the English equivalents, would be refugee or asylum seeker "so I say *hijrah*" because "It could be me in their place." As Niziri explains it:

> These guys are like, every one is normal, if you understand me correctly – normal guys who were professors, teachers, etc etc, doing their job, studied their profession, and then they have just an ideology if you name it so, or life philosophy, and also the relation to the Hizmet, and then they have this accusation and you see yourself this trouble.

In the interviews that the author made with some of what, within Naziri's framework, are called the *muhajir*, as a fellow human being one got a very clear sense of the profound trauma and suddenness of what happened to them (see Weller 2022, Sects. 4.5 and 4.6). As an example of this, Tekalan has attempted to interpret his own experience of becoming exiled within this hermeneutical framework of *hijrah* as, follows:

> In history, there so many cases of *hijrah*. Our cases, for those who had to leave the country, are also within the frame of *hijrah* where we must keep our patience and turns it toward active patience which means not to stay passively but to try to achieve many goals in addition to having patience. It could be voluntary or involuntary, it does not matter.

In relation this, Yeşilova has noted that "*hijrah* is a big emphasis in Hojaefendi's life. But we realise it's a part of Islam too." Thus, since the events of July 2016 and what followed, Fethullah Gülen has spoken about the contrast between those who, in the past, undertook *hijrah* as a voluntary activity understood within a framework of it being a *hizmet*, or service, but that now much of the migration in which people from Hizmet are involved has become involuntary. When asked specifically about 'involuntary *hijrah*' and how far it could be likened to the classical sense of *hijrah*, Gülen's own perspective was:

> In a sense this movement out of Turkey can be likened to *hijrah* but of course there are substantial differences. First, we should recognise that Muslims in Mecca were not given any chance to live in Mecca as a Muslim. So, they had to leave and when they arrived in Medina established a new kind of government, a new kind of state, a new kind of civilization, but people of Hizmet are integrating relative to their new societies. But, depending on their intention in their hearts, their movement with the right intention can be likened to the hearts of the people who migrated. So, in some sense it is similar to *hijrah*, but in other sense it is not similar to *hijrah*.

As illustrative of Gülen's perceptions of the impact on people in Hizmet and hence the poignancy of its impact on Gülen himself, one can refer to his 21 February 2018, reflections on "Living Abroad: Migration, Martyrdom and Service." These reflections give a sense of the humanity behind the numbers, including the feelings of earthly homesickness that accompany this, but also the attempt to set all of this within a more eternal perspective:

> A home a place they are used to…
> Their street, a place they are used to….
> Relatives and neighbours they sat and talked with….
> Parents, relatives, children, forced apart, forced to be away….
> Travelling to the Hereafter.

The frame of reference within which this needs to be understood is not that of an overly pious religious belief that superficially glosses over the challenges and the sufferings of the present in an easy perception of a coming eternity. Rather, it is one that while taking pain and suffering seriously also seek to learn from what has happened when exiles have sought help and other Hizmet people have generously responded. Thus, Gülen notes of some within Hizmet that, "When they saw the deprivation and the suffering some took out their house keys from their pockets and handed them over" and "If there were no keys, they would say 'rent a place somewhere and we will pay the rent'." But beyond learning from responses coming from within Hizmet itself, Gülen notes that countries that do not have a Muslim majority population, also felt moved to offer support citing, among others, the examples of Canada, France, the USA, and Germany. As for the 'Islamic world,' Gülen articulated the sharp critique that: "a majority they just slept" and "How shameful it is to sleep next to the one who acts, one moves to offer support."

Drawing still wider lessons from this in terms of the relationship between one's beliefs, identity, and actions, Gülen argues that "There may not be things that are required in your set of beliefs, but there are the attributes of a believer" and that "God does not look at your appearance or your identity whether you say 'Allah', 'I am Turkish', 'I am Kurdish', 'I am Albanian', 'I am Bosnian', 'I am Georgian' or any other ethnicity. He looks at your heart, the sense of humanity and the belief that resides therein." Nevertheless, despite these signs of wider humanity and of the encouragement that they bring both to people in Hizmet who have directly suffered in the aftermath of July 2016, and to Gülen himself, Ergene emphasises of Gülen that:

What has happened in the last three four years has probably deepened his pain even more. You are having this caravan that has been on its way with humble moves for over forty years and now some bandits come and destroy it. I mean this is a bankruptcy: imagine a boss or business owner who was so big, with this many amount of people around him, after all this collapsed, you would expect him to commit a suicide, you know, after all this huge loss. But you see him as an opposite pole: this huge spiritual power that keeps him alive, trying to motivate us, trying to still inspire us to stand and move forward. He is also very deeply suffering from not being understood. He's not accusing others for this, but he is questioning himself too: why have we not been understood?

Nonetheless, since Gülen is also a person of faith his approach to understanding any historical events is one that is rooted in faith and permeatively informed by a perspective of hope. In relation to this, Gülen himself explains:

In one sense I think people within Hizmet, these are people who believe in universal human values, human values that they believe could be shared by the vast majority of humanity. But have been, in a sense, concentrated in Turkey. And as Muslims they were not able to represent these values through their lives in other parts of the world. It appears that God and destiny pushed them forcibly to live in other parts of the world so that they can display this beautiful face of Islam and tell the world that Islam cannot be represented by ISIS or Al-Queada – but there are Muslims like these. This appears to be destiny's direction for the people of Hizmet: that they failed to do this voluntarily, in a sense, God pushed them involuntarily into the world. So, I see this representation of Islam in a positive and peaceful way through members of Hizmet as some good that came out of this terrible situation.

As an example from within Hizmet of the impact of the interpretive framework advocated by Gülen, while a pragmatic businessperson by profession, Fidan recounts that he has also learned to look at these developments on two levels, noting that:

As believers we look into events with prisms of two perspectives: how they look on the outside for apparent causes, and for what really is happening for some invisible reasons that are taking place behind the apparent causes. Apparently, what happened four years ago was the same government was caught red handed in corruption in the December 17th process as it is called, and since then they are persecuting our movement. But on the invisible side of things, which we also need to take a look into, it's probably because we did not fulfil our duties enough. For instance when a judge gives a verdict on you for a crime you did not commit and they sentence you to a certain punishment it is probably unfair, but you actually had committed something wrong before so you can see this balance being struck by destiny for the other crime you had committed on another occasion. So apparently, yes, the judge was unfair, but destiny was fair for the other crime you had committed. And in this case, our crime was, we did not go out, we did not leave our homes, although Hojaefendi had been telling us to leave our homes and go and spread around the world. Millions of us, we were stuck in Turkey, and now under the persecution of a tyrant, now our friends are fleeing Turkey to move to the rest of the world, some of them through very difficult means, even they have to swim in the Mediterranean for this. A family got drowned, actually two weeks ago. So, you see there are the apparent causes, and the invisible causes to things.

Ultimately, however, from Gülen's perspective, because he primarily looks at temporal things within an overall theological vision of the passing of all earthly powers, despite the suffering that he is very much aware of that come out of July 2016, informed by the conviction of faith, he can say:

> On the other hand, this persecution, all the oppression, I don't think it will last for very long. One scholar once said disbelief will continue to the end of the world because this disbelief concerns God. But oppression and persecution will not last in any location, in any particular context. When you look at the example of Hitler, at the example of Saddam, of Gaddafi, or others like themselves who persecuted people, they end up with terrible ends.

And from a reading of the signs of the times, Gülen still affirms with confidence that there can be a different future for Turkey itself too:

> So, I think their end is near and they will face a similar end like those people. Right now you can see the signs of their end, because the world has a perspective on them. They are recognising their persecution – the authoritarian, dictatorial nature of their leadership. In many respects, in many respects, in many dimensions, politically, economically, culturally they are going down.

However, both the background inheritance and impact of the 'Islam of Heroism,' and also the ways in which both many with Hizmet and Gülen himself try to deal with the trauma experienced by Hizmet post-July 2016 can coalesce into the challenge which Keleş calls the issue of 'religious causality' and identifies as one of the underlying reasons for why many people in Hizmet struggle to articulate what has happened and has also been going on since July 2016. This is the issue, as Keleş expresses it, that "If we ascribe post-fact everything in a positive way, if we interpret everything post-fact in a positive way, then we learn nothing from anything." And, as already noted in the first section of this chapter, when discussing the impact on Muslims of 'Islam of Heroism,' Keleş sees this as intimately being linked with the much bigger theological challenge that he believes observant Muslims in general can have with loss and defeat, the self-awareness which he does shrink from linking with the wider and big theological issue of the understanding of divine destiny, in relation to which he points out that:

> Nursi says look at the future as something that's always within your will-power. Look at the past as something that is determined by God's destiny,

so that you never criticise the past. In Islamic history there's significant wars after the passing of the Prophet, where tens of thousands of Companions died fighting each other. Ayesha, the Prophet's wife, leading one group against Ali, the Prophet's cousin and son-in-law, leading another. We gloss over this history. Hussain, the Prophet's grandson was beheaded by a Muslim, precipitating the creation of the first Islamic dynasty, leading to the Sunni/Shia split in Islam. But we don't teach this. Gülen doesn't teach this: according to Gülen, all of the Ottoman Sultans were saints. Nursi interprets the loss of the Uhud battle, waged during the time of the Prophet, as the future Muslims (the Meccans) winning over the present Muslims (the Muslims of Medina). In other words, Nursi says that this was not really a defeat because those that won would eventually convert to Islam anyway.

Keleş summarises this in terms of the challenge both in and to Islamic orthodoxy of the issue of causality of the danger of making after the fact justifications and rationalisations. In the light of this and taking, for example, the narrative referred to in Sect. 5.1 of this chapter that because people didn't voluntarily do *hijrah*—that it is occurring in an involuntary way as a kind of a judgement, in relation to which Keleş says, on the one hand, that "That might be the case," but also that:

It doesn't mean that there is nothing to be learned from this. This is the problem. We can chew our gum and scratch our head at the same time. It could have been that. But the unwillingness to discuss this and to think about this, it goes, I think, in part down to the way that we understand success and God's support, if you like, for want of another word, to be God-like or to be in God's way, must mean worldly success which goes back to the Calvinist type of interpretation, you know, if we are "Chosen People", so to speak, then we must be successful in everything we do.

Keleş referred to Lesley Hazleton (2012) who, in one of her *Ted Talks* talks about the Prophet's own account of how he received revelation for the first time and alongside that about the early accounts written about the Prophet's life. Of this Keleş summarises that: "She says that these early accounts presented the Prophet in far more humanistic terms than those that followed, which presented him in far more supernatural terms, making the Prophet less relatable," out of which, as Keleş says of the Prophet: "That's why his every action was not only ethically correct, it was also successful in the worldly sense – that's a very tall order. So, what happens when your ethical action may not produce a worldly success, what do you choose? And in the example of Hizmet it appears that we have chosen to bend our principles." Thus, Keleş summarises that "Altogether, such practices of whitewashing loss and basic human nature has robbed us of the possibility of exploring success in failure and triumph in defeat. In some sense, we have equated spiritual success and God's blessing with worldly success and worldly blessing." And it is this, which leads Keleş to the startling reflection, albeit not explained further by him, that "This is why the Crucifix is such a powerful symbol and teaching in Christianity."

5.4   Self-Criticism and Its Limits

The issue of post-fact religious causality issue is of considerable importance in relation to the question that will be explored in the final section of this book which is that of how far those within Hizmet are able to confront and process the events leading up to, in, and following July 2016, especially in so far as these not only impact upon Hizmet, but also raise questions for Hizmet about itself. While many in Hizmet public positions naturally want to put a clear distance between the tendentious accusations cast at Gülen and Hizmet as being responsible for having organised the events of July 2016, among some of the asylum-seekers interviewed, and for many becoming also part of the trauma, are existential and profoundly disturbing questions that the events of July 2016 and what led up to them have raised. With regard to these questions, AS1 says "I am always asking this: what has happened" in relation to which:

> There are many questions in our minds because of this coup attempt, because what I am thinking is that is organised very, very cleverly. And of course, someone from us connected, how to say, is in this coup, I am also thinking, because otherwise they couldn't get the people to believe we are engaged with this coup.

And also:

> People who we have seen as our friends being engaged with coup and still, unfortunately, in this Movement, I believe this. This is my opinion. And here, the same thoughts I can see also in their minds in the diaspora who support the Hizmet movement – and because of that they have hesitations about what we do or what we didn't.

Even if one does not, as this book does not, accept the narratives of those who ascribe the events of July 2016 to an attempt organised by Gülen and/or Hizmet as such to take power in Turkey, such questions and issues are real for those who are burdened by them and, if the trauma is Hizmet is to be overcome, need to be dealt with more honestly and openly by those in public positions within Hizmet who are sometimes reluctant to do this, precisely out of a concern that doing so might seem to justify and give comfort to the Turkish authorities' continuing unjust treatment of Hizmet people within Turkey. But Keleş significantly argues that not doing self-criticism sufficiently, rather than helping the people in Turkey or those who have fled from it is actually "prolonging the pain of the persecuted people in Turkey" because such self-criticism would then "allow people to complexify Hizmet's composition." Keleş said:

> People are saying this to me: that they are afraid to stand up for Hizmet, because they feel that standing by 90% of it may seem as standing by 100% of it, including aspects that appear suspect and problematic. So, I mean, the status quo is a decision, it has ramifications. This is why I keep on: indecision is not an absence of decision.

As Keleş, for example, points out, although in its earlier development, Hizmet managed to keep a good distance from political parties, as things eventually developed in Turkey:

> The movement supported the AKP by distributing leaflets for the AKP in Turkey, correct? We heard about this: going door to door. You don't get more supportive than that. Whether it's strategic, whether it's this, that's not our principle. Why is Hizmet the most hated group in Turkey, apart from the demonization of the AKP? Why is there so much hatred? – because we said one thing and did another, and in doing so, we enabled and empowered the AKP regime. This goes back to what Hizmet stands for. If Hizmet stands for itself, then it has made itself sacred and in doing so, has become extremely pragmatic. That means, to survive, today's "wrongs" become tomorrow's "rights" and that is what "pees off" a lot of people, and rightly so.

Of course, it is not that Hizmet is, as some try to construct it, especially guilty. As Keleş articulates it: "Every group in Turkey is guilty. There is no innocent – I mean you start from the Kemalists, they have no leg to stand on. They created this mess by persecuting pious Muslims for so long, they created the AKP." In relation to this, even Keleş while critiquing Hizmet on the basis that "I'm not saying all these external factors are to blame, yes you should have overcome this, you should have overcome that" nevertheless acknowledged that Kemalists "created Hizmet's mindset. Gülen was jailed in 1970s, he was sought after in the 1980s" and because of this, Keleş also says of Gülen himself that "He has a securitised mindset." Nevertheless, even Keleş acknowledges that, overall:

> If you look at the Turkish religious landscape, Hizmet is in fact the most advanced of those, I mean it is more open, it is the more dialogic, it is engaging with other people. If the Kemalists outdid themselves as much as Gülen outdid himself, and the movement outdid itself in the religious landscape, we would have a different kind of world here. The Kemalists did not outdo themselves. So, nobody is – I mean, the Kurds as well, I mean, I hate that Salahattin Demirtas is in prison, but has the HDP party been able to deal with the PKK past and its history? Has it been able to differentiate from that, publicly, sufficiently? The left wing, I mean, the social party, the CHP Party, was it able to deal with its Kemalist past, has it been able to offer public self-criticism and embrace the other half of the population. At every critical juncture, the CHP party supported Erdoğan in entering parliament, in securing critical votes, in legitimising his presidency etc. No group is free of political guilt in Turkey, and that includes Hizmet.

Nevertheless, Keleş also argues that:

> The fact that others also have much to apologise for does not exclude Hizmet from doing so also and coming to terms with the mistakes it made and why and how they came about. But can it change? I don't know because if we constantly find ways of justifying failing as, in fact, success, then what is there to learn from.

In terms of understanding what has happened to Hizmet post July 2016 and in the run up to it and what is currently happening in relation to internal debates within Hizmet, it should be noted that many of the relevant debates are conducted in Turkish and can be found over a range of weblinks. Of relevance to such debates is that throughout Gülen's own teaching the note of self-criticism—that a key role of Islam is that it should bring about real self-examination and self-criticism, coupled with an understanding acceptance of the weaknesses and failures of others—is very strong and very consistent. Tekalan said of Gülen that:

As someone who's known him for over forty-eight years, if you ask me what I've learned from him in the meantime, I can say two things. First, do you shape your life according to the Qur'an and according to the *hadiths*? Second, you have to be other people's lawyers, but you have to be your own prosecutor.

Interviewee Ercan Karakoyun (see Acknowledgements) from Germany, says that his reading of Gülen's teaching is that "no matter what happens to you, you have to look for the mistake in yourselves. So, what did I do wrong that I am in this situation now? And if you are always point to the others' mistakes, you won't get one step forward." On the other hand, when an initiative has been around for a period for of time, there is always a tendency towards solidifying a particular status quo which Karakoyun explains in the following way:

Well, the point is there is no – how would you say it – no proper discussion going on because we have the problem that people that are engaged in Hizmet for many, many years and who are in influential or in higher positions they, of course, are very much trying to focus on keeping the status quo, because they say, it's not our fault: it has to do with Turkey and Turkey is guilty.

However, HE3 (see Acknowledgements) from the Netherlands says "My own observation is that Fethullah Gülen is a good guy, and people on the ground here, and in other countries also, they have a good sense of contribution to the society in which they live." However, in relation to what HE3 from The Netherlands calls the 'middle management' around him, he sees this as "still too 'Turkish and Turkish-oriented'" and that in communication with Gülen, "the signals from the people have not been properly analysed, managed and told to Gülen to get his ideas and advices." In relation to this, Keleş also notes that "the people around him have a preference for the status quo," while HE3 in summary commented that:

I think the coup in 2016 in Turkey has so far forced the 'middle management' that they have to think and act in another way. And this is why I say that Erdoğan did it something – which is painful, which I say, because there are lots of people in jail in Turkey and who are suffering many things. But the coup that Erdoğan did towards the movement has a huge impact on the middle management and how people now think about their role in the movement. Internal criticism and critical thinking among *Hizmet* people have increased enormously. Erdoğan does not know this, that he has done a 'good' job for the movement.

This is sensitive and difficult territory because, on the one hand, especially for those who have been with Fethullah Gülen and Hizmet for a long time, there is naturally a strong wish to defend him and the wider Hizmet and, not surprisingly also themselves, against what are seen as unjust accusations. And this is particularly so on the other side of July 2016 and what many thousands of Hizmet people have experienced in terms of persecution, loss of jobs, deprivation of assets, and exile. As one example of this, Haylamaz notes of his own experience as a longstanding close associate of Gülen that, "I have been tapped for four years, for instance, and I am now reading the indictment against me. The only accusation they are bringing is 'he is from Hizmet'. It is no different with other people. This means, they have not found anything to bring any reasonable charge against these people." What is more, as Haylamaz says: "When you look back at what has happened in Turkey, *Hizmet* is probably the most transparent and formally transparent group in Turkey and probably in the Muslim world." As noted in Weller 2022, Sect. 5.4 and its discussion about Hizmet and transparency: "This has not been in Hizmet's favour. Those who are now persecuting Hizmet has had easy access to everyone affiliated with Hizmet; they have all the lists of people. If someone has not chosen to remain less formal, this was mainly for the fear for despotic regimes they live under."

In relation to this, Haylamaz argues that "The basic dynamic of Hizmet is trust," while observing that, "I think some of the concerns that rise around informal structures and accountability are mostly related to financial issues." With regard to this, he underlines that "Hojaefendi has always mentioned that community leaders of Hizmet should never deal with financial issues: they should never 'touch' the money" and that "The example that Hojaefendi keeps giving to us is the example of Abu Bakr, the first Caliph. A jar was discovered in his home after he was deceased, and in the jar was the remaining of what he was given to him as a salary. He asked his daughter to give it back to the government." Especially in relation to Gülen's own family, Haylamaz notes that Gülen cites the example of the second Caliph Umar who many people advised him to select his own son who was very skilful and talented to be the next Caliph. However, he did not do so in relation to which Haylamaz reports that "Hojaefendi is calling himself 'I am Umari' – other words of the school of Umar" in that he never favours his own family in this matter. He keeps his brothers, he keeps his family away from any status within Hizmet. Hizmet is Hizmet, its servants." Because of this Haylamaz says of Gülen that,

> In one of his prayer books he actually prays against those who abuse Hizmet's resources for their own benefit or who seek personal gains out of the opportunities formed around Hizmet. He always discouraged people from making worldly investments for luxurious lifestyles. And, again, his own brothers said Hojafendi had this prayer for them that they shouldn't become rich; and how everybody can see in what circumstances they live.

And arising from all of this, Haylamaz notes, "This is why the AKP government actually went wild and crazy because they could not find anything. Some may have certain things from their families, but other than a few, the rest do not possess anything in this world" and, in summary, reports a former Deputy Prime Minister, Hayati Yazici as having said "Those who wants to take (or fill their pockets) come to us, the AKP party; those who want to give, they go to *Hizmet*."

Nevertheless, even bearing in mind all of the ways in which the movement is unjustly targeted, Keleş is one among those who have called for what he calls "an internal dialogue" within Hizmet. However, he says that reaction to this call has been "very enlightening" in so far as "our call for internal public self-criticism is being misunderstood by the movement." Explaining this further:

> The criticism that we level at the movement stems from a certain perspective and experience we have gained in part because Hizmet has encouraged us to engage in certain practices. For example, through dialogue, we have sustained social and intellectual interaction and engagement with the other, which has enabled us to better appreciate what Hizmet could be doing better, which is often the basis of our self-criticism. So, while I often remind myself of this, it doesn't necessarily change the validity of the point that we are making.

Keleş also noted of some of Hizmet colleagues, particularly in the USA, that "We found that they weren't sufficiently aware of the various levels of criticisms that were being levelled at the movement, some of which were, actually, well-founded. They weren't so worried about that, or some of them weren't even aware of that." As an example of this kind of issue,

Keleş refers to the role of the Hizmet magazine, *Caglayan*, which he describes as "Hizmet's sort of 'flagship' … and you could see it as the, sort of, official *Gazette*," Keleş recalls that in one of the issues, it published an abridged version of an article that had already been published elsewhere which criticised public self-criticism of Hizmet. In response, Keleş recalls that:

> So, I wrote on Twitter, I said, well I am glad that *Caglayan* has published this. This suggests they are open to debate and that they will be open to having a counter article on this, because you know, otherwise you are just beating a straw man, you know. And so, they wrote to me, you know, on What's App, saying we are open, of course we are…and they sent me their policy…and in their policy it says, "Original articles will be considered". And I said, "Well this isn't original, why did you publish it?" And then we wrote a bit more and then I said, secondly, I said, "Did this chap even ask for this article to be published?". It turns out that it was someone who read it to Gülen, and Gülen says "This is great" and then, so, it wasn't the author's request. And then the third point was the more we discussed, at the end of the conversation, the chap says, "you know what I don't even know – they said to us put this in, some of us even objected and I don't even know why they did it" – which goes to the heart of the problem.

Keleş sees this as very much illustrative of the key problem which is that "You can't create an identity around *Caglayan* as a magazine. *Caglayan* cannot create great writers and a new way of thinking and so forth if it is operating under a shadow, if it is unclear what it is." And this leads Keleş into wider considerations, "So, while I admire Gülen for many of his good qualities as you know, I reject this form of dualism in decision-making." And as he goes on, he makes a link with the previous section's discussion of religious causality in terms that, "If we justify everything post-fact, then what happens to accountability, what happens to those who repeatedly make mistakes with the decisions that they take?"

More recently illustrative of, and even more sharply focusing the tension present in these issues is the debate around the November 2018 *Joint Statement on Hizmet's Decision-Making Processes* (20 November 2018) which was prepared for signature by:

> A group Hizmet participants, primarily engaged in Hizmet-related dialogue activities in Western Europe. We prepared this statement of our own free will without consulting or informing Hizmet's senior participants. The aim

was to publish this statement in the last week of November with the support of at least one hundred Hizmet participants from diverse Hizmet backgrounds – dialogue practitioners, academics, community organizers (*bölgeci*), mentors (*rehber*), *mütevelli* (donors) and so forth – from around the world. In doing so, we aimed to contribute towards the process of Hizmet's renewal through critical self-reflection in the form of a public joint statement, which drew attention to four specific points of concern (and recommendations) regarding Hizmet's decision-making processes.

The statement itself is accessible on the blog site of *Ozcan Keleş: Musings of a British Muslim Academic Activist*,[1] together with a more recently published covering comment from Keleş himself entitled *The Suppression of Hizmet's 'First' Self-Critical Joint Co-Option of the Right to Self-Criticize*, and from which the above explanation is taken. In the original statement, the intended signatories speak of being "positively moved by Hizmet's demonstrable achievements" worldwide in the fields of "education, dialogue, social responsibility and citizenship" and that "In many respects, Hizmet has been a pioneering faith-based movement both within and outside of Turkey." And on the basis of this that "We feel compelled to issue the following statement," which focused specifically and narrowly on Hizmet's decision-making processes "because of, not in spite of, our support for Hizmet's values and its many achievements in the public domain."

In relation to this, the putative signatories expressed that they were "united in the view that any form of hizmet practice that cannot be conducted in an open, transparent and accountable manner should not be conducted at all." And although one reason for not being transparent is not to be so vulnerable to external attack, rather more importantly "Opaque decision-making processes mask failure and incompetence in both strategy and people" and that "its work ethic and mindset has been influenced and shaped by the Turkish socio-political landscape and cultural mores," albeit that its "work ethic and mindset has been enriched by what Fethullah Gülen refers to as the 'give and take' of cross-cultural fertilization" leading into it being possible today to "speak of hizmets in the plural" in relation to which "It is important that this emergent heterogeneity in Hizmet is embraced and not inadvertently reversed."

But the statement then quite challengingly argues that "We suggest that those who do not wish to contribute to Hizmet's decision-making processes in the manner described herein, or struggle to do so, should not hold formal or informal decision-making roles in Hizmet altogether."

And, even more specifically, "without casting aspersions of any type," that "Hizmet participants who in recent years held key decision-making roles in Turkey should not hold or be seen to hold any role of similar bearing outside of Turkey," with among the reasons cited for this being that:

> While Hizmet's grassroots reject the Turkish government's accusations about Hizmet, an increasing number of Hizmet participants and supporters consider some of these key decision-makers to be morally responsible for Hizmet's failings and mistakes in Turkey, such as its domineering practices which alienated almost all sections of Turkish society.

And that going forward:

> It is imperative that Hizmet's decision-making processes, especially those pertaining to Hizmet's general positioning, include male and female participants from a range of Hizmet practices including dialogue, education, relief work and media as well as participants and external advisers with a range of expertise and scholarship with a particular emphasis on the social sciences and humanities. We find it disappointing that, at present, the Hizmet movement appears to be failing to meet this obvious need.

Of what happened to this, Keleş' explanation is that, "Alas, despite the lapse of time, Hizmet's senior leadership, for the most part, appears to be focused on maintaining the status quo" and that therefore:

> We chose to communicate our concerns through a joint statement to ensure that it was no longer ignored. After all, the issues raised in the statement had been aired countless times before behind closed doors. However, the statement was leaked to Hizmet's senior participants days before its planned release.

In Keleş' evaluation, "what followed was the organised suppression of the statement by an opaque and unaccountable decision-making process(es), that is, the very point of complaint highlighted within the said statement." Referring to a similar statement issued by the Alliance for Shared Values,[2] Keleş said that "The AFSV's statement drew attention to the issues raised within our statement, albeit in a far more watered down and indirect manner. By publishing their statement before ours, they aimed to co-opt our criticisms and thereby undermine our ability to publish our own." In summary, Keleş explains that "I am not suggesting that all efforts to bring about change from within Hizmet are broadcast to the world in real-time. However, there are occasions when this becomes necessary" and that "Furthermore, defending Hizmet's positives requires us to call out Hizmet's negatives."

In having given space of this kind to both the original critique and to the later commentary on it, it should in fairness be noted that, especially since at the time of writing, the publication of these documents was very new, as far as this author is aware there was no form of written response to the points that have been made. At the same time, this author is aware that there are those associated with the Alliance for Shared Values who would have a different characterisation of at least aspects of the processes that are addressed in the commentary. And it may also be the case that there is a preference precisely not to make a response in open and written forms. If this is the case, then that of course both gives expression to, and underlines, some of the issues that have been at stake in terms of the varied and currently contested views within Hizmet about how to handle such matters.

In reflecting on self-criticism per se, as distinct from the matter of the arenas in and through which such are pursued, Keleş underlines that he sees the transcending of what has been in the past through self-criticism as having been one of the key characteristics up to now of both Gülen and of Hizmet. In also contributing on the question of self-criticism, Balcı cited both Thomas Aquinas and Said Nursi as part of a wider tradition that puts self-criticism at the heart of religious faithfulness and engagement, as examples of those who "have changed in their lifetimes, who have published their own self-criticisms and so on, and who actually made 'change' not only something acceptable or tolerated, but also something appreciated." At the same time, this self-criticism and change was complex because, in the case of Said Nursi, while he did change during this life, he also never said that he repented for being "the Old Said." Indeed, Balcı noted that "Sometimes he invited the Old Said to deal with confrontational issues and so on." But Nursi can nevertheless be contrasted with those who see the main characteristic of being the leader as that of never changing and that "they stand still in their position from day one to the end of the days." In contrast, "Said Nursi changed, and he was happily accepting that he changed." When it comes to Gülen, Balcı summarises that, "Hojaefendi changed in front of our eyes and he dragged the whole community to change" and that, as a consequence of that, in relation to Hizmet:

We became open to the idea of change. And, in fact, at some point we became expecting change. When we feel ourselves on edge, we feel ourselves not being able to produce anything, we usually look around and say something new has to be done; something we never tried until now. This is not Islamic, well it's Islamic in its authenticity, but the East does not like change, the East is conservative. I think this readiness, this openness to change, this openness to learn from our own mistakes, and so on, and to be able to say from now on this is this what I am doing is number one.

And Keleş also positively noted that:

On this point of self-criticism; if you look at Hizmet, it always transcended. In the 60s and 70s, the religious congregation versus the Turkish secular state: it goes into education, it just takes a different route, it avoids conflict, it transcends it. In the 90s there was another problem, in Turkey the movement is so big now, the state is ready to take over the movement, then in 1997 you have the post-modern coup. But in 1994 Gülen starts dialogue. In the 2000s, Erbakan is collecting money from Germany to found a party, and in Turkey Hizmet is collecting money in Turkey to found schools outside Turkey. So, it is constantly wrong-footing, if you like, the opposition by, if you like, avoiding those kinds of conflicts and transcending the issues even if it is at cost for him, a personal one. He was declared an apostate in the 1980s, because the schools that he opened were secular schools that had to abide by secular laws. He was declared an apostate then. In 1994 he was declared an apostate for dialogue. All of the religious Islamic movements disowned Hizmet then.

Indeed, Keleş underlines that in taking the changed directions that he did, Gülen himself was often misunderstood and faced internal resistance. In relation to this Keleş cites Ahmet Kurucan as recounting that when, in 1994 Gülen said, as discussed in Sect. 4.4, that democracy is not perfect, but it is the best system and we cannot retreat from it. Kurucan also says that he asked one of the senior *Abis* or older students what Gülen meant by this and the *abi* concerned said "Hojaefendi was ill that day, you know." While the records show that Gülen was indeed ill at that time, as Keleş emphasises, "Gülen was clearly saying something that didn't resonate there and then with his followers, he was moving beyond them." Taking that as a lesson, Keleş argues that "So, when some say, 'why are you engaging in self-criticism', we say (a) it is the ethical thing to do, and (b) because it is also the thing to do to transcend the framing of the movement. The movement transcended the framing in the past" when people tried to tie it down to being either a religious movement or a social movement. Therefore, as Keleş starkly asked in one of his tweets, "If Gülen were thirty-year old volunteer, would he be part of this movement, would the movement allow him to be?" At the same time, while some of the challenges identified by Keleş may, as he says, be to do with what he calls "the internal dynamic of the movement," he also notes additionally that:

> It may be to do with Hojaefendi's age. I believe that Hojaefendi also has a preference to avoid that diversification, that type of self-critical approach that we are suggesting. I think he is now more in favour of a more traditional approach – traditional in the sense of Hizmet's practices. I have my theories as to why that is, but ultimately he is now 80 years old. Before he was in the public, he had two different channels of communication. He was doing the sermons, that was really important, to meet people. And Gülen is someone who learns from people, you see that. But those channels of communication are shut down and he's a bit like an Oxford professor in Oxford all the time that only sees his students. There is something that is in his speech, his demeanour. It's very contextual for the people that he's speaking to. But when he was giving a sermon, he was very different, he spoke differently. Even today, if you look at the two speech patterns, and the lexicon, and the speed, it was a different thing. He doesn't have that communication channel open to him. So, it's very archaic, it's still very esoteric in some ways.

Summatively speaking, in relation to these kind of ongoing discussions about the future of Hizmet, Karakoyun speaks of "some fractions" that he sees as "poles." On the one hand, he identifies that "a lot of academics from Hizmet say that everything has to be changed." On the other hand, "the people who are the decision-makers in Hizmet at the moment, their position is to say no, we won't change anything. We are beaten by the big Turkish state. We are wounded." Overall, the anonymous interviewee HE1 thinks this is a challenge for the Hizmet people more broadly in that "they have really to get together and to change things, change direction," but also that a social scientist friend of his "made an analogy of a ship, like an Atlantic liner with thousands of people. And if you change the direction in a sharp manner then the system of steering breaks. So, you have to do you it in such a way." Of course, the positive thing that one can about transitions is that, only living things transition. If things or movements are dead, they are no longer in transition, and it is the argument of this book that this is not the case with regard to Hizmet. As Keleş put it in an interesting analogy:

In organisational studies there is that organisations need different types of leaders and different types of work ethic in relation to its socio-historical environment and development. Take, for example, the Kodak camera: it was all based on print pictures, and actually the founders were not from that technology, they didn't come from that background, they spent a lot of time, a lot of energy creating that business model, which was great. Now the chap that eventually went to Sony and created the revolution in cameras at digital Sony, before he went there as CEO he was the deputy CEO at Kodak, and he said that he just could not convince them. He saw that photographs would be stored digitally rather than printed and advocated the need to change the entire business model, but he failed to convince them and they went out of business not being able to change....and the guy who failed to convince Kodak went onto Sony where he steered the company to great success by leading the digital camera revolution. And now you've got iPhones and Apple, and they digitalised music, when it was not their industry, and in that, Sony failed to adapt on time, despite it being their core business with Walkman's, CD players etc. So, they asked Steve Jobs, how could that happen? – and he said they could not conceptualise music in software.

The anonymous interviewee HE1 says, "There are lots of signs of life inside the community, but it's for sure that lots of people are confused. And Fethullah Gülen is also not giving any concrete directions. It's like he is waiting for something." Naziri commented that in the context of Hizmet's present trauma, Gülen is primarily trying to maintain unity. This should be understood against the background of every movement—religious or otherwise—that undergoes a major trauma, given that such trauma can expose fundamental fault lines that may have previously existed but which now cannot be avoided.

While interviewee Ramazan Özgü (see Acknowledgements) from Switzerland, thinks that Gülen has, perhaps, fundamentally completed his work except for holding unity, Keleş poses the question of whether he might still be able to go further, saying, "I mean he's a great man, he's far greater than me personally, but I mean can he do that final thing? It's the final trick, I mean will he be able to allow for that, and I don't know." In fact, with reference to the future, Gülen himself says that "They will not understand me anymore, and they will do their own thing," of which Keleş comments:

It's a very Islamic thing. The Prophet, he could say I am following in the footsteps of the Prophet and he would be right in some ways, because the Prophet does not determine a clear successor politically. He doesn't. He does inferences, but you always think to yourself, my God, because other than one of the successors of the four Rightly Guided (they call them), all three were murdered by schisms. I mean we never recovered from that: the Shi'a Islam, Sunni Islam, is based on that. And Nursi, I think as well, Nursi creates a sort of a group [*shura*] for consultation to lead the Nur movement after his departure. But I guess that at some level you can't do this at the end – you have to have created that culture of independence while you're alive and many years prior to your death.

As anonymous interviewee EH1 says:

I mean there are a lot of questions and critiques right now going on in Hizmet, and there are people who are reflect on it. I think it is a very good thing although there are some comments on which I don't agree and other comments with which I partially agree. And it's quite an issue right now that we are discussing these things.

NOTES

1. https://www.ozcankeles.org/the-co-option-of-the-right-to-self-criticize-347/
2. https://afsv.org/values/

REFERENCES

Hazleton, Lesley (2012). Seeing Muhammad – And Each Other – Whole. TED Talks, https://www.youtube.com/watch?v=9aC7bUTBKv0

Weller, Paul (2022), *Hizmet in Transitions: European Developments of a Turkish Muslim-Inspired Movement*. New York: Palgrave Macmillan.

Yavuz, Hakan (2003). The Gülen Movement: The Turkish Puritans. In Hakan Yavuz and John Esposito (Eds.) (2003). *Turkish Islam and the Secular State: The Gülen Movement* (pp. 19–47). New York: Syracuse University.

CHAPTER 6

Inheritance, Methodology, Integrity, and Creativity

6.1 Evaluating Gülen Interactively with Hizmet

In trying to undertake an evaluation of Gülen's life and teaching, there is a question about how far it might or might not be appropriate to attempt to do such in more 'Western' registers of what might for key figures in other religious (and especially Christian) traditions be called 'theology' and/or 'theologising'. This question is pertinent partly because of the lack of direct equivalence that exists between *'Ilm al-kalam* in Islamic traditions and wider understandings of theologising. But it is also important to bear in mind the implication that Gülen is not, in any generally accepted sense, a systematic theologian. Rather, as highlighted by Thomas Michel in Sect. 4.2, Gülen is more a figure who combines spiritual direction with also being a preacher, poet, and inspirer of a movement.

However, one can certainly enquire about what might be called the 'formative anchors' in Gülen's teaching and discuss the relationships between his teaching and that of classical Muslim scholarship of Islamic sources and biography. In this, the challenge confronting a traditionally formed Islamic scholar is that of whether and, if so how, such a scholar can transcend repetition to achieve the creation of what might, if not a systematic theology, truly be called a 'constructive theology.' In relation to this, it is the argument of this book that the dynamic that enables such a 'constructive theology' to be found in Gülen's reception, development and transmission of a living and authentic tradition rooted in Qur'an and Sunnah is precisely in its ongoing interaction with the reception and

© The Author(s) 2022
P. Weller, *Fethullah Gülen's Teaching and Practice*,
https://doi.org/10.1007/978-3-030-97363-6_6

further development of his teaching in a hermeneutical circle of engagement with Hizmet that ultimately connects back to, and also challenges, Gülen himself.

Change has, in fact, been an important constant in Gülen's life, thinking, and teaching, with Tekelan saying that, "As a medical doctor, as someone who likes psychology, psychiatry and observation, I've learned a lot from him, and I'm still learning. He regularly updates and develops himself according to where he lives, but also motivates people to integrate into the society in which they live." Kurucan has also pointed to the changing nature of Gülen's teaching and practice by explaining that:

> The centre in Hojaefendi's theology and practice of Islam is not one thing. It is something that is changing depending on time and space and conditions of the world. Take the example of the way he spoke about the issue of the women. If we go back like forty years ago, the way he approached the matter is never the same as he is now speaking today. The way he spoke in 1977 is never the same as he is speaking today. So, you can see the progress as he is interacting with the rest of the world, you can see that progress as he develops himself and his visions and perspectives in the way he approaches an issue. So, it's not a constant.

On the one hand, "Certainly, there is constancy in the way that, like, all Muslims have to approach…The main principles, the Prophethood, the methodologies, so that's there. But in the secondary issues you can see a huge progress." Or, using another image often used by Gülen himself, Kurucan says:

> Again, with the example of Rumi, there is analogy of him with one leg deeply settled in the centre, but with the other leg travelling seventy nations. Hojaefendi is the same Hojaefendi as he was 40 years ago in the fundamentals or essentials of faith, which are the uniqueness of the divine, the life after death, Prophethood and justice. These are four main principles of the Qur'anic message. But in the secondary social, political and cultural matters you can see his vision expanding since the 1970s.

One of the ways that Kurucan suggests one can frame an overall understanding of Gülen's life and thought is by reference to different key personalities of Islamic history and how far he reflects these in different dimensions of his own life and activity, thus:

This actually came out probably twenty-two years ago, that he used for a book (*Ufuk Turu*) that was published in Turkish, but not in English. It was a lengthy interview by a journalist, Eyup Can, and I helped him with the editing of that book. There they came upon three identities for understanding Hojaefendi: like Imam Ghazzali; like Rumi; and then like Nizam al-Mulk.

As Kurucan explains this: "So, there were three different personalities who were prominent in three different qualities." Working within this paradigm, Kurucan suggests that "Hojaefendi acts like Imam Ghazzali who was "a scholar and he taught generations of students. And this is how Hojaefendi really behaves when he teaches his students." And then, "He becomes a Rumi when he delivers this wider sermon to a wider audience which is distributed not to his inner circle only, but through TV now (and before through audio cassettes) to people outside his circle. He really acts like Rumi and he speaks to history in those sermons. And finally, "He acts like Nizam ul-Mulk, who was a leader, a founder of all those *madrassahs*. Hodjaefendi acts like him, like a leader trying to find solutions to problems; and he usually does that when his friends come to visit him." However, Kurucan also notes that one of the consequences of these different identities is that "people may misunderstand some of his messages in different settings." Thus:

When he is trying to be a leader to the community and to discuss some of the problems that are being brought to him, if any persons who are not involved are not really aware of the context, they may again misunderstand. Again, he is concerned that even many people from the inner circle of his quarters there from the early years still probably misunderstand him or are not up to that level of accurately understanding him. So, I really wish those blocks were identified much more clearly so that people would know how they should contextualize what Hojaefendi said at that specific moment.

The thinking of Gülen and the approaches of those inspired by his teaching are sometimes referred to as "Gülenian" or by those with a less sympathetic approach as "Gülenism." Whatever stances one may take on such usages, it is important to understand that Gülen would not himself be at all comfortable with either descriptor. As Tekalan explains it:

This is not Gülenism, he does not want something like that. Why? Because he tries to explain all the time the Qur'an and the Hadith, not his own ideology. Bediüzzaman Said Nursi who was a very famous scholar in Turkey, he said also similar thoughts: if you read my books and if you find out that these are a little bit opposite to the Qur'an and the others, you should take care all the time the Qur'an and the others instead of my books. Exactly, Fethullah Gülen says like Bediuzzaman. 'Everybody will be responsible for what he/she did, said in hereafter personally, there is no guarantee that everybody in Hizmet movement will be safe in the hereafter.

Understood from his own perspective, Gülen is not advocating, and does not wish to be seen as advocating, a new or idiosyncratic interpretation of Islam. Rather, his work is concerned with trying to uncover, develop, and apply in a way appropriate to the contemporary context, aspects of Islamic tradition that are rooted in the sources of the Qur'an and the Sunnah of the Prophet Muhammad. And while some observers such as Saritoprak (2003) have rightly identified a strongly Sufi flavour in Gülen's approach, albeit in a distinctive way, Gülen himself is more generally at pains to stress that Sufism is the inner dimension of Islam itself and is therefore not to be separated from the *shariah*. At the same time, along with evaluating Gülen against a long and deep Islamic tradition inflected by a Sufi inheritance, EH1 argued that it will be important in the evaluation of both Gülen and Hizmet to be even more open to external academic voices in terms of engagement and critique:

I think it is also important that we hear some of the voices from people – like from academicians – which are not Hizmet participants, in which they observe externally. I think we didn't hear enough yet. I think we should ask more the people who observe the Hizmet movement and who are academicians and who know the subject.

Over around two decades of engaging with Hizmet in both academic research and practical ways, it has always seemed to the present author that it is a phenomenon which—notwithstanding the internal voices of criticism from Keleş and others that it does not go far enough—in this author's overall evaluation does, generally speaking, make space at least for external people to interpret and critique it in a way that many groups from within all religions are not so often ready to so. Therefore, while it is possible to critique Hizmet for not always being as fully transparent as it might in that interchange, its relative receptivity to such critique is something from which other religious groups and organisations might usefully learn. Secondly, the degree of transparency that it does achieve is rooted in

Gülen's general encouragement for Muslims to undertake self-criticism such that one does not have to depart from Islam to welcome the engagement of the critique of others. Indeed, it is Gülen's approach that one should be open to embracing self-criticism precisely because of Islam. With regard to the kind of questions that can be and are raised by external academics, the present author can give an example of critiques that he offered in the context of a Hizmet-organised event as long ago as 18 July 2008, but which, it will be seen, are arguably also still pertinent to the situation post-July 2016. Just prior to travelling with others to Turkey on a study trip organised by the Hizmet-related Dialogue Society in the UK, participants were encouraged to write down their thoughts, observations, and questions in relation to Hizmet. What this author wrote at the time was, as follows:

As a critical friend of the movement, what particularly inspires and encourages me about it and about Fethullah Gülen's teaching which undergirds it, is:

1.] Its willingness, in thought and practice to engage with modernity, science and civil society
2.] Its members' commitment and its organisations' resources being devoted to dialogue
3.] For the Muslim world, Fethullah Gülen's unusually clear teaching about religious liberty

However, in addition to the above positive points, and taking the opportunity offered to be critical, the author also raised the following issues:

Also as a critical friend of the movement, I would pose the following questions in a spirit of dialogue:

1.] The movement is involved in grassroots dialogue in the UK, Europe and beyond, where Muslims are in a minority. Fethullah Gülen has had some high profile national level meetings with Christian minority leaders in Turkey. But in the light of Gülen's teaching on dialogue and religious freedom, to what extent does the movement engage with minority Christians (and not only those of Greek heritage, but also more Evangelical Christians) at a more grassroots level in Turkey, and support their rights to manifest their religious beliefs and identity in worship and other activities based on their religion? It is understood that this minority is only a very small minority in Turkey and therefore not with a widespread presence: but there have been reported difficulties, for example, for some Christian groups in gaining permission to open church buildings and also on occasion when individuals from a Muslim background (but who were perhaps not practising Muslims) have become Christians.

2.] In a lecture that I gave in Texas at one of the conferences on the movement, and since published as a (2006) book chapter on "Fethullah Gülen, Religions, Globalization and Dialogue", I highlighted the question of how, in relation to Lerner's (1958: 405) observation about there being dichotomous alternatives for Turkey of "Mecca or mechanization", the movement might or might not be able, in the end, to: ".....navigate through the insistence on these alternatives that can often found among secularists, religious traditionalists, and new Islamists alike is a central part of the challenge facing Gülen and the movement associated with him, and especially so in his homeland of Turkey.....It is arguable....that Gülen's teaching represents an attempt to find an alternative path as reflected in the title of Ahmet Kuru's (2003:115–130) essay "Fethullah Gülen's Search for a Middle Way Between Modernity and Muslim Tradition." Of course, steering a middle or third way is a project that is fraught with difficulty. In politics, third ways have often been viewed with a certain scepticism on the basis that, in the end, they have turned out not to have been third ways after all, but rather variants on one or other dominant ideology. There remains a possibility that this may become the fate of the movement initiated by Gülen. At this point in time the outcome cannot definitively be known." The question is, therefore, what strategies the movement might have for avoiding, as far as possible, what appears generally to be the historical fate of "third way" movements, notwithstanding their "third way" intentions?

3.] While rejecting political "Islamism" as a blueprint for the transformation of society, does the movement sometimes at least give the impression of being relatively uncritical in relation to capitalism which, arguably, on a global scale, can be seen as an economic and political system that has brought immense suffering to large numbers of people, while offering possibilities of growth and development to others. Might an apparent reluctance robustly to criticise capitalism be one of the reasons that some are suspicious of the ideological orientation of the movement? – including of whether it may be being (either wittingly or unwittingly) "used" by political and economic forces whose main concern is to ensure the continued dominance of what is ultimately not a "natural state of being", but is the product of a specific and historical configuration of a range of choices, forces and power.

With the benefit of hindsight, it seems evident, in fact, that all of these questions asked at that time had both a pertinence then as well as one that has persisted beyond 2008. In many ways, post-July 2016, they may now also have a newly relevant intensity. The first question underlined how, at a level of granularity within Turkey, despite Gülen's teaching on religious freedom and the courageous stances taken by Gülen himself and by organisations such as the Journalists and Writers' Foundation on a number of issues that affected religious minorities in Turkey, Hizmet was perhaps still not at a grassroots level sufficiently engaged with such issues. And perhaps one of the consequences of this has been that, in its own time of need, Hizmet has found itself more isolated in Turkish society than it might otherwise have done had it managed to build stronger, deeper, and more organic relationships across the religions both internally and internationally.

The second question—which was concerned with the fate of movements which seek to chart a third way—is particularly poignant in retrospect and, given the context of the events of July 2016 and beyond, arguably needs no further explanation. In relation to the third question, Max Farrar, a sociologist and formerly of Leeds Metropolitan University (and which university, in 2010, awarded Fethullah Gülen an honorary doctorate, wrote about the same visit, in an *Open Democracy* article (Farrar 2008) on "Anatolian Muslimhood: Humanising Capitalism?"

In relation to critiques of Hizmet as being a sheep in wolf's clothes, Farrar clearly stated that, "In my view, the movement is what it says it is." However, he also went on to critique it for being what he called "yet another effort by spiritual people to humanise a monster. It is probably the best organised and most coherent effort yet; but, as with all the world's religions, this movement seems unable fully to confront the massive injustices and inequalities that capitalism engenders." This criticism is one that perhaps has some connection with the now emerging questions being articulated among some Hizmet people concerning the movement's tendency not to have engaged with some of the political and economic roots of the injustice that has, in turn, led to what this author (Weller 2022, Sect. 6.4) has noted as a 'development' of one of the three keynotes of the movement—namely that concerned with the relief of poverty. Although Hizmet's own post-July 2016 experience of social marginalisation and active persecution does seem to be leading many within it into a broader concern and engagement with injustice, at least in terms of individual human rights, Hizmet has not yet and, in fact might never, further develop into a fully systemic critique of capitalism of the kind referred to by Farrar. Political scientists perhaps not surprisingly tend to argue that the main hermeneutical key for both understanding and evaluating Fethullah Gülen and Hizmet can be found through an analysis of their positioning within the interplay of socio-political forces. By contrast, while this book recognises that such forces play a part, its central argument is that the Hizmet inspired by Gülen comes out of a deep rooting in a "traditional" Islam, in the proper sense of the word, in terms of the distinctive inheritance which that religious tradition brings into the world and offers to it, and is the product of a dynamic interplay between the outward expression of service (*hizmet*) in the variety of activities focused on dialogue, education, the relief of poverty and the further development of that. Indeed, as Ergene argues, it is such a rooting that enables the resilience of Hizmet in the face of persecution:

> What convinces our dedication, our commitment, is that we are right and whoever oppresses us like Tayyip Erdoğan is wrong because using the state resources and millions of dollars, and bribery and gifts and offerings and investments and the other things, he was unable to convince the world community to shut down these schools. Yes, he managed to shut down or stop our running institutions in a few countries, three or four countries in Africa, through bribery, you know, through personal offerings and other so-called 'investment offers', but then out of one hundred and seventy countries if we say that one hundred and sixty countries, you know, didn't buy this, then it also shows that we are right and he is wrong. So, this makes us more hopeful that people of common sense and intellect and conscience will not buy into such cheap and empty offers.

Nevertheless, in relation to the inevitable ambiguities that affect historical and organisational forms of movements whatever their ideals, and with particular regard to the potential of mistakes having been made by Hizmet in Turkey, AS2 said:

> When I see something nonsensical and illogical I can quit, I can finish the relation and connection. For now, it is also like that, I am of the same opinion when I see something illogical, I can finish, or can try to correct them. If I cannot correct them, then I sit and watch. But for an organization, there will always be some problems. There is no organization without

problems. For me the most important thing is to minimize the problems and to be transparent.

Recognising that all human beings and organisations have their limits, their boundaries, their ambiguities, and their failings, the same interviewee also pointed out that but arguing that "you have to look at the, how can I say it, the main idea. You have to look what can be done for humanity, for education, for good things. And you can continue after that."

6.2   DISTINCTIVE NORMATIVITY
AND ORDINARY 'NORMALITY'

In the literature on the movement inspired by Gülen's teaching one finds many and varied attempts to categorise it, such as in terms of "social movement theory" or as "Muslim puritans." However, as emphasised earlier, Gülen himself and those closely associated with him and his teaching would not wish that teaching to be seen as anything other than Islam, or those associated with the movement as anything other than Muslims or other people of good will.

Within Islam, 'innovation' is often seen as being equated with departure from normativity and yet within Muslim tradition there is a legitimate form of 'innovation' which is not only a reform in the sense of 'calling back' to something seen as originally more pure, but also as a trajectory that is primarily about a contemporary and future 'renewal' of tradition. In such a renewal, it is arguable that what might be called 'distinctive features,' born of particular geographical and cultural receptions and temporally situated engagements, do not necessarily lead to a departure from normativity.

Thus, in Gülen's teaching the Turkish, Ottoman, and Sufi heritages are all important, as is the context of globalisation and of Islam in the modern world of cultural and political pluralism, science, technology, and education. As Ergene in his foreword to Gülen's book, *Towards a Global Civilization of Love and Tolerance*, explains (in Gülen 2004c) Gülen's model is "the essence of the synthesis created by the coming together of Turkish culture with Islam"; that "This tolerance was initiated by Muslim Turkish Sufis"; and that "Muslim Turks have practiced tolerance and concurrence, which are the essence of the contemporary democracy, over a vast geography for centuries. Islam has been interpreted in this geography with the same tolerance for thousand years." (p. viii). In similar vein, it is the argument of this book that Gülen's vision of Islam, rooted as it is in its fidelity to Qur'an and *sunnah*; drawing upon the rich synthesis developed in the Turkish appropriation of Islam; and translating that into action via a community of transformative action and a pattern of civil society initiatives, is an example of what can perhaps best be described as 'distinctive normativity.'

Thus, Gülen's vision of Islam is not that of a 'modernist' or 'liberal' project which could easily be dismissed as a betrayal of true Islam by Muslims who have a more traditionalistic approach. Rather, based on his wide and deep knowledge of Muslim, and especially of Ottoman, history, the approach that is taken by Gülen is one of a *tajdid* or 'renewal' of Islam that is rooted in the common Islamic sources of the Qur'an and *sunnah*. But it is one which also seeks positive engagement with the contemporary world and, within that, with people of religions and none. As Ergene (in Gülen 2004c) again, explains it, Gülen's model is one that "re-generates this tolerant interpretation and understanding of Muslim-Turkish Sufism within contemporary circumstances, albeit highlighting a broader, more active, and more socially oriented vision…. Gülen opens up this framework and vision to all societies in the world, transforming and broadening it" (p. viii).

Coming back to Gülen himself, Ergene says that, "Hojaefendi's thoughts, actions, the way he looks into the universe and the human, the plurality and diversity in existence should be better revealed, for the profile he displays is very much needed in the Islamic world," although he also emphasises that "this is an opportunity for both the East and the West." Expanding on this, Ergene argues that:

> For the Islamic world to break through its constraints, it needs to adopt such a vision, which is represented in the ideas of Gülen, and this could be any other name; our focus here is on the ideas, not the name of a person. Otherwise, there is no way for the Islamic world to save itself from the reactionary mode, nor would it be possible for them to understand the age and modern times. Without such a vision they will continue to exist in the pit they have been buried and will remain in constant conflict with other countries. So, it is very significant, the role, the mission Mr. Gülen, and other scholars for it is not him only, who are following such a path where they still keep their values and approach the other to understand them rather than refusing them.

In relation to the Western World, Ergene argues that is "important to present his ideas and vision as bridge not to the Muslims as they are today, but to the real essential values of Islam which, he believes, could be great reconciliatory pathway." Nevertheless, in relation to these opportunities, Ergene gave the stark summative evaluation of Hizmet that "we have failed in both directions."

Looking both backwards and forwards, Alasag reflected that: "Gülen started this Hizmet. For us, in Turkey, growing up, when I was in Turkey, it was very unique what we were doing" and also "When we came to Holland, at first, I also felt we were very unique." However, Alasag noted that Gülen's own methodological approach has been to use many examples from history and that, in so doing, Gülen himself, through his own practice, underlined that what he has been contributing might not, after all, be so unique. Therefore, Alasag's overall evaluation in relation to Hizmet is that: "In history there were many groups. The longer I am here, the more I see that in this country there are so many groups that are doing exactly the same things" and that "You see many of these kind of activities and organizations, voluntary movements, they are everywhere." In the Turkish context, though, "which was under direct rule of the army, every ten years a coup, and no freedom or democracy" and where "as a child I was put in jail a couple of times – I thought this is so unusual, so big, or so important, whatever, I don't know. Under those circumstances it was very big, very unique, very different."

The question of uniqueness, distinctiveness, and normality strongly interplays with the question of the future with and without and/or beyond Gülen in the sense that, as Alasag says, "Whenever you have the idea that something is unique, this is the only movement doing this, the focus is on the leader." However, because of Hizmet's global spread and coming into contact with other similar initiatives "it makes you kind of 'normal', a very normal, very humble, a very small group which is trying to be a part of the solution and not a part of the problem." This, in turn, opens up the question of wider connections between Hizmet and other initiatives, both in relation to Hizmet's own experience and future trajectories, and also in terms of its positioning in relation to other religious (Muslim and other) and secular initiatives concerned with human challenges and human need. In connection with this, Ablak also points to an ongoing tension between the movement's inner dynamic and its outward expression:

So, I think Hizmet is a way of living. We shouldn't fit it in organizations or in formal things. And I think that in the last few decades that that was the problem within Hizmet: that we got more and more organizations and that shouldn't be the main purpose of Hizmet. It is a way of living, or a way of being a good person. I don't say about being a good Muslim because Hizmet is more than for Muslim people. It is about...the human...about what would be a good human and doing good for others. And so, about the universal human values. So, you don't need to be a Muslim to be part of the Hizmet movement. It's about my new way of living.

A particular challenge for Hizmet arising from its inheritance was expressed by Ablak in the following way: "The mindset with lots of *abis* and *ablas* was to build our own organization, but why? We could co-work with other organizations. We don't need our own organizations." As an example, Ablak says:

It is wider, and we are part of the Dutch women's organization – which has been around for 125 years now. So that's where the opportunities are, and so I didn't agree with lots of organizations that were founded by Hizmet volunteers. And still they are setting up new organizations against the decision we made that we don't want new organizations! – only if the Board would be diverse with non-Turkish or non-Hizmet people, with women and men. And still there are persons with Hizmet who found organizations and they say that those are Hizmet-inspired organizations. I don't agree with that!

In relation to Hizmet's own experiences, AS1—whose Turkish roots were in the Cappadocia region, and whose ancestors had come from the Ukraine and were Ukrainian/Crimean Tartars reflected in the following way on the recent fate of Hizmet in Turkey in relation to that of his ancestors: "At the end of the Ottoman time they had to flee from the Ukraine because of the Russian invasion. And now that history again repeats, having to flee from Turkey to other parts of the world." So, because of this, he says:

I don't believe everything is clear in this world. Hopefully, hopefully it will happen, but actually I don't believe it, because what I saw from my father's life, my grandparents life, these coup d'etats always happened, and the people had only their suffering and had only just themselves know it, and the other parts of the society had no idea about it. Because I didn't know the sufferings of people before me. Now I can understand them – Alewites, Armenians, or you can say, the left side people. Maybe I saw them previously as "others", as "the others."

And now in the Turkish post-2016 context, he concludes that:

What is happening now is – many of my friends have said – that never in history has anything happened like this. But I don't see it like that. It was every time in history. If you have a goal and idea, it is fighting of the good part and the bad part, or ugly how do you call it. Maybe we didn't know, or the history didn't write everything. Because of that we didn't know or we couldn't say. But I am sure the same things have happened to previous ones of our ancestors or your ancestors, doesn't matter whether the Islam part or the Christian part, if you have a goal and especially if it is about religion, the people, especially the politicians, control the society using the religion very easily, especially in the eastern part. And no-one, no politician gives this power, this useful tool for them, to an NGO, if you can say, to a special society.

In relation to Hizmet's ongoing work, close associate of Gülen, Muhammad Çetin (see Acknowledgements) explained that "Since July 1, almost one and a half years ago, a month before the coup d'état, I came to the USA for Ramazan. So over here I am with Hojaefendi," and he underlined that, in contrast to any sense of exceptionalism, and especially in the light of what had happened in its Turkish land of origin, Gülen was heavily underlining the importance for Hizmet of its future outside of Turkey:

And he's from that day on – he was saying before and then comes an urgency and immediacy now – he says that there are three things now: successful integration wherever you are. He is just insisting on this one. But he says that you should preserve your values which makes you this thing or proper Muslim, without losing your own true sense of identity but you should be in such a way integrated that people pick you up, choose you, elect you to head of institutions etc. He says I know that this is completely contradictory, and this is three ends of one paradigm or a stick, but you should manage, you should learn how to do this. In short, to be such a Muslim that you are truly sought after.

In saying this, Çetin also explained that Gülen acknowledged with regard to such matters that:

The older generations might be an hopeless case, but your children are being educated and being raised in this country so focus on that. Make them, for example, American-Muslim, make them British-Muslim, adored, looked up to and admired by the local people. Integrate as successful Muslims but not alienate or detach yourself from the main society because you are a Muslim...this is not only the US or the UK: it could be whichever country you settle in/wherever you live.

Reflecting on Hizmet in the context of Spain, Naziri noted that "Your activities should be do whatever it is normally, and if they ask, explain it, like who you are, because they are interested and ask you" and "There are many people who are very interested because they want to learn." Reflecting on this in relation to his own engagement, Naziri said in relation to the nature of Hizmet that:

> Like for me, being a Muslim, it's something unusual, unique, like a movement from an Islamic – you know, in the Christian world, you have many of them, many denominations.... But in the Christian world you have some *corfradia*, or brotherhoods: Hizmet is somehow a *jamaat*, but it is more than that, it is different. I think being Muslim, having a Muslim identity, an Islamic identity, that's why it is more interesting for me – the phenomenon of Hizmet, I mean.

And also that:

> Well it has also some particularities that, probably, those Christian groups or *corfradia* don't have, but we have to investigate what are they because I believe that every individual is different, is not similar. So, what you have to do is to discover that singularity, that uniqueness within it, and I believe the same thing happens within different groups. Whether it could be positive or negative, let's see.

And indeed, both sociologically and theologically speaking, it is often the case that what is distinctive about an individual and a group can be a strengths that, on the 'flip side', can also become a weaknesses and vice versa. In the final analysis, this is to do with being human, whether on one's own or in community with others. In Karakoyun's evaluation, going forward:

There can be different models of Hizmet. If an aim of Hizmet is to serve humankind then, depending on the local situation, Hizmet can do different things in every country of the world. It can be in Egypt fighting for the human rights of the Coptic Christians; in Ethiopia it can be fighting against poverty; and, I don't know, in Kyrgyzstan it can be different things; in Germany it can be different. So, this is what we have to learn: Hizmet can be different in every country of the world. But rooted in the principles that we stand for.

At the same time, if such a degree of localisation happens, then the question is posed of how, in the future, communication, mutual challenge, and the mutual sharing in different contexts can be maintained—both now and into the future, and especially when Gülen is no longer in the world, the potential issues and challenges arising from which are explored in the next section.

6.3   Gülen and Hizmet: Now and Beyond

The personal figure of Gülen continues to be important within Hizmet. As anonymous close associate of Gülen, CA1 expressed it as follows in terms of his own personal testimony: "When I don't go and visit him for a few months I can feel something missing and need to see him so that I can see that connection is there, that possibility is there, that quietness is there." In the period before Gülen settled in the USA, when there were disagreements, people within Hizmet travelled there to consult with him in person to find a way forward. When asked for examples of such disagreements in relation to which a way forward was found on the basis of consultation, Haylamaz responded that "There are many examples," explaining that: "When I offer something to him for instance, he usually says, 'it looks good. Go speak with friends, ask their opinion'." Haylamaz also says that "Hojaefendi positions himself more like a consultant. There are other situations when he asks us to do something, but which we cannot do, simply because circumstances are not good for that thing to happen." As a concrete example of such, Haylamaz recounted that:

> For instance, I travelled all around Turkey for eight months for this Contest on the Prophet's life, and with the exception of one place, everyone disagreed with the project. Only one person said "let's try this at least in one place, maybe we will have a beautiful outcome out of this. Let's not just say 'no' at the onset." And then it became a very successful example thanks to

that one person, although Hojaefendi had said that's a very good idea, people did not want to do it. It depends on times and conditions and sometimes there are other priorities; there are economic constraints, there are many reasons. So when Hojaefendi gave an alright, gave a go to things, we were unable actually to do it because we not ready for it or did not want to do it. And he is also keeping himself, much more than before, especially these days, like a consultant, giving advice rather than ordering things. He might say, this looks like a good idea, go and speak with others and if you can materialise it, then go with it.

At the same time, the fact of looking to Gülen personally for guidance and advice raises practical issues and not only for the future and, but also in the present circumstances. Thus, Haylamaz acknowledged that:

This has become more difficult since he moved to the US. But those who are able to do it, has come on behalf of others to get his advice and prayers. And if not, they consulted among themselves. So, there was this network of consultation. Unless there are disputes, action to be taken is determined by consultation. Everything comes to fruition by people who are in the field; they learned together, they collaborated. Hojaefendi's role is mostly to show a direction, to turn the lights onto a certain path.

Similarly, the anonymous interviewee HE1, said:

I think that in a more concrete or administration way, Fethullah Gülen doesn't have executive power; he doesn't forward the activities that are on the grassroots level, I think it is more symbolic right now because people like and respect him, and this is one of the most important things that the Hizmet movement or Hizmet community gather around – this is important. The second one is his principles, his ideology, his example that shows and this is, I think, almost all the Hizmet participants agree that we don't completely understand him or we don't completely, we cannot follow his example.

Out of all of this, of course, the question of what might happen following the eventual death of Fethullah Gülen is an important and a sensitive one, in relation to which Naziri asked the author, "Did any journalist ask him about this question, or did you know what he said?" Certainly, a number of people have asked Gülen this in interviews. In summary, one could describe his basic response as being that Hizmet is not even if individuals may have taken something from his teaching,

Hizmet is not something that comes from him. In reflecting on the question of what comes after Gülen, Tekalan says that:

> So many people ask this question at different times. All the time he has said, "I cannot speak for the future, but I am here now. I can speak about the issues of today. In the future, the people who will be present in the future will decide themselves." I think that for the future after Fethullah Gülen, the Hizmet movement will continue. There are so many young people all over the world who didn't even see Fethullah Gülen, but they know his ideas.

As commented on by Naziri, even though he acknowledged that Gülen might be described as "a charismatic leader," nevertheless in his evaluation "I don't even really have a time of thinking another name after Fethullah Gülen," although "I don't mean it doesn't interest me." In relation to what form or forms Hizmet might take when Gülen is no longer there, Naziri expressed the view that he thought it might go forward "in a somehow democratically" way, but in relation to within what precise organisational structures Naziri said, "that part doesn't interest me." But Naziri also emphasised that "What interests me, and what I am really concerned with" is "whether every and each participant of Hizmet is aware; is informed." Even more so, Naziri asks "Did you incarnate it – I don't know if I am using the good and correct word" or, "Embody it, embody it, embody it, that's it! ... Into your personal life and then if it is so, then no problem, there are many, many individuals who are working for the good and they will go on doing this, they will continue doing this, I suppose so." For Naziri, then, it is this core service orientation of Hizmet that brings hope for its future beyond Fethullah Gülen's earthly life:

> The serving sometimes brings you pain, brings you discomfort, I don't know, many, many other things that normal people do have, and could have, and they are having, but you are, like, dedicating yourself to the basic philosophy and what it should be. Whether we are doing it 100% or not, at least this is the philosophy and the way in which you have to work on. And so this is a good place. And if this consolidated, so I think even if Fethullah Gülen passes away, somehow this will work.

When trying to take into account Gülen's own perspective on this matter, as Özcan explains, if you ask Gülen:

He uses the pen name 'nothing' – *hiç* – which means 'nothing' and he always introduce one kind of term, a jargon into Turkish: that is 'zeroing of oneself'. And whenever he was asked he never assumes any kind of leadership or ownership of the services and he says I am just an ordinary guy, I am just the most sinful among you, and I have nothing done than trying to encourage you and I am not sure if I am sincere on this or not.

In relation to any achievements that may have occurred, Gülen says "Allah did it, because there is a verse in the Qur'an that says all your work and your handiwork is from God. You cannot assume any positive thing about yourself, but the negativity has come from you, that is the point, because we are interfering with all this, God's progress system."

One of the reasons that questions about the future of Hizmet without Gülen can be sensitive to pursue is because, while it is an important and appropriate question to ask in its own right, and particularly in the light of the historical and sociological analysis of other movements that have emerged around a charismatic figure, it is also important to understand that there are those who are actively using the question to attempt to disrupt Hizmet and to create internal dissention. Thus, in referring to what he explains Hizmet people call the 'tarmac media' in Turkey (meaning the media under the control of Erdoğan), Özcan says "So, in that, just to cause chaos within the community, they are saying that Hojaefendi is about to die and now a couple of his students are competing and fighting amongst themselves who would be the next person."

Such a perspective is rooted in what this book argues is the mistaken, if not tendentious, critique that Hizmet is a kind of mafia like semi-business empire controlled by Gülen and that, once he is gone, there will inevitably be some kind of a fight for control of it. In contrast, as Özcan argues, "Hojaefendi is not inheriting any physical property or wealth to people. What he is handing over to us is a meaning, a message, a system of thought." Because of this, "there is nothing to fight for this wealth like in the dynasties or, you know, rich families. What he is leaving to us is a proper relationship between God and his servants." Therefore, also as Özcan says, "This is not an issue of a man, this is an issue of the message. So, the message will be conveyed to other people. So, the sincere followers, or the committees, or the, you know, group or people will take up and continue."

With regard to Gülen's close associates, Özcan states that "no one is aspiring to be Hojaefendi, because we cannot be," and this is because, apart from anything else, Gülen has pointed out that, in the first place, "you are all married," and therefore, as Özcan says, "So we lost the chance to be like him." Overall, then Özcan underlines that "Hojaefendi never assumed any kind of leadership, ownership of, or any kind of status for himself and he teaches to people exactly the same." Özcan also cited Nursi who held that "Eternal fruits cannot be built on a temporal, transient human beings" and that "Hojaefendi drew our attention to one fact that each and every action, and whatever we base our understanding should be Qur'anic and *sunnah* based. So, he referred us to the text again, the original and authentic text." Overall, as Özcan says, "The truth is always eternal but the human beings are temporal and transient, finite. So, the infinite truths will prevail and if people pick up those truth in the principles, they will continue the service." Nevertheless, while Gülen remains alive, as CA1 puts it:

I refer them also to Mr. Gülen. He has also, I think, too many questions in his head. He tries to motivate the people always during these last two years, always about the next world. But they also ask him questions about this world. People are still here because they couldn't find an adequate alternative, I believe, and they also know this is the true one among others.

In relation to the limits on Gülen's human life, EH1 says:

So, this is going to continue after, let's say, his death. That Hizmet was gathered around him – this is not going to go for many years. He is an old man, so we know that after a certain time he is not going to be there, and so what happens then? I think I see all this trauma and this incident of 2016 as a good opportunity to be more sustainable in Europe, or in America, or in – I don't know if we are going to see Hizmet in Turkey anymore, but let's say in the West – so it's really important that there is an opportunity for us to create sustainable institutions and sustainable models that this movement, Hizmet movement, can last long after Fethullah Gulen is passed away.

With regard to those who have been receiving teaching directly from Gülen, Kurucan explains that "There are more than 100 students, I don't know the exact number who studied in his circle. But I don't see any single one of them who could really have the authority really to continue this heritage as Hojaefendi has been doing to us." At the same time, Kurucan notes that "there are certain individuals," citing as an example that of Enes Ergene, who Kurucan says "has that really deep understanding and scholarship of those diverse disciplines of Islamic sciences – not to the degree of Hojaefendi, but as much as he could, but he has that capacity." Kurucan also has noted that that while Gülen is alive:

> Hojaefendi's presence, for that matter, is an opportunity to be able to maintain that heritage because he is alive. And, if you have any deduction out of any argument you can correct yourself by going to him and asking him directly whether that's how we should understand his message. But since he is also there as the authority, people do not really take one step forward to come to the front and deal with those matters individually on an authority that doesn't really violate the presence of this teacher there, who is already there. You see there is that paradox.

Karakoyun, from Germany, offered the following assessment: "So, this is what I also think about Hojaefendi. Of course, everybody still benefits from what he is saying. He is still the one who with his teaching and what he says gives good ideas to the people. But the main activities, the institutions, the people, they are doing the job." As Naziri has said, where people have taken an inspiration it has a value, and people continue to work with it. And, as Naziri emphasised "all the things he teaches, he says, is Islamic" and indeed "you probably can find it, and also other scholars saying that." But, and significantly with Gülen and Hizmet, what has been at stake has been a combination of "the charisma, and the actions and the example, the life example."

At the same time, as with many in Hizmet, there is a strong personal dimension to the question of the future loss of Gülen—as Özgü put it, "I would be very sad as a person, because he has been an authority for me." But at the same time, Özgü realistically evaluates that "every person has to die and that is part of life and that's why it's a thing which is very normal." Özgü says that "Now the people in Hizmet they talk about the situation of Fethullah Gülen, but after his death they will talk about it more. Many people will say, Fethullah Gülen was just a normal man, a human, a normal person. And I think there will be a discussion of this in Hizmet." Overall, Özgü's evaluation is that "I think he is a normal person who has good thinking and good ideas about Islam, and that's very important for me."

Interestingly, Özgü adds that "And he has done his job I think." In other words, in relation to the question posed by Keleş towards the end of Sect. 5.4, Özgü does not expect particularly creative advances from Gülen himself, but at this time of great stress for, and debate in, the movement, Özgü says does see a special and unique role for Gülen in terms that:

I think now his most important job now is to keep the people in Hizmet together because many people had this thinking, now Hizmet is over and we have to go our own way. But because Fethullah Gülen is alive, he is our leader, he is the leader of this community and he is alive, and we will wait for what he says. Within the movement all these people who said we are going to have to go our own way, they say now we have to be active in Hizmet. That mission is to integrate the people together, to put them together, but after that I think he has done, in the case of the Hizmet ideas, he has done his job. Now we have his books. And if we want to start another project or found a school we don't have to ask him. We have now his work and his books and we can also listen to preaching, and that is enough now for us.

However, although the role of a unifying figure is important, from the historical example of Said Nursi, it can be seen that there is no guarantee that such an influence can be maintained beyond the death of the individual concerned. As EH1 puts it:

So, when I asked the social scientists, they say that communities like Hizmet, eventually after when the leader dies, the community dissolves or it divides. So, this is like an extinction of a movement. But, I mean, we should really ask these social scientists how can we continue this movement without the leader? But I mean this is a transition for Hizmet.

As noted earlier, when Nursi died on 23 March 1960, the Nur community was uncertain about the way forward. Among the *Nurcus*, some wanted one leader to be identified, while others wanted a consultative council to be established, and still others wanted to set up a political organisation. A number of the longstanding members elected Zübeyir Gündüzalp as leader, but that did not end the debate. Already during the life of Nursi, there had been those known as the so-called writers and those as the so-called readers and, following the 27 May 1960 coup, the "writers"—who had copied the tractates (*risale*) of Nursi by hand— became an identifiably separate group under the leadership of Hüsrev Altınbaşak. The "readers" preferred the printed version in Latin letters. Others thought that an armed struggle was the way forward. Thus, reflecting on future possibilities, the anonymous Hizmet participant observer HE3 notes that:

One scenario could be similar to that of the Nursi movement – the fragmentations and the leading persons. It is one scenario. But when the leading persons in the movement, such as Abdullah Aymaz who is living in Germany, and some other people, if they have no more position in the movement because they are old and have no more energy.

Against such a background, and in the face of the uncertainties of the future beyond Gülen's earthly life, Kurucan articulates the unanimous view of those interviewed: "May he long live and that's what we pray for. But, that's our faith, and everyone passes away." And, in the end, Kurucan thinks that:

> Afterwards I expect that certain people will choose their own way of understanding and interpreting his message and follow that path. So, there will, perhaps, be diversification in the way that his message is inherited by the following generations and that's in the nature of human being anyway, and that's in a way inevitable.

In the meantime, Kurucan invoked the relevance of a traditional Islamic model, as follows:

> Well, I mean, the challenge is, first and foremost we cannot live up to the model, the friends of the Prophet actually portray. There is this very great example of when the Prophet was sending away as an envoy one of his companions – Muadh bin Jabal – as a governor to Yemen. And he asked him, how are you going to give your decisions? He said, well, I will look up in the Qur'an. If you cannot find it in the Qur'an what are you going to do? Well, I will look it up in your example. And if you don't find anything in my example? Well, I will develop my own reasonings and come to my deductions out of it. And then the Prophet praised God and said I am grateful to God for giving me such friends who can use their own deductions.

At the same time, although this is the ideal, Kurucan acknowledges that:

> We are not up to that model. We don't have that courage to come forward with our own individual reasonings. That's probably because of the 'neighbourhood pressure' (we have that concept in Turkish, probably 'group pressure'). People may come forward and say, look, we still have Hojaefendi, the mighty teacher here, who are you to teach us what to do in a certain context, you go and ask him and that's it. I don't want to use the word 'cult' but for some people that may really be the case as they see him

as the ultimate authority in all issues and just you go and ask him in all issues, as if you cannot come up with your own reasonings. So that may be a pressure on certain individuals not to be able to come forward courageously enough.

In a similar vein, Keleş also makes the following observation that:

It's so unfair that we ask so much of Gülen. I've asked his students this: how are you going to avoid the pitfalls of Nursi's students? Have you got some methodology in place for training? Look, Nursi was in the 50s/60s right?...Clearly Hizmet is far more advanced and has far more resources than they did, what's your research man? Come on, you know we still expect Gülen to tell us everything, and you know what, I don't care if that's what Gülen prefers, because Gülen is open to be challenged, so long as you do it respectfully. I mean his notion of respect, I mean, we overdo it. He doesn't want that and you can tell him.

Of course, how the death of Gülen might feed into the development of Hizmet itself in the future can only be responded to in a speculative way, although some idea might be gained from projecting forward things that are already happening in Hizmet. In relation to what will happen to Hizmet after Gulen's death, interviewee Özgür Tascioglu (see Acknowledgements) from Belgium says "Nobody can answer this question," while Özgü thinks that the challenge for Hizmet will be that:

I think that after his death, it's like now we have to show we are not just a movement which is person-centred. And then we will have to show that Hizmet can also be without Fethullah Gülen. That will not be so easy, because the people in Turkey who are now coming to Europe as asylum-seekers, they are very connected to Fethullah Gülen, not just as an authority. So, people ask me if Hizmet is a cult, and there are people who for them Fethullah Gülen, and Hizmet is for them very person-centred. But for the people in Europe that's not so. He is a very important person, that's right. But we can also live without him. We can also have our associations, our foundations, our schools without him. I think it's good to have him, yes.... it will be a great shock for these people.

Özgü notes that, for many people:

After the death of Fethullah Gülen he would be for them a 'holy person' like Said Nursi. Right now when the people talk about Fethullah Gülen, he is a normal person who is an Islamic scholar, who is a really good authority, but he is not a holy person now for most of the people. But after his death he will be a holy person maybe.

Özgü also explained that, although "I know many people who are really very interested in the health of Fethullah Gülen and who say he should live longer than me and things like that, but I am not the kind of person who says things like that," from his personal perspective, he underlined that, "For me I think that can be very dangerous because Hizmet should not be a person-oriented movement."

Ablak, from the Netherlands, takes a similar position and, as she put it, says "Fethullah Gülen is important, but I don't see him as THE important person in my life. So, lots of people of people don't agree with me on that" and some say, "What are you talking about, and that you shouldn't say that." I think that isn't the case. So, also after Hojaefendi I think that Hizmet will go on, and I don't think then that some other *abi* will be in his place. I don't think so." At the same time, she acknowledged that:

> Not everyone within the Hizmet movement have the same thoughts, and we have a free society! So, that's my own opinion. And, as a person, I try to help, to yeah, change the mindset, so that's why we talk about the Dutch Hizmet more. So, the Hizmet movement is, from my own understanding, it's about education, it's about being good people; it's about charity; it's about dialogue. So those are the pillars of the movement...

In thinking about the future, others draw attention to other possible framings for these matters beyond that of a more sociological analysis of potential change: namely, in terms of the traditional Islamic understanding of time and people of which HE3 explains that is a perspective in which:

> There will come another person, and it was Said Nursi, and after him it is the person Fethullah Gülen, will come someone else, and he is born somewhere else in the world, I don't know. And after him he will take the job to tell Islam to this age, and he will continue the activities of Gülen or the activities of the Hizmet movement. I don't know what it will be. But this is another story.

Regardless of that wider question, with regard to the future of Hizmet itself, as Karakoyun expresses matters "It is difficult to speak about this issue at the moment because there is a lot going on at the moment."

Nevertheless, his own position is that "changes in civil society movements are not possible from one day to the next. It needs time." But Karakoyun also thinks there are some points of consensus, such as that Hizmet has to become on the one hand, local, and on the other hand, transnational, and that the issue is of finding "something like a balance" in that.

6.4   LINGUISTIC DEPOSITS, INTERPRETIVE PROCESSING, AND INFORMED APPLICATION

Sunier and Landman (2015) identify tolerance, love, and compassion; dialogue, peace-building, and co-existence; and responsibility, civility, and citizenship as being at the heart of Hizmet. While noting that such concepts can be found in "the standard discourse of many global organizations," Gülen's achievement has been that he "integrates them in his theological worldview and explains them as Islamic principles." Finally, and significantly, they point out that "The clusters of concepts are connected to one another through Hizmet" (p. 92). But as Çetin says about the actual current position of Hizmet USA as distinct from the integration emphasis of Gülen that was previously mentioned "Unfortunately, the message is not taken yet properly/adequately. But each and every few days he reiterates this message: successful integration without losing your true essence and the values, and the message should be taken to people in the best way they can understand." And for going into the future Çetin underlined with regard to Gülen that, "The issue is not him, but what needs/ought to be done. It is not the man, but it is his intention and action," and that Gülen himself insists, "It's not my word, it's not my work."

With regard to the splits into which the Nur community fell after Said Nursi's death through the formation of what are now up around 20 different Nur groups, there is the perhaps equal but different issue that also emerged following the death of Nursi in terms of his followers becoming 'guardians' of his writings as a kind of 'fixed deposit' rather than taking his inheritance forward as contextualised appliers of it. As Çetin expressed it, "The Nur Cemaat unfortunately failed in this. They said we can only read from the original, we can only interpret, we should interpret, no new versions, no abridged versions."

In reflecting on Nursi and the *Risale-Nur*, Keleş points out the irony that, in contrast with such an approach, what Nursi wrote was "not passive book, it is an active book, it's not a textbook. It is a book written on horseback. It is not an academic text. It's a wonderful, it's a wonderful thing, but they have now solidified that dynamism by refusing to have an abridged simplified Turkish version" also highlighting that: "Nursi's *tafsir*, religious commentary, is actually a break from the classical religious commentary that was written at the time and prior, and many of the Nursi followers credit their faith to Nursi's extraordinary style, and his name is Bediuzzaman, 'extraordinary', his nickname." And as Keleş summarised it:

> Nursi was a phenomenal thinker, and a phenomenal person for his time – in every respect, extraordinary. I mean he said things that were just downright weird, in the sense he would say this '*bu sarik bu bas ile cikar*', that is, 'this turban, would come off with this head' [in response to The Law on Headdress and the regulations on dressing at the time] but he was clean-shaven. So, you think why do you say that? What's the logic of refusing to abandon one *sunnah* (the turban) but abandoning another (the beard)?

In contrast with the reification of this extraordinary text written on horseback that has occurred among Nursi's immediate followers, Çetin emphasised that "Hojaefendi is encouraging – take the message and you yourself do something: it's not my work, you process it." Çetin also explained that one of the reasons for this is that Gülen says of himself and his teaching that "I know that the younger generations will not understand me, will not understand my books, will not have that language capacity. So then, make simple versions or the versions they will understand so that they can follow the message." Once again, this contrasts with what has occurred in relation to Nursi's writing, with Çetin pointing out in relation to his Nursi's followers that: "For years they simply cannot simplify the language there was always a conflict within the Nur community. We understand and we read, but the younger generations cannot read and speak the same language, they do not have the same vocabulary."

In interview, Gülen himself recognised something of the challenges involved with human linguistic diversity when he spoke about how coming generations of Hizmet in the USA are not likely fully understand his words. And, indeed, one of the challenges for Hizmet people of diverse ethnic backgrounds and even more modern Turkish background is that Gülen himself writes in a style of Turkish which even Turkish first language speakers can find challenging and this is one of the reasons why English translations of his work can sometimes feel rather 'flowery' or 'circumlocutory.'

Hojaefendi speaks, delivers sermons once every week, and that's broadcast on the web. But especially younger generations since he uses this very sophisticated classical Turkish language, younger Turkish generations, especially if they are in the West are really unable to understand, even if they think they understand it is deficient in many ways. Some of his students said if one could please come forward and annotate and interpret Hojaefendi's intention or meaning in his sermon, that would be very useful, but you cannot have any certain person coming forward and taking that initiative on his own to interpret Hojaefendi's message.

As already noted, asked if it would be possible in principle to play back one's interpretation to him and say have we got that right, Kurucan ruefully commented "We are not as courageous." Similarly, when asked about the responsibility of taking forward Gülen's teaching Ergene answered that, "Our heads are down unfortunately."

Of course, apart from the question of generational vocabulary, it is the case that the Hizmet movement has to wrestle with the relationship between the Arabic language of the Qur'an, the particular Turkish style of Gülen, and the indigenous language or languages of the countries in which Hizmet has taken root. As Ablak from the Netherlands explains, the hermeneutical challenge involved:

So I see the work of Gülen as that we have the Qur'an, the Sunnah, the Hadith, and the *Risale-i-Nur*, and those are important things. And the work of Gülen is important to understand these. I don't speak Arabic, I don't understand that. I can read the Qur'an, but I don't understand what's in it. So, Gülen helps me to understand what's in the Qur'an and in the Hadith. So, I am thankful for that. But my main source must be, and is, and will be the Qur'an.

But although Gülen's work has achieved a global spread into translations into many languages, Ablak highlights that:

There isn't much translated into Dutch, so I helped translating two or three books, and that's a big problem. So, I was reading them in Turkish and also listening to the weekly sermons on You Tube. And we also had on Monday mornings lessons, and we read the *Risale-i-Nur*, and also the Qur'an, and new sermons were put online, and you took one on one day in particular. That was when we came together and talked about the sermon and together with others read the books, and then discussed how we could reflect that to the society, and to our jobs etc. But that was very, yeah, it wasn't deep. At the Dialogue Institute Platform INS, all our work was about Hizmet, was about dialogue. So, I needed to get more information about that, and I then stopped working for the Erasmus University so I got more time to read the books, to listen to the sermons and so on. So, it wasn't easy but I have a background of working in a large organization so I was used to come on time and that kind of stuff, which Hizmet people aren't.

Interviewee HE3 says that, "It tells you something about the situation at this moment – what they want to say, and I also support the literal translation of what he says in the Dutch here is not always the best way. You have to adapt it to the cultural understanding level of the people here." And, of course, the more global and transnational a movement like Hizmet becomes, the more challenging becomes the issue of faithful translation while retaining intended meaning and, as HE3 also points out:

> Most of Gülen's published thoughts are translations and I have given this to some text writers here, in Dutch. And they don't understand some of the parts of Gülen's thoughts about Islam. And I say "Why?" And they do not have the basic knowledge here, about Islam and Islamic culture. And I gave them the task to rewrite the texts so that the Dutch people here understand what he said and says in his books. And they have changed lots of things, not the meaning, the content of the text but the way of saying in the Dutch language and Dutch culture. And I have asked people in the US, to people there, can I do this? can I change the sentences of Fethullah Gülen so that the people here can understand what he says? – and people (young people especially) who do not have Turkish proficiency and they think in Dutch, they are not able to understand Fethullah Gülen very well. So some ideas of Fethullah Gülen, it could be a problem within the Netherlands, if we translate it as he said. But I understand him, and what he wants to say.

In relation to his own approach as a scholar, Gülen (2002) himself explains that, while "Taking the Qur'an and Sunnah as our main sources and respecting the great people of the past," one should also proceed "in the consciousness that we are all children of time" and that, because of this "we must question the past and the present" (p. 118). Put simply, Gülen summarises the challenge thus: "We must review our understanding of Islam." And as he then went on to further explain his aim to be that "I'm looking for laborers of thought and researchers to establish the necessary balance between the unchanging and changing aspects of Islam and, considering such jurisprudential rules as abrogation, particularization, generalization and restriction, can present Islam to the modern understanding" (p. 118). With regard to the question of how and what to take from all of this to inform Hizmet developments in the future, Kurucan said of Öztürk and Ergene that "They actually have started a bit the first steps for formulating how to maintain that heritage of Hojaefendi's scholarship, and there were some, you know, steps back in Istanbul as I remember, but that was again very immature" but also that although there were "very big ideals":

> I think it didn't really move forward to anywhere other than perhaps training a group of students in the same way that Hojaefendi taught the Islamic disciplines, but that's another issue. But here I hope they will come forward with a certain technique that can develop that scholarship of Hojaefendi's teaching.

Here Kurucan's use of the word "technique" is of particular interest and relevant, relating as it does to the overall notion of 'methodology.' As one example of the kind of development that has occurred from the applicability of Gülen's methodology, Kurucan cited Gülen's (Gülen 2004a, 2004b, 2009, 2010) four volumes on Sufism, the *Key Concepts in the Practice of Sufism: Emerald Hills of the Heart* collection, "which I believe and argue is very unique in the Sufism literature from the very early beginning onwards until now." And this is, he says, in ways that are worth quoting at length here:

> Because, you can see Hojaefendi – it's a big compendium or glossary that Hojaefendi has done with Sufi concepts – where you can see him taking a concept like *zuhd* (asceticism) and he basically compares and contrasts the way this concept is being presented in the Qur'anic scripture; and then in the way the Prophet taught us and practised it; and then how it was implemented and understood throughout the tradition of Islamic Sufism; and then, finally, how he understands the concept as a scholar himself; and how we can enact that concept in our lives in the modern times. So that Sufism collection is a good example of it.
>
>   But, also, the way he introduced those concepts to us in his specific way of teaching is the methodology, but we are not yet there how to understand his teaching. For example, Imam Azam (Abu Hanifa) and Imam Shafi, who were among the four pioneers of the schools of jurisprudence in Islam, but actually their students perhaps two hundred years later, developed a

methodology of how Imam Azam brought out solutions to some of the issues in that scholarship. Their schools of thought have actually developed later on. But it's a responsibility on our shoulders not to make that a hundred years later, but now, in how Hojaefendi is teaching us and handling those concepts.

Methodology is perhaps a longer-term project, but we have perhaps the means to do it in our lifetimes and it's a responsibility on our shoulders. Also, that we need to recognise the fact that as time passes, new conditions arise and however we may develop, Hizmet theology will certainly be affected by the time. The analyses will be done on his methodology.

...when we can hopefully formulate Hojaefendi's methodology of teaching we may also come forward with new concepts and additions on how we should understand his teaching.

As another example of methodological application this book has already noted (see Sect. 4.3) that Kurucan cited the addition of 'freedom' to the classical formulation of the five purposes of Islam being related to the protection of one's faith, life, family, property and mind. But Kurucan suggests that one way in which it may be possible to work within Gülen's trajectory but go beyond it will be "when we will develop a certain methodology," then within that "just as Hojaefendi added a sixth principle," then also "we should add a seventh one, which Hojefendi does not focus too much on, which would be on the protection of nature and environment. So, perhaps not now, but as we are working on those, or formulating that methodology we should have that liberty to add the seventh which I consider very significant."

6.5   THE METHODOLOGY OF LEARNING BY DOING

It is the understanding of Gülen as a person of action as well as being someone who is clearly located in the classical scholarship traditions of Sunni Islam that is so important in understanding both him and his relationship with Hizmet. HE3 emphasises in comparison with Nursi that "Nursi focused on writing some religious books and texts, but Gülen is also a man of action. And I think that people will continue developing many many projects and programmes for the societies in which they live" and that this will be "With or without Gülen himself as a guiding leader." Unpacking this in more detail, HE3 went on to say additionally of Gülen and of his relationship with Hizmet that:

He is a man of action, he is an entrepreneur, he is a writer, a teacher, but fore and foremost he is man of action. He is a person who initiated this whole. It is good that at this moment he is alive. And after him, the movement is now in an actualisation process, if the current political pressure finishes in a healthy way, the movement will not need him maybe any more as a leader and will act in the societies with his philosophy. The movement can exist from now on without Gülen and continue its existence without him.

To the extent that one takes such evaluations and judgements seriously, they point to the possibility that the most appropriate way of understanding Gülen's inheritance might not be so much to do with the substance of a body of his teaching that then gets passed on. Rather, it could be something which, despite its rather 'clinical' sounding tone, might be closer to that of a *methodology*, a way of understanding, developing, living out the impulses from Islam in the world, and therefore, as something which is more to be inducted as a way of living, being, and acting rather than simply received in the sense of something that is "passed on." As Keleş neatly expresses it, this is: "The difference between internalizing the methodology of your teacher, or the methodology of a particular line of thought, versus reproducing the product of that methodology that is time bound." Gezen from Denmark says of Gülen that he is "a man of action, and most of the initial activities of the Hizmet has been initiated by Gülen himself. I really respect and like this part of Gülen."

> He's not an academic as we know academics are. The way he lives, the way his environment has formed, the way the movement has grown certainly are not allowing him to pursue such a lifestyle where he can sit down, write, formulate and produce work that can easily be transmitted to other people. But he's a man much more engaged with the people who are visiting him, he's much more engaged with his prayers, he speaks, but he's not a person like an academic.

In other words Gülen, is in the full sense of the word fully 'inter-active' with the sources, with himself, with those from within Hizmet who seek his advice, and with the challenges of how to '*do hizmet*' in the specific times and geographies of the world than abstractly systematic in his thinking and teaching. As Gezen goes on to say of Gülen:

> And also if not personally and perhaps as a mission too, he perhaps cannot constrain himself to that academic systematism anyway, and perhaps it's not

fair to expect from him. That's perhaps like expecting the Prophet or Jesus or any other great leaders of our history to be following a certain academic discipline. People like Gülen take Prophets as their role models.

And, indeed, what is striking in relation to Gülen is that there is a sense of this dynamic of being rooted in the sources, but also always of contextual engagement with new things that present themselves. At the same time, this is not a methodological approach that is completely abstracted from substantive content, but rather a methodology that itself reflects and embodies a core content that is in one way or another to do with the primacy of divine love and of the human within what is believed to be the revelation of the Qur'an and the example of the *sunnah*. Therefore, at the heart of this is a vision of Islam and a methodology in which people are called upon to manifest the revelation of God in the world in a way in which theological ethics is at its heart. Thus, Gülen (in Ünal and Williams 2000) teaches that:

> An Islamic goal can be achieved only through Islamic means and methods. Muslims must pursue Islamic goals and adopt Islamic methods to attain them. As God's approval cannot be obtained without sincerity and a pure intention, Islam cannot be served and Muslims cannot be directed toward their real targets through diabolic means and methods. (p. 99).

Practice based on the foundations of the Qur'an and the Sunnah is central to the understanding of Gülen and of Hizmet in which there is a practical call to a 'doing of the truth' which leads to transformative understanding that in turn can inform new 'doings of the truth.' Indeed, this is why Balcı makes so bold to argue that "I believe that Hojaefendi has a duty, to a certain extent he has done, but it is not yet completed, to start writing a liberation theology that not only gives lip service to human rights issues and so on, not only says the Farewell sermon is the thing." As an example of the kind of thing that might be developed, Balcı cites a *You Tube* video which he and İsmail Sezgin and developed and which worked with the story of Moses as a leader of peaceful resistance. Concerning this, he said that many Hizmet theologians responded that "this is a unique commentary of the Qur'an, we never thought of Moses as a leader of resistance and so on." Drawing a wider lesson from that Balcı says:

And I realised that there is a still a potential of re-reading the Qur'an from within your own experience. And in fact, this is the whole uniqueness of Said Nursi and Hojaefendi. They have not written full commentaries about the Qur'an. They are always referring to the Qur'an from within everyday life situations. And that makes the Qur'an living. And now we are passing through something that we have never passed through and that is an invitation of, if you say, faith, to look back to our own holy sources from a different perspective, to read the Qur'an and the life story of our Prophet from the perspective of oppressed peoples.

In this one can see echoes of the kind of liberation theology approach developed by a number of Christians some decades ago in Latin and Central American countries in which they were going behind the inherited interpretations of the scriptures and bringing together in a circle of action and reflection in which the scriptures and the everyday experience of poor people were brought into a new hermeneutical interaction. In doing so, the pioneers of that approach were sometimes criticised for the lack of balance or otherwise in the conclusions that they reached and the actions that they undertook in comparison with the overall history of textual interpretation within Christian tradition. But what they tried to do was at least grounded and rooted in experience and gave rise to concrete actions.

As another concrete example of the kind of thing approach to the Qur'an of which he is thinking, Balcı cited the Qur'anic verse that advises Muslims not to go to war all together, but to leave somebody behind to study the religion. In relation to this, Balcı says:

It does say to take care of the elderly or the children. But it does also say leave some behind. And it says why. It says so that when those who go to war come back, they are going to advise them. So classical commentaries always deal with the human resources dimensions of it and say many people would be killed, so if you all people of the religion go to the front then you would lose all the people, the scholars and so on. So, they look at the human resources perspective. I'm looking at from the human nature perspective: fighting – whether it is war on the frontiers or it is a political struggle it changes human nature. And the Qur'an says there has to be somebody back who will drag your natures back to the normalcy, back to the ideal nature. But if you all go to the frontiers you will all become the same.

Linking this with his personal experience, Balcı explains that when he was in Israel/ Palestine and used to write about that conflict, he criticised suicide bombing operations. But he used to receive messages from many Turkish readers who argued that if his mother or sisters had been raped, he would do the same in relation to which, however, he had responded:

> Yes, yes, that is precisely the reason why I am writing this. That is precisely the reason. I am out of the ring. I always gave the example of these boxers in the ring – when they receive the first blow, it usually turns into animal instincts, they forget the rules. Somebody outside has to say, keep aside, keep aside, otherwise you will have the second or third one. He will lose. Somebody has to take us back.

In offering their views on what they see as the main hermeneutical keys for appropriately interpreting the teaching of Gülen and the practices of Hizmet, Hizmet interviewees have consistently highlighted one or both of two key themes. One is that of love as explained in Gülen's own teaching and embodied in the actions of Hizmet. The other is that of the human. A connection between the two can be found in the Sufi concept of the Perfect Human. This is not perfection in the sense of an 'impossibilist' interpretation of the Christian tradition which human beings other than Jesus can achieve. Rather, it is meant in the sense of a more open and dynamic trajectory. As an interpreter with Özcan explained it, "A true human being as God wants and wills … means that keeping the 'truth' and being a human, and preserving that one and expanding, enhancing your skills and abilities with the physical, with the spiritual, as God wills. It is this being a true human being." Enes Ergene further explained this as:

> When we started the discussion you asked about Gülen's theology I said 'human' is the centre of his theology. The human being is the centre of everything. Although Hojaefendi is saying this by looking at the Qur'an, his reference is the Qur'an, some people, radicals are not happy with this teaching. At some point he was accused of creating a new religion, a new faith, by bringing in different parts of the religions and faith: they used the term of 'soup'. No, it is not a new religion. The essence of all religions are the same. Of course, world views have changed, and there are nuances, but what he points at is the spine, the main core of all these traditions. Over time, other components like art, science, politics, etc. intervene, but that main core remains the same.

An illustrative example of how this hermeneutical circle between Gülen's teaching and example with regard to the primacy of the human and of love as it works out in 'inter-action' with Hizmet is the back story to an invitation the author received, while on a visit to Australia, to speak in Sydney at the 2018 launch of an initiative called Advocates for Dignity.[1] In the initial correspondence about speaking at this event, the provisional title for both the event and for the organisation was to have been "Victims of Turkey." But ahead of the event itself, the name was changed. This was significant in at least two ways. First of all, there was no evidence, as some have charged, about the relationship between Gülen and Hizmet being that of a 'cult-like' organisation or a paramilitary-type command structure in which somebody makes a decision which is then transmitted to everybody else and has to be implemented. Rather, as consistent with the author's general knowledge and experience of Hizmet over many years, and notwithstanding the critiques of Keleş, relative to many organisations of a religious character, Hizmet is more often than not a space of genuine and lively debate. And, therefore, the name of the initiative changed to the one actually used at the launch.

In addition, the substance of that changed name is important because it does not contain the passive word "victims" but instead settled on the active word "advocates." This is, of course, not to gloss over the very real victimisation that thousands of people connected with Hizmet have experienced. Rather, the name "advocates" was chosen so that, in terms of both its substantive focus and its external projection, it would be more consistent with the positive ideals and teaching of Gülen. This is because, as already noted, in Gülen's teaching, what comes first is not that one is a part of Hizmet, or even that one is a Muslim, but rather that one is first and foremost a human being, and from that humanity one then works out what it is to be a Muslim in the contemporary world in engagement with the Qura'nic sources and all that makes for that.

Therefore, the focus was not on "victims," but on "advocates," not focusing only on "Muslimness" or "Hizmetness," but on dignity—human dignity. In addition, the original country focus of the title on "Turkey" would not have been quite right because, although there are shared responsibilities for what occurs in each individual society, it would not be correct in any undifferentiated way to put at the doorstep of an entire country or people what is being perpetrated by a particular power structure and its active supporters, even when many others are passively complicit.

In addition, a geographical focus on "Turkey" alone would also not be quite right because people have also been suffering outside of Turkey by virtue of their association with Hizmet. And furthermore, by calling the initiative Advocates for Dignity, the new name universalises the aim of the initiative. That is to say it is not only focused on (which would, of course, be entirely legitimate in socio-political and legal terms alone) the self-interest of a group of people who are suffering greatly at this time. Rather, this initiative had both a proper focus on the injustices to Hizmet occurring in Turkey and linked with Turkish developments but was also seeking to connect those experiences with other injustices in other contexts.

As connected with what has happened to Hizmet in Turkey and responses to that of the kind just described, Kerim Balcı has outlined a series of examples of how a methodological commitment to learning by doing through the embodiment of love as a verb into concrete actions—including into things that have sometimes diverged from and/or conflicted with more 'normal' understandings, stances, and approaches found within Hizmet—came about, and has discussed what has been learned from this, in the following ways. The first example was of what began to happen among Hizmet in Turkey itself in response to the growing sense of authoritarianism in the country, even before it began so directly and seriously to impact upon Hizmet itself beyond the 2013 closure of many of its educational initiatives. As Balcı recounted this:

> Actually, it didn't start with our own people, but we already realised it was going to come to us. So, we started to join sitting protests in front of what became the infamous Silivri prison where I think that more than 5,000 members of our movement are in jail now. At that time there was none, but left-wing journalists were being jailed. So, we started to go and sit in front of the prison as a show a solidarity.

But the authoritarian developments did start to affect Hizmet directly, and especially in December 2014, when both the editor-in-chief of *Zaman* media group, Ekrem Dumanlı, and the *Samanyolu* TV Manager, Hidayet Karaca, were arrested. Balcı explains that initially the protest involvements of Hizmet people were not co-ordinated, but advisory messages were being sent on What's App. But when the above arrests happened, "Everyone was in front of Çağlayan – the Palace of Justice in Istanbul, protesting about their arrests. Eventually, Ekrem was released, but Hidayet Karaca is still in jail. He will, if this continues like that, he will die in jail." Later, when in the USA, Balcı was involved in organising a small protest of around 40 people involving friends from the dialogue activities in the Chicago square. This was small in number and with every speaker needed to speak to agreed printed texts, in order to minimise the risks of negative spin-offs in Turkey.

These protest actions were not one that were centrally co-ordinated with leaders in Hizmet and had not been discussed with Fethullah Gülen before they were carried out. In relation to the action in Chicago, Balcı explained that he later account took advice from people who are close to Fethullah Gülen, acknowledging that he and others had taken this action "without asking him" and that "if he didn't like it, we shouldn't continue." However, following that it was reported back to them that when Gülen had seen in on TV he had asked, "Do we have only forty people in Chicago?". Encouraged by this, Balcı organised another event with 2000 people in front of the United Nations, where he was also one of the speakers.

Of that event, Balcı said "When I returned back to Turkey, Ekrem Dumanlı said to him, 'Kerim you were speaking as an opposition leader, there, I assume, there?' and I said, 'And you were speaking in front of Çağlayan as the leader of the country, actually.' " Explaining what he meant by this is Balcı said, "Well, the point is, that when we started these moves, we didn't realise that people outside Hizmet were looking at us as possible political actors of Turkey." In relation to this, he went on to say that:

> Many people from the CHP and the MHP – these are radically different, but both nationalist parties, one is a left wing and one is a right wing nationalist party – both of them wrote letters to Ekrem Dumanlı inviting him to come and become the leader of their parties. This said a lot of things. First of all, this said that Turkey had a lack of opposition leaders. Second, at that stage, we were not seen as enemies of the public, you know. Many people, from CHP for example, you know – this is a Kemalist, secularist party – invited me to their meetings to give a speech and so on after that event. This was 2014, a year after the graft investigation. So already Erdoğan had decided to seal our fate, exterminate the movement and so on. But the left, and even nationalist right, was able to stand with us, invite us to join their ranks – actually not to join their ranks, but to become their leaders – but this also says a lot about the movement.

Nevertheless, Balcı said that "None of us took this seduction. None of us said, 'Why not do politics, people are leaning to us, people are inviting us,' and Ekrem is a tall guy, handsome, not like me, so if he wanted he would be quite a successful politician. He didn't." Because of this, Balcı thinks there will need, in the future, to be some retrospective reflection on what might and might not have been done, with contributions from Hizmet, before matters had gone too far:

> A generation later that question has to be asked also. It's not only that we are suffering from a persecution. It's that we, also, rejected an opportunity, a political opportunity. Now, when people ask me questions like, were you involved in this coup attempt and so on, I am saying, "Why don't you ask me, why this movement didn't try this in a political way? Why – you had the opportunity. You had the largest circulating newspaper of Turkey, best watched TV channels of Turkey and the support of almost all opposition groups, and yet you didn't appeal to power?"

And even though in relation to politics Balcı says that, "I still believe in the motto of Bediüzzaman Said Nursi, '*Şeytandan ve siyasetten Allah'a sığınırım*' ('I seek refuge with Allah from Satan and from politics')," he insists that there is a real question to be answered. Of himself, he explained that "Even in countries like the UK – I am a member of the Labour Party, I always felt myself a Fabian – but, I am not interested in making politics, or appealing to power positions. I'm a student, I'm learning, and I want to contribute to my society, to my new home, yes, but not as being a leader." In relation to civic society protest, it was still that, "at that stage, we started to learn how to protest, how to write slogans, how to chose slogans and so on. I remember, I don't know who said this, but this was a left wing person who knew protesting and said 'These Gülenists are newcomers but they are learning fast'."

However, Balcı thought they made the mistake of believing too much in social media, commenting that "Twitter particularly, might really be a good place to promote an idea, but 'likes' do not count, you know." So, what they were not able to do was "how to turn that public protest energy into change in society." They were unsure of how to move from 'likes' to real engagement and "At that stage I can say we put eighty per cent of our energy into social media activism. Street activism was only twenty per cent."

In relation to such actions, Balcı says that "many people, even here, are still critical of my activism," citing the example of when he first organised a protest in front of the Pakistani Embassy in connection with when a Hizmet-related family were seized by Pakistani police officers and deported to Turkey without any due process, but in relation to the invitation to protest, "Many said no way, we are not going to do that, this is not

Hizmet, and so on." Balcı acknowledges that such critics "might be right." However, he explained, "I asked myself the simple question, 'What can I do?' " because, although a journalist, in practice, he could not get into *The Guardian* newspaper or the BBC to be interviewed which he might otherwise have done, similarly with the politicians, but…what was ready to listen was Amnesty International "so I have spoken in several Amnesty events all around the United Kingdom," but also "the streets were open, so I did that." In other words, in Hizmet tradition, Balcı was identifying what was "the opportunity space," and of which he commented that "This is true for all kinds of new areas of activity in which Hizmet is being pushed towards."

As expressed by Keleş when reflecting on the past, present, and future of Hizmet in relation to the teaching and practice of Gülen, there is an important "difference between internalizing the methodology of your teacher, or the methodology of a particular line of thought, versus reproducing the product of that methodology that is time bound." Or, as Kerakoyun has expressed it, reflecting on the more traditional forms of Hizmet initiatives in Europe "If you 'copy and paste' and if you don't have people who are brave enough to start something new, it won't work. So, I think also Hojaefendi is very open, but many people in Hizmet are not brave enough to start something new."

6.6   LOVE, THE HUMAN, AND ECUMENICAL *IJTIHADS* IN ACTION

In the process of coming to terms with the impact of its own recent trauma and suffering and with what might be learned from this, it is at least possible that a new opportunity could be opening up through a shared human experience of suffering and injustice, to focus more clearly than ever before on the centrality of love and the human, and in working together with people of all religions and none in the development of inclusive ecumenical *itjihads* in action.

For example, despite his previously noted critique in relation to Turkish nationalism and its impact, including within Hizmet, Naziri agrees that Hizmet is "in my opinion one of the, if not the most open-minded society or group in Turkey" and that as a consequence of what has happened to it post-2016, Hizmet has become "more open to know other societies, other languages etc etc....to make an empathy, to learn to make an empathy in relation to many aspects – in language aspect, in ethnic aspect, in religious aspect." As Naziri says:

> What I think is that I am now evidencing the huge transformation, the huge transformation, yeah, of the Hizmet, like, in different ways and in different modes. Now, every problem is bad, but it could be again a good opportunity. Like the Hizmet was not anti-democratic, never ever I suppose, I guess and I believe. It was not anti-human rights, but yes, after these events it has become more pro- these values and embracing many, many other values and, you know, like, sticking it or putting it in a very solid way, like, this is mine, this is what I want, these are my values. If these bad things are happening and I am still who I was, even you know like, despite all of these bad things, I think that these things are happening are helping in consolidating, let's say, the Hizmet attitude and philosophy.

Reflecting more broadly on this, Naziri opines that "what happens to us should, at least, give us some lessons, and you have to...they give us the lessons and the question is whether we learn from it or not." And, interestingly, in echo of what other interviewees and informants have said, this is also now beginning to be extended from within Hizmet to "every group which was persecuted, no matter what ideology they had" with Naziri, for example, arguing that this is extending not only to ethnic Armenians, and to include the suffering of political leftists, but also that "it could be LGBT, it could be everything, you know."

As Naziri describes this process he says that "generally speaking, I think that many, many Turkish citizens who are Hizmet participants and are subjected to these problems are learning positively and, like you know, it is affecting them positively, this part at least. They are being able to convert it into an opportunity." To some extent, regardless of whatever position is taken by individuals in relation to internal Hizmet debates on how to interpret these events and what their implication is for the future, in many and various ways, Hizmet people are all having to learn:

> All of these things are teaching us all Hizmet participants whether we are persecuted or not directly or indirectly, to accept, to learn, and to embrace many values which we find, let's say, implemented and working here in the European societies and the western countries, and which are, probably all of them, or most of them, Islamically-based. To believe on them, to embrace them, to receive them, to accept them, again and again thinking and making

a permanent compromise, doing good and serving the people, in order to please God, if this is the main point of Hizmet, and it is, if everyone really believes on it. So this is the time to consolidate this philosophy and to put it into practice, instead of talking like me, showing it in action!

One of the things about which there does seem to be agreement in principle within Hizmet is that Hizmet can no longer simply be Turkish. As Ercan Karakoyun from Germany puts it, "Hizmet is not Turkish anymore. I am not Turkish like the Turks in Turkey. And the people who finish our schools in Pakistan, in Ethiopia, and in Tanzania, there are also not Turkish." Indeed, "We everywhere we have to have different local approaches to Hizmet and a transnational aspect is, of course, well, although we are German Hizmet, Ethiopian Hizmet and they are Pakistani Hizmet, we have the same ideas. Our ideas are transnational, we have the same values that we stand for all round the world."

When he was himself asked about what he saw as being at the heart of Islam, Gülen said, "I think if you are going to name one thing that lies at the heart of Islam I would say that is love. Yes, there have been circumstances which necessitated conflicts and sometimes violent conflicts. But that is exceptional, that is not what is at the heart of Islam." Indeed, he went on to say that "You can see this love-centred spirit of Islam in the writing of some of the famous scholars of the past. For instance, one said don't hurt or harm a single life. It is equivalent to demolishing the high seat of God" (by which Gülen was referring the Throne of God, or the authority of God). Gülen went on to say that, "In the writings of Rumi you can find similar verses," and in reference to one of Gulen's early and very influential spiritual teachers, the Anatolian-based Sufi Muhammed Lutfi of Alvar (also known as Alvarlı Efe), who was also based in Erzerum and who said what in English translation might be approximated as: "The lover with a pearl-like skin says: Don't be offended by the offender. The one who allows himself to be offended is lesser in maturity than the offender."

The emphasis here on the universality of love in combination with the emphasis on the human both allows for, and can also actively facilitate, the emergence of what one might call ecumenical *ijtihads* in action—in other words, *ijtihads* that, in practice, are not done by Muslims or Hizmet people alone but by them in dialogue with others. As a concrete example of this, for example, in relation to the challenge of dealing with trauma in Hizmet, Balcı says that "I am very much open to the idea of involving Jews and Christians into an *ijtihad* body" and also argues that ecumenical *itjihads* between Hizmet Muslims and Jews would be able to draw on the Jewish experience in Europe where many Jewish people have been burdened with trauma that has gone through generations and has arguably, at least in part, hindered the potential of the Jewish people to offer the gift that is in the Jewish tradition to the benefit of the wider humanity. But as also in Jewish experience, out of trauma can come learning of theological depth.

Even more broadly, Balcı explicitly argues that it is necessary for Hizmet to take up the challenge of 'ecumenical *ijtihad*' in action for the future because the nature of the main human challenges of the future are global in scope, and have impact not only on Muslims and Hizmet but also on people of all religious traditions, and indeed on all humanity. As an illustrative example of this challenge from beyond Hizmet, Balcı referred to a talk that he recently gave in a liberal Jewish synagogue, noting that "when it comes to Judaism many of the people think that, you know, theology, it's done, you can't add anything, it's already a complete book," and Balcı says that because of this:

I spoke about the challenge of artificial intelligence and genome editing. I said you might think religion is altogether finished, you know, written, we have the Mishnah, Talmud, and you know, what do you need further, but I am going to ask you a few questions. All these driverless cars, they are not learning from the code. They are learning from themselves, from observations, and in critical situations they are making decisions to kill this person and not this person. And they are actors: for the first time in human history, somebody other than a human being is an actor [agent]. We don't have theology for non-human actors [agents], you know.

In Islam, especially, we don't have much place for non-human actors, we altogether erased everything other than human being and *jinn*, from theological discussion, you know. We simply say that animals do not go to heaven or hell, finished. I have problems with that. But robots – is there a place in Paradise for robots, or hell? Or if a driverless car kills somebody, who is going to pay for it. Do we just switch it off and that's it? How many people were involved in writing of the code? Are we going to go back to the coders and so on? People buy code from a code library and use code from there. Are we going to go back to the code library? It's a challenge.

And already in China, people started to play with the human genome. What if we have – and we will eventually have that – human beings that can live under water, then what will we do with ablution, you know, if they are living under water? And, you know, in Judaism, a bit in Christianity, but in Islam, spiritual ablution is so much so important, and so on.

These observations by Balcı have echoes of, and resonances with, Kurucan's references to the discussions with Gülen's close associates concerning how, in two very different times and contexts, one should assess the appropriateness of the sources of water for ritual ablutions. But these examples take those intra-Muslim discussions even further in underlining the need for inter-religious and inter-human dialogical engagement if such issues are going to be engaged with in a creative and productive way. In relation to such opportunities and challenges, what Gülen's methodology offers can perhaps be characterised as an ethical theology or a theological ethics that bears witness to the revelatory truth that it claims to have received and which translates that into a style of Muslim living in a religiously plural world in which modesty and integrity are combined with realism and distinctiveness. Such living gives Muslims, but also people of all religions and none, the social and theological space to witness their own understanding of truth as well as to be free to make their response to what is shared with them by others, within which the praxis of ecumenical *itjihads* in action can be engaged with as part of a better understanding of truth as well as a means of effecting positive change. In relation to the challenge of doing such ecumenical *ijtihad*, Balcı quite startlingly and challengingly says:

> This challenge is a huge challenge – only Muslims, or only Christians or only Jews cannot deal with this issue, particular ethics of genome editing which will happen, you cannot, you cannot just say, we are against it, that's it. Yeah, we are against homosexuality says the Catholic Church, but how many Catholic priests are homosexual? You cannot undo things by just saying this is non-Christian or non-Muslim, and so on. It is a fact. It is a fact. So, we have to deal with that, and I believe that Hizmet is uniquely positioned to deal with those challenges. And that is one area that is going to give us an opportunity in Europe, in the West.

6.7   GOING BEYOND GÜLEN?

When asked about the future of Gülen's heritage after Gülen's death, Ergene said, referring to his 2008 book *Tradition Witnessing the Modern Age*, "I wrote one book, but we could have written five books. But I am a lazy student. I was to about to finish a second book, but these new bandits of Turkey confiscated everything. All I wrote are gone. We had to leave everything behind." Reflecting on the challenge of how this heritage might nevertheless be taken forward, Ergene confessed that, "Our heads are down on this," while noting the scope of the kind of challenge that this presented given that Gülen is, as Ergene expressed it:

> He is a person with so many dimensions. It is hard to convey all of those dimensions and provide a framework for this. In the past there was a tradition of annotation where students used to write notes and expanded on the literature that they had inherited from their teacher, systematized his ideas, and if that has become a school that was thanks to the efforts of the students. In this case, then, this responsibility really falls on us here and several others and surely there is a need for that. Perhaps in the last twenty years, I have working on him as a spiritual person, as a scholar, as a thinker, as a renewer, as an authority in law. But I have to say it is a very difficult job to refer to all of these personalities. We need to start first perhaps by systematizing his way of thinking. For his discourse is pretty much encyclopaedic. You would find him speaking about ethics at one point, but then moving from there to *kalam*, to Sufism, to philosophy, to current affairs and then connecting them to social realities. He makes very rapid transitions in between disciplines. This is usually how founding personalities are; they have things to say in every domain. His discourse has to be processed in an intellectual analysis.

In the light of the impact upon him as a person and his teaching of changing social, political, geographical, temporal, and religious contexts, Gülen acknowledges that his own perspective has now broadened to such an extent that, as he put it in an interview with the present author:

> I've always believed that Islam, Muslims, Christians, Jews, Buddhists, Shintoists, you name it, members of all these religions can live in harmony, and people in Hizmet believe this. And you can say that the schools that were established around the world were the first steps toward our contribution toward this goal. And now with this push these further steps are taken. In a sense some seeds are placed in different parts of the world. At some point these seeds will bear, produce, trees. So, they will represent the bright face of Islam and Muslims in a more beautiful way, and these people in their localities recognise the same thing that I believed all along that yes we can live in harmony and embrace each other. This embracing of all humans around the world, each other, has been my dream throughout my life. It is so strong, so fundamental for me that it is almost a prejudice that I certainly believe that this will happen one day.

In adding to the question of the future of Hizmet beyond Gülen, HE3 also notes one of the key differences between Hizmet and the Nursi movement is "the international perspective of the Hizmet compared to the Nursi movement," as a result of which HE3 speculates that:

> This dynamism can make it that the movement will be managed with a group of people, internationally but also locally in each country. After Gülen, I see such a kind of managerial leadership structure in the movement in which everyone, in whichever country is free, and this is the collective of the movement. And they will listen to each other, they will look at each other's activities, but the ideal view of the ideas of Gülen will be at the centre. They will still be the main guiding ideas and principles.

Gülen himself has even talked about a wider *shura*, or consultative council, although Gezen thinks that "a big *shura* of European Hizmet or worldwide Hizmet that is giving directions to a local Hizmet" is unlikely to happen since it "would be utopian, if you ask me." But apart from the question of its likely viability, Gezen expressed his own personal position about this as being that "I don't think I would want to be a part of a thing like that – simply because the purpose is not to establish something, but to establish life after." Noting that Gülen is over eighty and that when he will not be here anymore, "it's only his work that will stay, through his books and speeches, in which there is a lot to take from," Gezen went on to say that:

> Gülen is a very, very influential figure. He has inspired a lot of people. So, for me, if I still am alive the next twenty or thirty years, my main resource and inspiration will be Gülen's writings. So, I will be talking about Gülen as an inspirer, and because I am able to write and read probably I will write things inspired by Gülen. And the idea, the vision is the same. It does not die when Gülen dies. That is the philosophy. It's totally misinterpreted if someone feels that, if Gülen dies, then the Hizmet will die although some people will stick with the ideas. That's not the case. The issue is pretty straightforward. It is that while you are alive you try to get God's acceptance, which is a life-long endeavour. It being a life-long endeavour does not change with Gülen dying. So I think the vision will continue.

But in addition, Gezen commented that he also thought it would be "inevitable that there will be Hizmet people in Denmark in the future that are inspired by new scholars, maybe scholars who are developing Gülen's works and are saying that the ideas and the vision are still there." Thus, Gezen's evaluation is that it is more likely that no one person or group will emerge, but rather there will what he called "local trajectories" and therefore "local Hizmet." Indeed, Gezen's own preference is that "I would focus on local issues, with a group of people who are having the same vision. So, local associations will continue and in twenty or thirty years from now."

Karakoyun explained that it is difficult at the moment to come together because "everybody has a lot to do with their own problems." However, Karakoyun also says that, in terms of the 'Western' world at least, there nevertheless remains "good co-ordination with Berlin, Brussels, Rotterdam, Paris, London, and New York" because many of the problems and issues are still similar. But unlike Gezen, although he also thinks that "globally it's not possible at the moment," Karakoyun is still of the view that "I think Hizmet has to work on this *shura issue*" on the basis that:

> If you have circles and decision-makers that come together and discuss properly; share their ideas properly; then going on from then, decide which way to go, then I think that Hizmet will do very well in the future because this is, by the way something that Hojaefendi always says: instead of having one genius, it is better to have three average ladies coming together and discussing and working on a consensus, because there are then better solutions. So, if we can establish these *shura* circles, there are democratic consensus-finding bodies in different countries, then we can have a future. Otherwise, I think I fear that we will have a lot of different hizmets, maybe as many as there are countries. So, the transnational idea will maybe get a little lost.

Keleş links the question of the future of Hizmet with what he identifies as having been a key characteristic of the movement since its inception, which is that:

> One of the things that defines Hizmet is "momentum". This is the idea of *helmin mezit* in Hizmet (is there not more I can do in Hizmet)? This is like, to never be satisfied with what one has done, but also always to look beyond, which is why it became so expansive, both geographically but also sectorally.

Nevertheless, Keleş he also evaluates the present position of Hizmet as being one within which:

It's almost as if we are experiencing the clash of two Hizmets. Hizmet (values, ideals, and principles) versus movement (reality, interests, practicalities). Will the movement allow us to practice Hizmet's values. And it's not just "us" verses "them", it's inside everyone, you know. It's fascinating from an organizational studies, sociological, social movement, religious movement point of view – it's quite interesting whether or not that will happen.

Pressing this further, Keleş makes the observation that "I mean you have a very sophisticated, educated movement with doctors and so forth in it" before, and from his perspective somewhat rhetorically asking "Can we not see this? Can we not take part in it?" before providing his own rather downbeat response "I guess we can't?" albeit with inclusive of a question mark. But as with the previously discussed question of the application of post-fact causality thinking to a hermeneutic of Hizmet's trauma, once again, Keleş links and broadens the questions that he poses to Hizmet with ones that are wider and deeper than those that he poses to the movement alone, as when he asks: "Can the Islamic culture and civilisation achieve a form of social responsibility and accountability and independent institutions? Can we institutionalize this? So now I am questioning this?" Citing examples of others who have sought to be creative in this regard, such as Hamza Yusuf, as an indigenous Muslim leader in the USA, Keleş comments that he and his group of people "have failed spectacularly in the face of what is happening in Turkey and other parts of the world and their inability to stand up to it"; and Tariq Ramadan, of whom he says that is "an intellectual, but not much more in terms of that."

These wider observations and questions therefore also led Keleş on to a question that connects both Hizmet and Islam more broadly which he framed as follows: "If Hizmet is one of the most sophisticated, widespread, culturally enriched Islamic movements in the world, if it can't do this, who is going to do it?" For all his critiques of Hizmet in recent practice, the in principle still positive evaluation of Hizmet's creativity expressed here by Keleş was also echoed by Balcı who expressed his conviction that, "I believe our Hizmet people are the most open and well-attuned to open the gates of *ijtihad* and the Muslim world, the whole world needs this." This is because, as he says, "Hizmet might not be extremely original for Christian or western civilisation, but it is so much so unique for the East, for 'the Muslim world': unique in the sense that it never happened in the fifteen hundred years of our history."

Balcı says that "maybe at the Prophet's time there was this level of openness," although he quickly also acknowledged that perhaps this is "only because I don't know his time very well." However, he is clear that since Muhammad's time "it never happened again." As illustrative of this, Balcı recounted that, on the day before the interview, a friend and he had been speaking about the situation of 'the Muslim world' but that he had pressed upon his Muslim friend the position of "Don't call this 'the Muslim world'. We are in the age of *Jahiliyyah*, you know. We have turned back to this Age of Ignorance, pre-Muhammadan ignorance." In relation to this, Balcı went on to explain:

> My benchmark is not the west. I am not looking at the Western civilisation and saying – yeah, we are backward compared to the West – but I'm not happy with where the West is going. My benchmark is the Prophet, and we are backward compared to our own Prophet. We are not four hundred years back, we are more than fifteen hundred years back because I am looking at the farewell sermon of my Prophet, and we have failed him in every single advice he gave to us. Every single one of them, and this is his last will, you know. So 'the Muslim world' is a complete failure.

Balcı testifies that he learned much on these matters from a respected non-Hizmet Muslim in the UK who he acknowledges "is a bit critical of Hizmet these days" but from whom Balcı sought consultative advice when first came to the UK in 1993 with the task of establishing dialogue institutions all around Europe and was uncertain about how to proceed. Balcı recounted that this respected Muslim initially did not seem particularly interested in what he was talking about until, just before the conversation was drawing to a close, Balcı mentioned that Hizmet was being quite harshly criticised in Turkey for its dialogue activities, to which the response came, "What, Muslims are criticising you?!" to which Balcı answered "Yes...*imams* and so on." And it was this which evoked the further response, "Write me, I am going to be your volunteer." When Balcı expressed his surprise at this outcome and that he had not even been asked about the basis for the criticisms made in Turkey, the reply was:

> Look at the 'Muslim world', and if someone is criticising what you are doing you might be doing something right, there is a chance you might be doing something right because 'the Muslim world' is altogether a failure and I thought you might be one of those Muslim organizations that are repeating what you have been doing for fourteen hundred years.

In many ways, this interaction was, as Balcı said, "a critical point where I have realised the value of being criticised. He said, we have to be criticised." And, of course, one is only criticised if one *does* something to be criticised for!—in relation to which, Balcı says:

> And that is a challenge for Hizmet nowadays, because some of us have entered into – you used the term paralysed – into a 'survival mode' because, even if they have the capacity or even the view to do something, they are keeping silent because this is an animal instinct: if you are hunted, you behave as if you are dead. But we have to stop it, you know.

Quite startlingly, in reflecting further on the implications of this challenge not only for the wider Hizmet and the circle of those around Fethullah Gülen, but also possibly for Gülen himself, Balcı says "maybe Hojaefendi may behave like that" and perhaps even more startlingly that, if that is so, "we shouldn't listen to it" because the reality is that "you can stop breathing only for some time. You will die otherwise." In another image, Balcı says:

> Hizmet is a bicycle. We have to move. We have to do something. It might be a mistake. It has to be something very different. That's precisely why I started the protests: it was something that we never did here, it was something different. And it also gave a sense of living, that we are alive. I think we have to continue with that. And it might be something different, you know, a Madrassah, you can say.

In relation to such an approach, Balcı thinks that what he calls the "beautiful expression" of İhsan Yılmaz's concept of "*ijtihad* by conduct" (Yilmaz 2003). In relation to this, Balcı notes that:

> There are some dogmas in the Muslim world that, when you pronounce them, it is a dead end, it doesn't work. If you say I'm doing an *ijtihad*, it is a dead end. Many people will come out and declare you an infidel and so on. But if you do it without saying so, everybody does it! Hizmet has been doing it; we are doing it in our daily lives, as Ihsan says, 'micro *ijtihad*'. So, this is a new phenomenon that never existed in the Muslim history. Action precedes the ruling. We do, we do it, and we do it. And in the end it becomes doable.

As an illustrative example of this in practice, Balcı recalled that a number of years ago some Deobandi leaders were brought to Turkey and they visited various Hizmet institutions including "our university where boys and girls are trained together." Although he noted that this gender mixing was "against Deobandi theology," after they had visited, "they started to do that. And they asked for advice, they said, let us build a school and why don't you come and manage it and so on." Balcı summarises the lessons that derive from examples as being that "largely, the revolution is an action, it is not a theory" and that "I think that Hizmet has taken this from Hojaefendi: action." And on this, he referred to Gülen's 1994 *Zaman* interview ("Reaching to the Horizon with Fethullah Gülen") with Eyup Can in which "there he said that for us, action is the fundamental. Only after a brief thought" but of which Balcı also noted that "This is completely non-Western" because "Here you think about something for six months before you are doing anything." But in terms of the 'Muslim world' context out of which Hizmet comes, Balçi says that, "we have passed through three hundred years of intensive waste of thought without any action," and that especially against such a background Gülen's impulse to action is truly revolutionary: "Hojaefendi brings action and says, you might have done wrong, but the fact you have done something is going to be the basis that next time you might do the right thing. If you do nothing, there is nothing to step on. So, that also gives a lot of courage to the Hizmet people, to do something."

Balcı therefore locates something of Hizmet's creativity as being rooted in Gülen's encouragement to Hizmet in effect to be willing to make mistakes as distinct from doing nothing. Reflecting on this, Balcı says that they "did grave mistakes back in Turkey" but also, "this might be paradoxical," since he says:

> Maybe we made those mistakes also because of the same reasons, maybe because Hojaefendi made us so open, so courageous to act. Maybe if we had come together and said let us speak this for six months whether we should support the AKP party or not in the elections, and then do it, maybe we would then have done it differently. And it might have cost us a lot, but in the end we did it. So, I believe this readiness to act comes with its own price. We have paid a lot of price about that, so we have to gather the fruits also. So, I feel Hizmet is quite ready to deal with the challenges of the Western world. But of, course, there is this question of whether we will be able to, you know, leave our baggage. All of us are carrying Turkey on our shoulders.

Balcı does see real opportunities for the future but cautions that "We still need time. It's like a divorce, you know: you cannot get married the next day you are divorced, you know. The pain is still there. The anger is still there. Also, the possibility of the reunion is still there." In this last sentence, Balcı was touching on what for some in Hizmet is still a live potential of the "myth of return" since "Some of us still believe in that, you know, returning back to Turkey" and "That hope is still there," before adding from his own perspective that "I don't believe in that, but some of us do."

Returning from these considerations of what has been and could in future still be in motion as produced out of the interaction between Gülen, Hizmet, and their respective historical and geographical contexts to attempt an overall evaluation of the role and place of Fethullah Gülen within this, Gülen's close associate and interviewee Enes Ergene (see Acknowledgements) summarises that "Well, certainly, the space, the environment, the place he was born, the place like Erzurum, certainly does have an influence on him," given that it "was a very, and still is, a very conservative part of Turkey.... where people are, you know, by definition, very conservative. So that has had a lot of influence on him, obviously. Yes, he was born into that environment, and some parts of his life reflect that conservative culture." And, as Ergene put it in reflecting a common perception in Turkey about the context of Gülen's origins, which is that "from that part of our Turkey, one really does not expect much of a person who grew up there to break through and have an understanding of a world where he is welcoming any other person." Therefore:

> We have to give credit to the way he was formed. Many people can become leaders, even in mystical terms or social terms, by changes in the dynamics of the environment, by economic and other factors that are involved, by the support that comes from society, by the push that comes from his family, one may become a leader.

But in addition to exploring the interplay between life and thought that is the more standard fare of a book that would aspire to be understood primarily as a biography, this book has also been concerned to identify and explore how a traditionally formed and rooted Islamic scholar, while remaining faithful to what he believes is revealed truth, has also found other ways of transcending the closed circle of sterile repetition in order to achieve what might be called a 'constructive theology.' And it is the argument of this book that this 'constructive theology' has been generated in and through what is the still ongoing hermeneutical circle of mutually interactive development between Gülen and Hizmet.

What is always affirmed by Gülen and those inspired by him is that he is not advocating a new and idiosyncratic form of Islam, but rather that what he sets forth finds its origins in what is believed to be the Islamic revelation in Qur'an and Sunnah; through its geographically, temporally, and existentially situated reception, translation, and onward communication through the life, teaching, and practice of Gülen; via the dynamic learning achieved and questions posed through the attempt to put those inspirational impulses into personal and corporate practice; and back again into a reflective engagement with the originally believed revelation in a way that brings about a richer illuminative and wider communicative possibility than would be possible without the operation of this hermeneutical circle, which this book argues is central to understanding Gülen's life and teaching.

The multi-faceted complexity of this kind of hermeneutic interaction has been evidenced and demonstrated through a recent examination by Keleş (2021) of the "interplay within and between Hizmet's doings and Gülen's sayings over an expansive temporospatial axis against a range of issues" (p. 141) in an as yet unpublished but important doctoral thesis that focused particularly on Gülen and Hizmet's handling of, and engagement with, human rights questions and issues around apostasy and of the role and place of women. As expressed by Keleş in theoretical terms, "this form of knowledge production ensues through two basic movements." As described by Keleş these two "movements" are those of "internalization and externalization" with an organic linkage between the two being posited as occurring through "cognitive compromise and cognitive dissonance," which Keleş then conceptualised in terms of a "symbiotic relationship between the internalized-tacit and the externalized-explicit form of knowledge" within this hermeneutic circle.

In more narrative terms, Haylamaz describes the relationship between Gülen and Hizmet in terms of what Gülen himself calls a "coming together around what makes sense," the concretisation of the varied expressions of which has, as Haylamaz put, enabled "many people from different backgrounds to find a place in this Hizmet." What, however, is not visible in Haylamaz's formulation are the notes of "dissonance" and "compromise" through which, in different combinations according to the issue being examined, Keleş' thesis argues are at the heart of the complex way in which new developments take place within Hizmet.

In summatively evaluating Fethullah Gülen's person, practice, and teaching, as Ergene points out, according to the influence of external environments alone one would expect a person who is more constrained within his inherited culture, but "What you notice in Gülen's life is that he was able to 'break through', and he did that with unbelievable measures." However, Ergene is also of the view that the interaction between Gülen and his changing environments cannot provide a fully adequate explanation of the phenomenon that he became because:

> However, there is so much in his life that you cannot relate to the environment he was born into. The way he behaves, the way he speaks, the things he did. I mean he was an *imam*, he became a preacher. What can you expect most from an *imam* other than telling the history of Islam, worshiping God, the Prophet's companions? But he is not saying "mosque"; he says "school." From late in mid-1970s onwards he starts speaking to his congregation and trying to have an influence on them for education, in a time when education was perceived as something out of religion by religious circles, you know: that's very secular, that's what the state wants, that's not within the domain of religion. And you have this *imam* who constantly insists on education, schools. Because you would expect an imam to speak about almsgiving, about charity, about prayer, you know, and nothing else.

Therefore, Ergene also seeks to interpret this via theological reflection and Islamic perspective through invoking the example of Mecca:

> There is a verse in the Qur'an, God chose Mecca as the place where he sent his last Messenger. Why? That's a place in the middle of the desert. So there is certainly a relation with the divine message and the place and space God is choosing for his specific person that he assigns – in this case a Prophet, but it's a very barren place, nothing living there, it's a rocky place, a desert, so why? So, there is certainly a relationship with the place a person is born into and where he grew up and the inner aspirations he's having inside.

In terms of this, Ergene commented of Gülen that "searching for the divine was perhaps always in his nature, or certainly very early in his age," and that "when you look into the life of Hojaefendi, you know in his early ages in his youth that he didn't really belong there, you know, he always had a similar aspiration to go beyond the boundaries of that village."

Overall, this author and this book concurs with Ergene's summary evaluative judgement that what is particularly remarkable about Fethullah Gülen's life and teaching is indeed that "he was able to 'break through'," and furthermore that "he did that with unbelievable measures" as illustrated and explored in this book especially with regard to secular-political taboos, national-cultural taboos, and religious boundary taboos.

In addition, given this book's emphasis that, fundamentally speaking Gülen and Hizmet cannot be properly understood without taking into account their fundamentally religious self-understanding, in concert with Ergene it is also important at the least to leave open explanatory space for the possibility of the unexpected being at work in ways that cannot be completely accounted for in humanly and historically reductionist terms.

At the same time, with regard to what it is possible to analyse with the tools of scientific academic disciplines, it is the argument of this book that Ergene's evaluation of the remarkable thing about Gülen being that he has been able to 'break through,' and "he did that with unbelievable measures," is that this was possible not only because of the interaction between Gülen's person, practice, teaching, and life contexts—even if one were to add to these that religious dimension referred to above. Rather, the extent that to which this 'breaking through' was able to happen in the past was also because of the contribution made to Gülen's life, practice, thinking, and teaching of the varied and now also globalised expressions of Hizmet that are themselves also increasingly 'breaking through' the cultural and historical constraints of Hizmet's Turkish origins, a concrete and specific case study of which can be found in this book's companion volume on Hizmet in Europe (Weller 2022).

The extent to which such 'breaking through' might be able to continue to happen in future remains an open question. This is especially the case given the traumatic impact of the events of July 2016 and their aftermath on both Hizmet and Fethullah Gülen himself in terms of the ambiguity and unpredictability of the outcomes arising from woundedness that has impacted both. In the light of this, it is uncertain how far their shared condition of woundedness might impair the possibility of renewal through the application of the degree of "dissonance" in terms of historical and contemporary self-criticism that might be necessary for facilitating a full renewal of Hizmet in truly global terms; and/or how far that shared woundedness might be a basis on which "compromise" can be found, out of which a new shared commitment to ecumenical *ijtihad* in action might in turn emerge for addressing the pressing global and human issues of our time.

Evaluated according to sociological or anthropological criteria alone, the impact of the trauma has been severe and, if assessed purely in temporal terms, the prospects at present remain uncertain. But, once again, as this book has continually suggested, and now emphasises again in closing: in order properly to understand either Hizmet or Fethullah Gülen, it is necessary to apply to an understanding of them, what is also at the core of their understanding of themselves. And that is the need to keep also in view what is the, at least in principle, unboundedness of a religious vision which, because of its rooting in a conviction about the infinite creativity of the divine, can offer to those who allow themselves to be shaped by it, a horizon of creativity that can generate the courage and vision to risk the development of new *itjihads* in action.

This book has argued that, in the final analysis, the creative inheritance of Gülen will not be found so much in the substantive body of his inherited teaching, pregnant though that remains with matters that will remain important into the future; the veneration of his person and/or practice, inevitable as that is likely to be, given the inspiration that he has brought to so many lives; or the copy-pasting of historical Hizmet initiatives, as valid and important as they have been for their contexts and times, but rather is that of a dynamic methodological call to continuously renewed and contextualised engagement with religious and spiritual sources centred on love and the human. If this argument is correct, then Gülen's and Hizmet's interactive contribution to the emergence of new ecumenical *itjihads* in action which, importantly, can only be undertaken in collaboration with others beyond Hizmet, could yet offer something important and still distinctive, to addressing the shared global human problems of our time, as a by-product of which further internal renewal might also be found.

NOTE

1. https://www.advocatesfordignity.org.au/home/homepage. The author's keynote lecture at this event can be accessed, c. 38 minutes into the recording of the whole event, via You Tube at https://www.youtube.com/watch?v=Eq0ejJM0CYk

REFERENCES

Ergene, Enes (2008). *Tradition Witnessing the Modern Age: An Analysis of the Gülen Movement*, New Jersey: Tughra Books.
Farrar, Max (2008). "Anatolian Muslimhood: Humanising Capitalism?" 29.10.2008 (https://www.opendemocracy.net/en/anatolian-muslimhood-in-search-of-a-humanised-capitalism/)
Gülen, Muhammad Fethullah (2002). *Essays, Perspectives, Opinions*. New Jersey, The Light.
Gülen, Muhammad Fethullah (2004a). *Towards a Global Civilization of Love and Tolerance*. Somerset, New Jersey: The Light.
Gülen, Muhammad Fethullah (2004b). *Key Concepts in the Practice of Sufism: Emerald Hills of the Heart. Volume 1.* (revised edition). New Rutherford, New Jersey: The Fountain.

Gülen, Muhammad Fethullah (2004c). *Key Concepts in the Practice of Sufism: Emerald Hills of the Heart. Volume 2.* (revised edition). Somerset, New Jersey: The Light.

Gülen, Muhammad Fethullah (2009). *Key Concepts in the Practice of Sufism: Emerald Hills of the Heart. Volume 3.* Somerset, New Jersey: Tughra Books.

Gülen, Muhammad Fethullah (2010). *Key Concepts in the Practice of Sufism: Emerald Hills of the Heart. Volume 4.* Somerset, New Jersey: The Light.

Keleş, Ozcan (2021). *The Knowledge Production of Social Movement Practice at the Intersection of Islam and Human Rights: The Case of Hizmet.* Unpublished Doctor of Philosophy in Human Rights. January 2021. Sussex: University of Sussex.

Saritoprak, Zeki (2003). Fethullah Gülen: A Sufi in His Own Way. In: M. Hakan Yavuz and John Esposito (Eds). *Turkish Islam and the Secular State: The Gülen Movement* (pp. 156–169). Syracuse, New York, Syracuse University Press.

Sunier, Thijl and Landman, Nico (2015). Gülen-Movement (Hizmet). In: *Transnational Turkish Islam: Shifting Geographies of Religious Activism and Community Building in Turkey and Europe* (pp. 81–94). London: Palgrave Pivot.

Ünal, Ali and Williams, Alphonse (2000). *Advocate of Dialogue: Fethullah Gülen.* Fairfax, VA: Fountain Publication.

Weller, Paul (2022). *Hizmet in Transitions: European Developments of a Turkish Muslim-Inspired Movement.* London: Palgrave Macmillan.

Yilmaz, (2003). Ijtihad and Tajdid by Conduct: The Gülen Movement. In M. Hakan Yavuz and John Esposito (Eds). *Turkish Islam and the Secular State: The Gülen Movement* (pp. 208–237). Syracuse, New York, Syracuse University Press.

Index[1]

A

Ablak, Selma, x, 129, 166, 199, 200, 212, 215

Adalet ve Kalkınma Partisi (AKP), 2, 91, 93, 94, 119, 143, 175, 176, 179, 238

Alasag, Alper, x, 123, 199

Alevi, 64, 99

Alliance for Shared Values, 182, 183

Ankara, 41, 50, 62, 130

Anti-religious, 29, 137, 140

Armenian, 36, 93, 96, 97, 163, 201, 228

Asylum-seeker, 53, 167

Atatürk, Mustafa Kemal, 61, 62

B

Bahá'í, 30

Balcı, Abdulkerim, x, 161–165, 183, 220–227, 229–231, 236–239

Belgium, x, 43, 160, 211

Businessmen, 35, 38, 39, 103, 130, 143, 157

C

Caliphate, 6, 62, 119, 128

Cemaat, 33, 67, 68

Central Asia, 48, 90

Çetin, Muhammad, ix, x, 6, 87, 91, 104, 105, 201, 213, 214

Christian, 10, 35, 36, 52, 94, 99, 100, 103–105, 107, 109–111, 127, 132, 134, 139, 140, 149, 189, 193, 194, 201, 202, 221, 222, 229, 231, 232, 235

Civil society, 13, 93, 94, 128, 138, 143, 193, 198, 213

Cold War, 2, 47, 64, 87

Colonialism, 85, 115, 141

Communism, 87, 125

Companions of the Prophet, 28, 117

Conflict, 8, 32, 37, 47, 52, 64, 67, 101, 118, 120–122, 128, 165, 166, 184, 198, 214, 221, 229

Conservatism, 28, 30, 76

---

[1] Note: Page numbers followed by 'n' refer to notes.

© The Author(s) 2022
P. Weller, *Fethullah Gülen's Teaching and Practice*,
https://doi.org/10.1007/978-3-030-97363-6

Printed by Printforce, United Kingdom